Dream

"You entered into life through the veil of the Dream, because your reason for being here must be kept secret from you until you find your way home. You don't know who you are, but one fine day you will remember."

LYNN ANDREWS, POWER DECK.

To Jen,
You are bodacious!
May All your horizons
Be in Beauty!
Laura Marie Parker
Love to you!

The Year I Lived Dangerously

- A traveling memoir

By Laura Marie Parker

Illustrations and Cover by
Jacob J. Norris

Contribution by Tony Topoleski

Dedication

*To my ancestors for traveling deep waters to get here,
To my mother for giving me life. To my father for
raising me. To the one who gave his seed and spirit.To
my sons for teaching me what it takes to bring my
creations to life just as I imagined and dreamed. To my
beloved Jacob...for believing in me. A special thank
you to those friends who have been on this journey
with me from the very beginning, thank you for all your
encouragement, my mother for lending me her part of
the story and to my friend Anna for being my Tribe.*

.

This is a true story real events. The names have been changed to respect the privacy of those involved.

CONTENTS

Templates

"Snorkels, we weren't going anywhere without those"

"The day has already begun" Laundry hanging in Naples

"Red Martinis at Castel del Ovo"

"Lugging the ridiculous luggage"

"In Hats"

"Vendor carries beachwear with poles"

"London Bridges"

"Amsterdam"

"Gnome with duck"

"Tango"

"On the Ferry"

"Singing Gnomes"

"I could hear everything the earth wanted to tell me"

PART ONE

The Tango

Is about tension. There is never a balance; balance only happens the moment that you die.
The Tango is
Life. It is emotional, nostalgic... The Tango
Is a walk with your partner; the most difficult
Part of the dance,
And it is beautiful when you
walk that way with some-
one.
Sometimes the dance is
over in a song or it may
last a life time.

The Tango.

        lives in our hearts and is remembered in our bones.

{1} - PACKING DAY

"Where is my Snorkel?" my mother asked me.

It was time to start packing. We had spent months shopping for all the right outfits to wear; each outfit was hung or lying out, mixed and matched for many options to get the most variety out of the least amount of baggage. Somehow still, packing light was an understatement.

The room was a whole rainbow of colors thrown over chairs and hung on bedposts. There were a few dresses, a slew of skirts, and multiple pairs of shoes. Tilted hats, sweet necklaces and slinky swimsuits posed like beach bimbos against the bars of the metal bed frame. So many choices to make.

There were checkered cottons, silk polka dots, and sheer: Sheer black, blue and white, sheer silks and light-woven cottons, sheer underwear and bras. On the dresser were bags of cotton swabs, cotton balls, shampoo and conditioner bottles, toothbrushes and paste, a box of zip lock bags to avoid spills and even little bottles of antibiotics, antihistamines and sunscreen.

Thrown in with a terrycloth after-swim robe was an elephant-like snout poking its pink trunk out, searching for its sister snorkel among the avalanche of clothing. Somewhere, with its cracking rubber and prescription goggles, was a misplaced black and orange Snorkel —

Snorkels. We weren't going anywhere without those.

My mother had happily invested in matching black suitcase and carry-on sets from K-mart for our adventure. The ridiculous sized suitcase had tiny wheels and a handle that pulled out for easy maneuverability. The carry on was a backpack with the same black leather patchwork and big stitching between each of the textured patches. In addition, she also purchased two black shoulder bags to use for travel books and CDs. We each carried a fanny pack with our passports and money inside. The two big suitcases took up most of the space on my mom's double bed, we filled the bags three quarters of the way full, with the intention to leave some space for things that we would buy along the way.

I piled a couple of travel books and my copy of Don Quixote on top of my folded sweatshirt and an extra change of clothes for my carry-on. In the bathroom I grabbed my toothbrush and a little bag of toiletries, then returned to my bedroom to retrieve my journal.

As I went to stack everything else onto my carry-on pile, my journal slipped off and landed in between the wall and the dresser. I had to get down on my hands and knees to gather all my sentimental loose papers that I'd stuffed inside. As I reached underneath the dresser, I saw my mother's portfolio that contained all of the photos her lover had taken when she was a model. I sat down on the ground and began to flip through. The pages were filled with pictures of my mother in different lighting, in nature, wearing fashionable eighties animal prints, fur coats and high-hipped swimsuits. In a pocket in the back there were some loose photos, some of them were nude and in a few she was standing among palm trees or in the ocean. As I studied her then thirty-four-year-old body, and looked for similarities between mine and hers, my mother came into the room.

"Oh, those are my modeling pictures that Reign took of me. These are from the trip we took together to Tahiti. "This one was when we went to Hawaii. It was so romantic there. I just love the tropics." I watched her body relax, remembering how it felt to be at ease in the warmth and humidity of the Islands. "The people were so sensual and spiritual about the land."

I looked at the picture she pointed at. She stood in the ocean, wearing a one piece swimsuit with large floral print. Her body was strong and posed like a model in a catalogue, with her arm wrapped up into her hair, and a striking look on her face. Her skin had a lovely glow of a fair redhead, with more freckles in the summer. The sun created a glare in the water beneath her, and in her eyes she looked as if she were in another world. It was like looking at a Goddess Spirit, emerging from the ocean, neither fully in her body or fully out of it.

"Mom, how did you convince dad to let you go?"

"I told him I needed a trip alone, I was always a more restless soul than him and he knew it so he didn't think it was weird when I wanted to go by myself. His mother helped out with you and the boys, she was always around to take you guys. I saved my money like we did for this trip."

"And dad didn't have any idea?"

"Well, after I got back from Tahiti he started to put it all together, then he realized I was having an affair, and we fought all night long about it."

Just as my mother was starting to tell me more, we both heard my father's footsteps coming to check in on our packing. I closed the portfolio and slid it back under the dresser, then tucked the rest of the loose papers into my journal. He peaked his head in at us.

"Hey, how's all the packing going?"

"Well," I looked behind my shoulder at all the mess of pretty fabrics, "I don't know how we're going to fit this all in."

"Ha! You're gonna need forklifts to get your bags on the shuttle tomorrow", he answered cleverly. We both laughed, my mother giggled in her high pitched laugh, the laugh my dad always said he could hear across any party, even with a loud band.   Dad stood in the doorway, watching us fold and tuck, zip and tie. After a few minutes he excused himself and went back to the catch the score on the game he was watching.

An hour later our bags were tightly zipped, with very little room for adding in extra things from our trip. We slid the suitcases off the bed. I threw my arms back and lay down, happy to be done with the packing. Mom disappeared to take out her contacts, remove her makeup with a little cotton ball of astringent, and brush her teeth. When she returned in her natural state, she asked me to go tell dad it was time to say goodnight.

Dad roused himself from a little nap in his recliner, and followed me to my mother's room. He sat down on the edge of the bed and kissed her goodnight. I leaned over and kissed her on the forehead, gave dad a hug, "Nite daddy", and made my way to my own bedroom, ready to collapse.

I lay in my bed, thinking about our long flight the next day.

After five years of saving money, making plans and searching for the perfect wardrobe, we were finally going to Italy.

{2} -THE ENDLESS SKY

"SECURITY IS MOSTLY A SUPERSTITION. IT DOES NOT EXIST IN NATURE, NOR DO THE CHILDREN OF MEN AS A WHOLE EXPERIENCE IT. AVOIDING DANGER IS NO SAFER IN THE LONG RUN THAN OUTRIGHT EXPOSURE. LIFE IS EITHER A DARING ADVENTURE, OR NOTHING." HELEN KELLER

Our flight was set at 4:30 pm standard time. The flight only took about nine hours, which would put us in Rome sometime around 11:00 am the next day. I sat, buckled and ready to take off, studying the cover of Don Quixote. It had a squiggled pen rendering of a man with a sword and shield sitting atop a horse. There was a sun at the top corner that looked like it had been drawn by a child, with a small circle and ten lines darting out to emanate light. I skipped through the various chapter descriptions and skimmed through part of the introduction. On page twenty-three I read, "The Libros de Caballerias recounted the adventures of valorous knights who dedicated themselves to lofty goals and to beautiful damsels for whom they were willing to risk everything"*.

"Hmm," I thought. "I wish Ahron would risk

everything for me, I can hardly get him to call me once in a season".

I put the book in the pocket of the seat in front of me and pulled out my journal. Tucked inside was a card Ahron gave to me when I left for college. The front of the card had a picture of a little boy carrying a suitcase through a train yard, holding a little girls hand to get her aboard the train safely. The two children were dressed in classy attire like they were already adults. Inside the card read:

Wrenna,

I really don't know what happened between us over the last six weeks, but I like it. You have made me pretty confused. I do know that I will miss you & I will be looking forward to our dancing & some more. Make the most of every day.

Thanks.

Love,

Ahron.

The Plane lifted off. I held Ahron's photo in my hand and looked at it hard, as if I could jump into it and change the moment that he drove away into one that could have made him stay.

My mother had fallen asleep next to me. I returned the card and Ahron's picture to its envelope. Tears dripped off my chin as I thought of Ahron and how I still couldn't let him go. I just wanted him to be with me. I cried and looked out at the clear endless sky and fell asleep to the hum of the plane's engine.

Laura Marie Parker

*Cervantes, page 23

{3} - ROME, ITALY

July 11th, 2002
Dear Ahron,

"You can't imagine what it is like here. I stepped off the plane in Rome and was carried by a stream of people to a conveyor belt, where I waited to retrieve our gigantic suitcases. I felt as if we were all holding tickets in our hand at the Kentucky Derby waiting for our horse to win. The Italians don't mess around, they found the strength and weakness of the current, passionately waiting for their bags, then darting out to catch a small carry-on.

Mom and I both felt a bit frantic in the city full of people speaking a different language after our day-long flight. We wandered around aimlessly through the train station until a friendly guy asked us where we were going. I told him the name of our hotel, something like, "Dove il treno per Pensione Panda vicino il Spanish Steps?" He didn't really speak a lot of English, so it was good I knew a little Italian, I got my point across. He pointed to a shuttle that took people to different hotels in the area for just ten Euros..."

We waited at the shuttle area until the taxi driver finally pulled up in a long white van. The driver was balding, his nose drove down off his forehead, ending abruptly and drawing back with a thick point. He was short, stalky, about thirty-five, and wound up like a toy; He seemed to be in a hurry, throwing our gear into the back of the van with a hyper pace, shuffling back and forth between the double doors and the pile of passengers luggage. There was little consideration for the contents inside. As he hurried back and forth, he asked each one of us where we were going, then hopped into the van ready to maneuver the freeways of Rome.

Everyone was hot and impatient and shoved their way to the front of the line to get into the air conditioned van, leaving me up front next to the driver with my face inches away from the windshield. The driver swooped into the flow of traffic, driving us away from the airport, and merging from lane to lane as he entered the freeway. His phone made a shrill tweet, and he reached out to the dashboard, picking up the phone with one hand and maneuvering the steering wheel with the other. I looked at the speedometer, which read 110 kilometers per hour. The driver suddenly jerked the wheel with his one hand while he shook the hand with his cell phone, yelling, "Vaffanculo!", as a moped darted in front of him going at least 120 kilometers an hour. I don't know if he was yelling at the mopeds or the person he was talking to on the phone. We weaved in and around tiny cars like a derby race. The cars were racing, not traveling.

In the rearview mirror, mom was smiling at me and taking it all in. I kept wanting to say something to the taxi driver to carry on conversation, but I thought better of it and chose to keep my mouth shut. After we got off the main freeway and onto the one-way streets, the thorough fair was packed with people jumping out of the way like bowling pins. We moved more slowly on the pedestrian full street, and finally we arrived at the Pensione Panda, where the entire block was one long building.

The driver dumped our bags on the sidewalk, got back into the van and drove away, leaving us standing in front of a looming hardwood door. It was cracked open just a bit, so we walked in. The floors and stairways were made of marble that cooled us off. There wasn't a soul around and nowhere to go but up. A soft natural light came in from a large window at the top of the wide first floor staircase. The stairway narrowed and the light dimmed. We climbed the stairs with our huge luggage in tow. After the rush of the taxi drive our adrenaline was pumping, and the absurdity of yanking our bags on tiny wheels up three flights of stairs made us giggle. We finally made it up and stood quietly for a moment catching our breath. The corridor at the top was dark, behind us there was an eerie, enchanting glow that filled the stairwell. We found the Manager's door and knocked. The Manager spoke little English and gestured that our room was one floor down, which made us laugh even more because we had to take our luggage down the same stairs that we struggled to climb up!

Mom put the skeleton key into the old lock, turned and opened the door. On our right inside was a tiny bathroom with a little old porcelain sink and a pull-string to turn on the light. After the shuttle ride, I was relieved to finally have a bathroom and was thrilled to see that the toilet sat directly next to a bidet. The toilet flushed by pulling a rope above me, and the bidet was very soothing.

Mom came in and we laughed about the rope flushing system as I washed my face and she had her turn with the toilet.

"I have always wanted one of these, ever since I saw one in Italy, when I went with my dad," she commented as she rinsed herself in the Bidet.

I was tired, but somehow still buzzing from all the movement in the last couple of hours. I fetched my bags from the hallway, where I left them in a hurry to get to the bathroom. I drug the big one in dropping it in the middle of the room between a single bed that was shoved up against one wall, and a double bed, that took up most of the space in the room. Our luggage seemed even more ridiculous looking at it in the tiny room. Once we opened up our bags and dug through for our toiletries and a change of clothes, the contents of the bags crinkled out like stiff legged passengers de-boarding a plane, ready to iron out their wrinkles. We were crunched in without a whole lot of stretching room and I was beginning to feel claustrophobic.

I decided to take a shower before I lay down for a nap. The shower was barely big enough for one person to stand, the door clasped with a magnet, and I was completely enclosed in a little steamy box; above me a slice of a window released the steam. Tears fell with the water. I wanted to be in Italy, but I thought it was going to feel different, more luxurious maybe. Instead, it touched into a raw place, a place of shadow within me, where, for the first time in my life, I felt a greater mystery, I was aware of spirits that I had never known before.

There was a similar feeling of dank, dark exploration in my basement as a child. I had grown up in a big old farm style house in a logging town that developed into a small city; my house was just across from the river. In the basement was an old heavy wooden door that I was scared to open, but with my brother one day, we peeked inside and found a string hanging down. We pulled it and the light turned on, it still worked. Inside a long narrow room there were a hundred mason jars lined up on shelves. The jars were full of peaches. Someone had worked hard canning them all, probably my grandmother. The ground in the root cellar storage was dust from broken rock that made me wonder if it had been laying there since the house was built. Something about those peaches, preserved life, waiting for twenty years already; something about them still contained spirit, whether it was a rot, or a spirit that stayed with the fruit, either way, I felt even in the dark basement, in a room that no one ever set foot, there was life pulsing.

I suppose that old house made me appreciate old things, though at times I think about how it also had a feeling that was unsettled and unknown.

As I lay looking up at the ceiling of the room on the second floor of the Pensione, I felt a new feeling of unknown. I traced the rectangular paintings with my eyes. The whole ceiling was adorned with a colorful design of pictures, bordered in strips of blue and filled in with yellow and pink swirls, flowers and shapes. I fell asleep into the dreams of my past, a place that was familiar, a place that I had already been.

July 11th, 2002 9:45pm
View from Our Window
    I took a nice long nap and felt funny waking up in Italy. I can't believe I'm finally here. Mom and I went to dinner at the restaurant we can see from the Pensione window. I nibbled on a little bit of bread and dipped it in soup that had little star shaped noodles floating in it. The soup was so

salty I feared I might swell up like a balloon and not be able to breath.

We ordered a litre of water that was served in a carafe, but I was afraid to drink it because mom told me a story about some ice cubes she drank one time when she was traveling in Europe that made her sick, and ever since she had warned me about the water in foreign countries, that you have to be careful. I was so overwhelmed I started to cry salty waterfalls down my cheeks and right back into my soup. I look up at mom and her mouth stretched taught and she started crying with me, wiping her eyes with the red and white checkered napkin. We were both so sleep deprived, finally coming down from a high we had been on since we boarded the plane yesterday that we left without finishing our food. I think it insulted the waiter, but I was relieved to get away from all the stimulus of new experience.

Now it's really hot in our room. There is an oscillating fan, which is nice, but only when it turns in my direction and hits me right in the face with air, so I opened the window to get some fresh air, it's even warmer outside. The window latch has this cute little metal buckle on it. Down in the street there is a little boy playing accordion with his dad, they're both dressed in black slacks and white button-up shirts.

It feels like a movie out there full of bustiers and corsets, Romeo and Juliet. I am sitting like Juliet looking out over this balcony, it's so romantic. I can see the outdoor tables that belong to the restaurant we just ate at. The tables outside are all covered with salmon pink table cloths. Inside the restaurant there were similar table cloths and one tiny candle lit in the center. The whole wall behind our table was a cupboard with wine bottles dating back a couple hundred years and they were locked in with dark wood slats. It reminded me of the true treasure in an Italian pirate ship, the wine that fueled the passion that flowed through their blood...

I finished my journaling and closed the shutters, and the sound of the accordion duo was silenced. A new kind of exhaustion came over me. My mind was blank, and all I could do was lay down on the bed with the fan blowing past my swollen feet every couple of seconds. It didn't take long before I had fallen asleep.

Our shutters on the windows shut out the light from outside, so when I awoke, I was disoriented about the time. I looked down at my hand and saw that my fingers were swollen and the ring my cousin had given me for my birthday was stuck on my finger. I began to panic. I got out of bed and went to the bathroom where I ran cold water over my fingers, and rinsed my feet in the bidet, then retreated to the bedroom where I looked for some water to drink. On the bedside table was a small bottle of water only a quarter full, and mom's watch which read 4 o'clock, still set for our home time, I calculated that it was 1 o'clock in the morning in Italy.

My thirst burdened me, it would still be hours until I would be down on the street where I could buy more water. Our Pensione was not a hotel with 24-hour room service. I didn't realize I should have planned ahead. I thought about drinking the water out of the sink, but remembered again my mom's warning about drinking water in a foreign country. I feared that I might get sick. Anxiety overtook me, I was afraid to drink the last of the water in fear that I would still be thirsty.

My mother peacefully slept in the single bed with her earplugs stuffed into her ears. I began to pace thinking about what I should do. I was afraid I might get dehydrated. The room felt so hot. I sat down in front of the fan letting it hum over me. I wanted to cry, but I was too worried and my throat just got tight. Finally, I stood up and went over to my mother's bedside, where I sat down. She always had a hard time sleeping; saying it was due to the many years of being up with crying babies. I was always hesitant to wake her because I felt guilty if she couldn't go back to sleep leaving her distant the following day. I looked at her face to see if she was truly asleep or if maybe she was just resting. I sat like that for a moment. Then, she sucked in a quick breath of air and her eyes opened wide. She looked frightened.

"Is everything okay?" she asked in a slightly high-pitched voice that was crackly from sleeping. I looked down at her with the same big eyes. My heart was fluttering and I felt sick and shaky.

"I'm thirsty". I said looking up at the almost empty plastic bottle of water on the table.

"Oh, you scared me. Are you okay? There's a little water in here," she said as she looked over and saw that there was not much left. "Oh. Oh no." She sat squinting her eyes, she was not totally awake or asleep. She and I both looked at the bottle of water. Suddenly I felt greedy for it.

"What should we do?" she asked me.

"I don't know. Do you want to share the last sips?"

"Sure." We both took sips until the bottle was empty. I thought that this must be what it's like when people are in the desert looking for an oasis.

"I'm still really thirsty," my mouth had a cottony dryness. I was frustrated about the salty soup, and as I looked at my fingers, puffing up like sausages, I wondered,

"What's going to happen to me?"

"I don't know about the water in the sink, if it's drinkable or not," mom looked stumped. I walked over to the window, unlatched the shutter and looked out to see if the answer might lie out in the darkened streets. There was a bar with a lit sign and a few dim lights about half a block away. Mom came and looked out with me.

"Do you think the bar will have bottles of water? I don't know if I want to go down there. Do you think it's safe?" mom gazed down at the streets that seemed suddenly much more dangerous without the meandering people going up and down.

"I don't want to go down there, especially to a bar. I think I'll just try to sleep". Having my mom awake with me calmed my nerves, I felt less alone, and after going over the option of entering an Italian bar at midnight, I realized that quenching my thirst could wait until morning.

"I think I'll just jump in a cool shower and try to get some sleep," I said. Mom laughed a little; the skin around her eyes was puffy and her eyelids were droopy.

"You freaked me out. Your face was about an inch away from mine, I didn't know what was going on". She laughed again, and I laughed along with her, it felt good after all the stress I had from traveling.

I showered and cooled off, then sprawled out under the cool sheet with the fan humming over me back and forth, singing its rhythmic lullaby until I fell asleep.

The night waned and I awoke again at four in the morning. Mom was wide awake too and we knew it would be impossible to sleep, so we went down to the crisp cobbled road and wandered a few blocks. We found a bench next to the road and sat down to feel the warmth of the morning.

As the sun pushed up, lighting the sky with soft pinks and purples, the street began to come to life. Delivery trucks wobbled down the road and stopped in front of restaurant doors. The smell of exhaust mixed with the scent of old stone, and summer pollen filled the already thick warm air. It was a cacophony of sensation. One service man stepped out of his truck and magically disappeared into an elevator built into the street. He came back up with an empty hand truck and the elevator disappeared back into the ground.

It struck me right then that I had finally arrived in Italy; the serenity of the morning allowed me to cuddle an ageless romance that people flocked to Rome for. The air was spicy, the heat sultry, and each building knew its own foundation to the depths of its soul. For a moment I felt I had arrived home, this peaceful place, on this bench, watching pigeons dive from rooftop to cobbled roadway. The quiet city morning was where I belonged.

Across the street, a man arrived at his vending cart. He sold water, juice, tea, and had a small fountain of water that trickled onto slices of fresh coconut. Mom and I noticed him and immediately remembered our desire for water. We made our way over and purchased three water bottles and a bottle of sweetened iced tea.

I noticed a pay phone across the street and we

figured it was the perfect time to call dad and tell him we were well, it was five a.m. in Italy, so dad would be winding down for the night back home, it was still yesterday there.

Dad had seemed nervous about our trip to Italy, he probably wondered if my mom might officially move to Europe and run away with some Italian. Mom had always fantasized about doing such a thing, but it didn't seem to go much further than that.

There was a card slot to put some kind of prepaid phone card into, but we could not figure out how to use the card we had. Finally, we just dialed the number and starting putting euros in the coin slot after the Italian voice prompt. Finally, the receiver made a drawn out beep. Another beep, then dad's voice came over the receiver.

"Hello?" The voice at the other end was surprisingly close sounding. I had expected him to sound an ocean and a continent away.

"Hi daddy." I said it perkily to hide the homesick feeling that came over me when I heard him on the other end. "We couldn't sleep so we decided to call you and tell you we made it here okay." I tried to sound like the twenty-year-old that I was, but somehow I couldn't help sounding like the little girl I felt like in such an unfamiliar, busy European city.

"How's it going, are you having fun?"

"Yeah, it's different here, it feels one hundred years behind, and we're experiencing culture shock. Last night we went for dinner and both of us almost had panic attacks in the middle of the street because of the mobs of people. Neither of us have ever seen so many people in one street before. The roads were so crowded the cars could barely get through. And when we got here we had this taxi driver that kept yelling Italian profanities and shaking his fist at people. Oh, and last night, I was so thirsty, because we forgot to get water before we settled in for the night. I didn't know if I should wake mom up, so I was looking at her face, seeing if she was really sleeping, and she woke up to my face like an inch away from hers, I think I freaked her out a little bit". I laughed. It felt good to share and feel connected to home through my dad.

"How's your mom?" he asked with a little sarcasm, knowing that when she travels, she wants to do everything and it doesn't take long before she's carried away in the spirit of things. "Off on a runner" is what dad called it. Sometimes it was hard to keep up.

"Well, it's never dull dad," I paused, "do you want to talk to her?"

"Sure."

I handed the phone over to her.

"Hi Carver," mom shifted to get a little privacy while I watched the light in the sky subtly swim through the remaining stars.

The buildings were splashed with sunlight, and long morning shadows grew then receded as the last of the sunrise faded. The city was one big Van Gogh painting with mysterious street lights, animated people and shady worn cobblestones.

Mom talked for a bit then hung up the phone and we strolled back down to the bench on the main drag. We probably looked a little out of place, but nobody paid much attention to us.

The doves on the rooftop were cooing like summertime lovers. The city's patience draped over us, elated, anticipating; waiting to open the curtains for us to use the streets as our stage and play out the fantasies that makes Europe famous. We watched the morning, the last star slipped back into the night traveling back to where I came from. Then, silently, in awe of it all, not sure what we would miss if we closed our eyes for even a moment, we watched.

***

After resting through the day and staying close to our Pensione, sampling sandwiches and salads from the nearby Piazza's, we made one last stop for a glass of wine and dinner. The Piazza di Spagna was packed with people, all the young people were out cruising the town on a Friday night. I sipped my Chianti and watched a pretty young man kiss his girlfriend. While they kissed, his eyes were scanning the crowd to see if anyone was looking. I laughed and told my mom to look.

"He reminds me of my dad when he was young, he had a shy side to him, but he was also very charismatic and good-looking," she surveyed the rest of the Piazza with me and we noticed similar behavior happening all over.

"This must be the hot spot," I commented as I scanned over a group of girls a little younger than me, who were obviously talking about a couple of Italian guys that were checking them out.

"This is what I was telling you about Wrenna, aren't the men so good-looking?" Mom followed one of the waiters with her eyes as she spoke to me. "When my dad and I came, they would come right up to me and whisper something in my ear. I was amazed at how much at home I felt when I came here last time, I don't know exactly what it is, but it just feels alive to me. The people express themselves, they don't hide their emotions, and everyone takes pride in their sexuality. I love the music, and the dancing, and the way the men are so attentive to the women," she looked off to the side watching a woman with a dress that hugged her round booty...she was pouting and turning her face away from the man who stood groveling in Italian, it seemed like a game they were playing.

Across the Piazza, a violinist performed with her case open for Euros to be offered. Back home we had an occasional bad guitarist playing in the breezeway expecting people to offer change, but rarely was there someone who had any talent. It seemed like all the street performers in Italy had known how to play for years.

"Do you think that woman is a gypsy mom?" I asked, taking in her jangling earrings and beautiful ragged clothes.

"She might be. You know, when I was traveling with my dad here, I learned that there were some gypsy's on my dad's side of the family. Some of them immigrated to South America and some are still living in Argentina."

"Really? That's cool. It makes so much sense actually, somehow it explains all the eccentricities that come out in Grandpa and you...and me. I do love soulful violin music and tango and accordion. I think of all the music in the world, that music moves me the most."

I finished my last sip of wine and nibbled on some olives and cheese. It felt good to be sitting down. After a little exploration and taking it easy, I was much more settled than the day before. Even our hot room seemed welcoming when we arrived back to sleep that night.

I sat in the window seat, feeling sedated by the wine, and watched the accordion players again. They were so fascinating, especially the little boy who was up late with his father. I tried to imagine where they lived, maybe in an apartment not far from there. I wondered if playing the accordion was all they did, or if it was just extra work on top of other work. The boy smiled jovially whether or not anyone passed by, he seemed to take joy in playing with his father.

I left the window open while I wrote a little in my travel journal, then finally closed it and washed up. Mom was already sleeping with her earplugs in by the time I fell asleep.

{4} - A NEW PERSPECTIVE

"Uncertainty is where creativity lives." JuJu

"I need an iced tea," mom announced, as she whispered her bangs around on her forehead. She wiped away the pink fangs that streaked up at the corner of her lips from her thick application of neon lipstick. Her head tilted down, with eyes looking coyly at her reflection in the tiny mirror hanging on the wall above the bathroom sink. She played in that way for a minute, practicing her look, like a model on the runway. She had her time walking the catwalk for a local boutique that sold expensive designer clothes. Her figure had always been beautiful, 5'4, 130 pounds, curvy hips, and breasts that filled a C cup perfectly. She'd been wearing the lipstick and short bangs look ever since I could remember, except in 1987 when she and I both got perms. My brothers and I used to have this joke about her lipstick whenever it would smear. If it was on her upper lip, we called her three lips, if she had fangs darting out from the corners of her mouth, she was joker, like in the Batman movie. If it somehow smeared on both the top and the bottom it was turkey-

The Year I Lived Dangerously

lips. On occasion she would drink from the opposite side of her iced tea cup than she had started with and end up with lipstick on her forehead between her eyes. In that case we just laughed at her. She always laughed with us, she found a lot of humor in her identity, even though she hid a lot of things behind it.

"We can go down to the little stand we went to yesterday to get some water and your iced tea", I said. "Do you have the book with the map in it for the walking tour?" I put a bottle of sunscreen into my fanny pack and looked around to find my sunglasses.

"Let me see..."she shuffled things around in her shoulder bag, taking out her
Oil of Olay, her wallet, her prescription glasses case...

"Here it is," she said as she flipped the pages to the picture of the center of Rome. The night before we were looking through the travel books and she came across a walking tour of the main historical attractions in the city, we both agreed that it would be a fun way to see Rome on our own time, instead of doing a guided tour.

"Okay, I'm ready." I put on my favorite floppy straw sunhat and we locked the door behind us. After a good night sleep, we were both refreshed, it was time to explore Rome, to drink coffee, eat pastries and watch the busy natives wander through their lives to the next destinations. We bought bottled iced tea and some fruit from a street vender then wandered up to the first landmark on our tour located in Piazza del Popolo. The heat of the day was already beginning to climb, soon it would be scorching. It was relieving after only eight blocks to reach the Church on the map and enter into the cool sanctuary.

We walked in and immediately dipped our fingers in the holy water, crossing ourselves. I pretended to mumble something.

Neither my mother nor I had been to church for ten years or more for anything other than a wedding or a funeral. She was brought up Catholic. I was too, but mom's experience was much more entrenched in the dogmatic expectations enforced in parochial school by the nuns. She often expressed that the shame she experienced as a young girl by the nuns influenced her feelings of needing to escape religious institutions and wanting to run away and be free to do whatever she wanted.

I remember hearing her talk about the nuns and her bitter experiences with them hitting her palms with rulers, making a scene and shaming her for having any kind of feelings for boys her age, or saying miserable and mean things to her when she was only a young blossoming girl.

When I was eight, my mother dutifully sent me to after school Catholic lessons that were mandatory for my ceremony of communion. Even then at the age of eight, I began to see through the false faces that rewarded us with money and gifts for being such obedient believers. Once the ceremony was over, I started to find ways to divert mom's attention from taking me to my Tuesday afternoon Catholic classes. Instead I convinced her to take me out for cookies at our favorite bakery, as I thought it much more fun to be with my mom anyway. She took the bait easily and I never went again. It was then that Sunday church going ceased, so when we found ourselves standing in the cool stone sanctuary of the Church of Santa Maria del Popolo, our tongues were rusty with the "Our Father".

We stood under the statues of Saints and the Mother Mary who hovered angelically above the podium. They all floated so gracefully.

Quietly praying, an Italian woman shrouded in black, stood over a table of tiny candles, lighting one and bending her head down. She looked forlorn, her eyes stared at the little fires, waiting for an answer to her search, waiting to be healed, waiting to be saved.

As we sauntered along by a row of paintings by Raphael and Bernini depicting numerous religious pictorials, I noticed the confessionals, which seemed to be in progress. I remembered wondering at my first confession if I should tell the priest that I had been masturbating since I was six, or if maybe I should tell him that I rolled around naked with a little black girl named Cassie when I was five, but I decided against it. I liked masturbating, it was my own secret, it belonged to me, and I did not want him to have it. So, I told him something about feeling guilty that I stole something once from a store. He told me to say two Hail Mary's and one Our Father. I never said the Hail Mary's because I didn't know the words and didn't care to.

I saw a man exit the confessional and thought for a moment about going in to confess something, since I was in Italy, the priests wouldn't even know me so I could just let go of something. But, somehow telling a man I didn't know something personal and intimate about me through a little window didn't feel right, even if he was supposed to be holy.

The Italian church did have a different spirit to it than the one at home, the cathedrals were powerful with their detailed art and towering ceilings, everything was adorned in gold; the bells rang out with a hypnotic symbolism.

We sat in the pews for a few minutes quietly, then made our way back to exit the way we came.

Outside we encountered four men with a casket walking up the steps toward us. The church's facilitators were emptying the church of tourists and shutting the doors to prepare for a funeral. We escaped just in time.

I looked behind me and saw a woman in a black babushka. She had just reached the casket and began to grab at the box throwing herself on top of it, she was moaning and wailing.

"I saw women do that when I lived in Chicago, the Jewish mothers and the Catholic women. My grandmother was like that, she showed her grievances and expressed them." My mom sighed.

"When I moved to the West Coast, it was so different, the culture of the Old Country just wasn't there. In Chicago, my Aunt and Uncle and cousins were all in one house. My father still spoke some Slovenian. My Grandmother made bread and cooked traditional Slovenian food. My family was very emotional, especially my father.
Everyone in my family was expressive".

Mom turned to see two more shrouded old women join in the wailing chorus. She turned back to me and I could see she was crying, she wiped away tears from the corner of her eye.

"I remember entering Washington, knowing I was going to live there, and I felt so sad, all the trees were dry, and the climate was so different, I missed my cousins. I can't imagine what it was like when my grandparents came to Ellis Island. They left their whole family behind, most of them they never saw again. It's different now because it isn't as hard to fly to see people, but there are still a lot of people that would never be able to visit relatives in America, they would have to save money for a long time to be able to travel. I think for my family they felt a lot of loss," she paused. "There was always a part of me that never felt totally at home after we left Chicago. I loved Carver and our family, but I always felt there was a piece missing. I missed my culture when we came to the West Coast. In Chicago there were more immigrants, and a mix of ethnic backgrounds. When we moved I felt out of place and misunderstood".

"Here in Italy you see people express to each other how they feel, and they really feel things, they are in life, like my grandmother, she never held anything back". Mom looked past the wailing women as if she was looking into a memory, "This is a part of life, our emotions are important, they are what makes us human".

We started walking away from the church, following the arrows on our map. Mom stopped as we came to an intersection that veered and sprawled out in many directions.

"Do you know where we are?" she asked.

I was used to everything being on a block system, everything in our city was square. We stood on a corner, where five other corners branched off in all different directions. If the intersection were a clock, there was a road at 11 o'clock, 12:30, 2:30, 4 o'clock and 8:30, and we were standing somewhere between 5 and 6 o'clock. We looked at our map and found the intersection, but couldn't figure out which direction we were actually coming from.

"I think we are here, oh yes, see the name on the store window? That's the address, this is the same name. Okay, we need to go that way." I pointed down the 11 o'clock road, and as soon as we headed into it, there was nowhere else to go but down it. We finally reached one of the tourist stops on the walking map, the Capuchin Crypt.

I read the plaque cemented into a rock wall that said, "What you are now, we used to be, what we are now, you will be."

"Are they warning us that we are going to die?" I asked. "Maybe they are trying to say that this is our only chance to live the life we want to live," I said answering my own question. "We used to be alive and now we are dead, this will happen to you too, don't waste your life like we did..." I snickered at my joke and I entered into a dark passageway built into the side of the wall along the city street.

The cool crypt was a relief from the pressing muggy heat of the city. We walked through the quiet dimly lit corridors of the underground tomb, and took in the arrangements ornately displayed along the walls of each room. One room had designs made completely out of skulls, another was all pelvises; there was also a wall of femurs and one of feet. I wondered why they separated all the pieces.

We didn't say anything to each other, just studied the preserved bones then retreated back into the bright daylight. I entered into a room where a heart was arranged out of pelvises. "Maybe the priests were artists," I thought.

"That was so interesting!" my mother commented and we came out of the cave.

"I've never seen anything like it. "

"It must have taken a long time to collect all of those bones and fashion them into such intricate designs". I said as I looked over the packet of postcards I bought in the little souvenir shop at the end of the crypt. I exited and saw the plaque again,

"What you are now, we used to be, what we are now, you will be."

Maybe it's about how nothing lasts forever, but that whatever we choose to do we take the lasting things and make something beautiful out of them. I wondered if the plaque was trying to say something about making choices, or about being present with what is presented to you. I wondered if each choice we make could be like a tiny death, and no matter where it takes us, we have the option to hold onto the past and continue to grieve our losses, or to see the opportunities that a choice to change presents. I remembered something mom had told me about her mother choosing to marry a Catholic man, and her Protestant parents disowning her for making that choice. She never seemed to regret her decision, she had chosen her own path, and from that choice she created a family and a life from it.

We walked awhile chatting and observing the culture around us and came down to a street full of shop windows.

"Hey look mom, the stores on this street all have sales, see the signs say 'Saldi'", I pointed to the word printed across a store window.

"Ooo, let's go look." Mom veered in the direction of a little boutique with the door propped open and Italian pop music blaring out of the store's rafters. We entered unnoticed, but *we* noticed the scene.

There were women everywhere flipping their hair, pouncing on the clothes that hung perky and flared upon the racks. Italian voices spoke quickly; decisions were made in half try-on,

One woman attempted a dress, and with only a second of consideration she tossed it to the ground; too small?

Another woman liked stripes, she strutted back and forth between the curtains, hugged by a striped tube dress.

A lady with striking and tough features, strong yet so comfortably female, let her body fat relax into a gliding jiggle. Her lover, filled with Italian coffee shots and sleeked up with black leather, fingered his way through outfits, picking out lace and stretchy leather. His upper eyelids hung down, as if squinting to watch the projector screen of his morning lovemaking session, or imagining her with all the garments walking through the streets saddled to his side.

She walked through the curtain from the dressing room to see herself in the mirror, he'd embrace her, rub his hand along her thigh, touch the fabric stretched over her perfect round Italian ass. Her European butt was full and sensual, made of all the real fats of real foods.

In the mirror her lover looked her over, with a half smirk and still shady eyes. A prostitute I wondered? No, just a lover. Her head nudges his chin, she shrugs her shoulder, and he tightens his grip on her ass again. Sold. The outfit is a keeper.

Another woman, placid faced, still as a pond with no expression except in her experiencing eyes was shopping with her daughter. For her, everything was too flashy, too see-through, too modern. She took her daughter by the hand, and made her way to the door.

My mother and I knew we were experiencing a happening-a sale at an Italian boutique. There was nothing slow about it, but it was timeless. A show of modern women in Italy. They think about men, they judge themselves, they look at themselves in the mirror to feed their hunger for attention, they create identities to match the personalities of the sexiest other half, they do mating dances in the dressing rooms. The dressing room was a hallway of curtains, and my curtain was at the back. I walked through each changing room to get there.

I puckered up and looked behind my shoulder; my bare ass was bobbing young and full right there. What is it about looking at full fatty fleshy surfaces that is addicting? Don't need to know. I slipped a stretchy lace skirt over my bottom, and pulled on its matching white flowered top. "This is hot," I thought.

"You look great, what shoes are you going to wear?" my mother asked smiling her manic, eyes full of icy fire-flared mischievous-creating matches-totaling discounts-loving every bit of it smile.

"I want to find a really beautiful pair of Italian shoes mom, ones that I can wear with anything."

I walked through the curtain past two large bubbly breasts, and a blue and red summer hat, big boots, a pair of panty hose, and flaming red hair. Next curtain, two girls, sadly moving through outfits, nothing quite right for their planned affair later that evening. The last curtain, long legs, calves wrapped in summer sandal straps, hairy armpits and short dark hair. A smile and a quick glance away.

We were shy in that dressing room. Out in the store I waited my turn for a mirror, except there are no turns. Everyone just dances in a reflective circus of fancy dresses and big hair. We twirl, we turn. We twist, we squint and pout, grimace, shrug, wiggle our toes. In the mirror my bush was a dark shadow beneath the thin stretchy lace and silky slip that stretched over my body.

I walked around to think about all the outfits I had tried on. I reached over to grab another piece of couture, and the rack of clothing shocked my finger. I found out later see through silk generates a lot of static electricity, (in the darkness in the middle of slipping my tongue in and out of cute boys mouths I would send green flashes of light beaming across invisible beds).

I was shocked back to reality. In my arms I held a pile of clothes with piccolo paper tags marked with E and slashed numbers. I was getting carried away. My mother would have stayed for hours watching that show, but she had other boutiques to look at, with clothes that might suit her everyday needs a bit more. And I needed shoes. We bought the see through skirt and matching flower shirt, and made our way out into the street with a bag full, just more clothes to add to our already overstuffed black suitcases.

***

We shopped a bit more then agreed that it was time to find a bite to eat. We found a little place with outside seating where we could people watch. It was a busy day in the city. A carafe of Chianti was served to us with two glasses, and mom ordered up some hors d'oeuvres.

I looked across the table at my mother, she wore a knee length skirt and a blouse with a sun hat, and she looked suddenly very young and free of responsibility. Her face was softer than her usual stony look, and her anxious drifting eyes that often avoided contact were now sparkling and bright. We were enjoying each other's company, and there would be no interruption, no going home for two more weeks. She took a sip of her wine, leaving a pink oil smeared around the top of her glass. We both started to laugh, pointing out all the Roman men that looked totally self-absorbed, dressed in tight pants and wearing cologne, they posed against walls, or scooters, they batted their eyes, they were pretty and they knew it.

Mom and I were both aware that our laughter rose above the crowd and attracted some attention.

"Do you feel like people are looking at us? I feel like they can tell we are having a fun time." I was aware of the looks we were getting from a table full of men nearby. "Yeah, I do." Mom looked pleased and rolled her eyes back like she was caught in a fantasy.

"Reign and I used to be like that, one time we went to Tahiti, and people would just stare at us. One of the native women told me that she'd never met a woman like me before. I came to find out that each morning some of the people that worked at the place we were staying would come and rake the leaves just so they could hear us making love. I wonder if that's what that woman meant, that we were loud, or I wonder if she had just observed our chemistry."

"Wasn't that the trip that he told you he was in love with another woman?"

"Yes, I couldn't believe it. He flattered me a lot, but then sometimes he would say things that hurt my feelings." She dipped her wine glass to the side and twirled the bottom in a circle on the table. "He'd look at other women obviously checking them out when he was with me. Sometimes he would make comments about my appearance, saying my breasts were saggy, or telling me that my hands were old-looking for my age. We had such an intensity together, but eventually it got to be abusive." She looked off at the sky for a moment, then shifted her attention to appetizers that were being served.

***

Back in our room, I lay in the dark, my legs aching and my mind buzzing. I was wired. The heat pressed on me like an unyielding lover and the fan blew cool air across the sheet tickling my skin and cooling me just enough to leave me wanting more, I was dancing in a sensual manage a trois of an Italian summer night. The day had been long and stimulating and my senses were still on overload. All I could do was feel the energy pulsing through my body, not sure where to go or how to evaporate. The fan's breaths were soothing, easing my ignited flame that made it impossible to sleep. I was no longer anxious about sleep like the night I arrived, but I felt a nervous sentiment the same a virgin might feel, wondrous of the unknown but melancholy for what would be left behind. There was so much to see in Italy, so much I had never seen before, and though I wanted more, another part of me was home sick.

There was so much uncertainty in me.

The movement through Italy stirred a part of my soul that had been sleeping. I started to imagine the thousands of love affairs that took place in our tiny room. How many lovers made love, or fought, or turned a cold shoulder, how many slept alone? If the room could tell you what it knew, it would say, "All of us fall in love, everyone gets hurt, and nothing lasts forever," but that room watched without attachment at the turning of the pages of each visitor's life. That room watched without judgement, at how, life and death are always dancing. That room had a deeper soul than any human being I had ever met and it scared me.

I tucked my hand onto the warm mound of hair between my thighs, aroused by the brush of cool wind ruffling my sheet, and I drifted into dreams.

{5} - NAPOLI, ITALY

"WHEN THE MOON HITS YOUR EYE LIKE A BIG PIZZA PIE...SCUZA ME, BUT YOU SEE, BACK IN OL' NAPOLI, THAT'S AMORE," DEAN MARTIN

"Banco di Napoli" it read on the top of the rock building.

"There it is!" We had walked in circles, and finally in front of us stood a large stone building with two intimidating uniformed men standing guard outside. Even the building was intimidating. A thick bullet proof door with greenish blue glass was used to protect the bank people from the busy street.

Mom walked up to the door and stopped abruptly, it didn't open, and there wasn't any way to push or pull it. Above the door was a red flashing dot, and beside the door there was a button. I reached out and pushed the button and the light above us turned green, the door slid open and mom entered, (there was only enough room for one person). I pushed the button on the door next to mom's and stepped into a tubular encasement that shut around me; I was only in the tube for a moment then the other side opened and I entered into the bank. Mom and I joined each other again, snickering at the cheap entertainment.

We found two chairs next to each other and sat down. I quickly realized we needed to choose a number in order to be served, so I pushed the little button on the machine that spit out my number, then sat back down. People entered in and out for a while and I watched the business of the huge city bank acting out their daily duties and taking it all very seriously. I looked at the analog clock ticking away above the security door, then my eye fell upon an old lady, moving slowly out of the entrance compartment. She took deliberate steps and held a cane to help make her way to the seat right next to me, where she plopped down like a water balloon into the chair and let out a deflating sigh.

She pointed to her shoes, "Ohhh, i miei piedi sono doloranti, le mie scarpe sono vecchie e irritabili come me". I was surprised that my translation of what she was saying came fairly easy. Mom nudged me and asked what she said.

"I think it was something like, 'my feet are aching, my shoes, my shoes, they are old and cranky like me'". Mom held back a loud toot of laughter, and looked around to scope out the old lady. She wore a plated skirt and her hips belled out under a short torso and a heavy set of breasts. She wore a buttoned blouse underneath a wooly brown blazer, with a silk scarf wrapped three times around her neck and a fedora hat.

"Queste scarpe, queste scarpe" she bent over, holding her cane with her veiny withered hand to balance herself. She looked over at me speaking Italian, hoping for a sympathetic response, but as well as I understood her, I was not nearly as good at speaking Italian as I was at understanding it.

"Devo comprare un nuovo paio, queste scarpe hanno fatto il loro corso", she looked abruptly over at the banker's little window and sent an irritated and impatient glance their way. Mom leaned over again and asked what she was saying now.

"Um, something about a new pair of shoes? And I don't know much after that.

"Oh, that's what I thought, that she was talking about her shoes," mom said, entertained by the old lady as much as I was.

"Bene, sarebbe bello per qualcuno aiutare una vecchia signora, aiutare una vecchia signora ad andare per prima, potrei morire prima di arrivarci. Eccomi con un pezzetto di carta e un numero molto piccolo su di esso, in attesa e in attesa, quando guardi questi piedi, guarda queste scarpe, che sono a brandelli, che stanno cadendo a pezzi. E devo aspettare, devo aspettare..

The lady kept looking at me talking and talking. I tried my best to understand what she said. She stopped talking for a moment as I smiled at her ranting in a language I could scarcely understand. I just kept nodding making facial expressions so that she knew I cared.

"What is she saying now?" Mom whispered to me.

"She's talking about her shoes I think. She wants a new pair...and she doesn't like waiting." I put together the few words I understood and figured the rest out from her body language.

"She keeps pointing at her feet," mom noted. I looked over at her then back again at my mom.

She stopped talking to me and stared at the board with the next number up. I continued to smile and nod and look around at all the slightly agitated crowd.

One man, covered in plaster and paint, held his hat with a grim expression, other people stood frozen in their place, a few were twitching, one man paced back and forth on his cell phone talking loudly and seemingly business like. A woman at the teller's window came away toward me and handed me a small piece of paper, it was the number 35, I had number 42; she gave me a short cut. I glanced at the number in the old lady's wrinkled hands that sat clutching her number in her lap. 56.

Just then, my number was called, the board changed, I was up, I didn't want to miss my chance I had been sitting for 20 minutes already. I approached the counter and shuffled through my fanny pack to find my passport and wad of American dollars.

"I would like to exchange these per favor". The teller, took the items placed out and immediately started stamping paper and writing notes, shuffling money in and out of boxes. Finally, she looked at me and counted in broken English the amount in Euro that I got to receive in exchange for $500 dollar notes.

"Grazie," the teller looked at me and gave a brief and faint smile, standing still, waiting for me to move away to help the next patron.

I folded the money into my fanny pack and tucked it down under my clothes. The old lady still sat with her umbrella and cane, now she spoke to another woman who had taken my seat, but the new lady ignored her, she stared into space as if the old lady was crazy. Maybe she was crazy, but I wouldn't know, she was a part of a different culture, I barely spoke her language.

I walked over to the chatty old lady and handed

her my number. She looked it over, and looked at me, "Grazie, Grazie" she said. I smiled.

"Prego," I replied, happy to make her day. The woman next to her shifted her stony expression to give me a befuddled look, a look of wonder at why I had chosen the crazy old lady to give my number to and not her.

Mom and I exited the bank, we had to go back through the security doors, first through one bullet proof glass door into a small room, then into another encasement and finally outside, into the busy city where we were ready to shop Naples.

It took us until well past noon to do our banking, and by the time we made it to the Galleria Umberto, I was beginning to get hungry.

"Do you want to eat somewhere around here?" mom asked.

"I don't know, all I see are cafes. I want to eat. A meal. Something that is going to fill me up. I don't want just a pastry or a coffee." I stood looking around at the scene inside the magnificent structure of glass and iron that curved up high above us. There were shops all over with the words, Prada, Fendi, and Saldi in the windows.

I had a desire to find Ahron a money clip. I couldn't think of anything that he could possibly use from Italy other than that.

"I want to check out a couple of shops really quick to see if I can find what I am looking for. Then, let's go and find a real restaurant."

As I was about to go search for money clips, a woman holding a baby in one arm came kneeling to my mom's feet and began to pat her shoes. She didn't say anything, but looked right into her face. Mom's hands fell at her sides in a gesture that I only saw when she was comforting someone. It was a sign of vulnerability and surrender for her. I could tell she felt something deeply about this woman. Maybe she remembered what it was like for her when she had a baby. At that moment the two women connected, far beyond my understanding, but I saw it happen. My mother reached in her purse and pulled out some Euros, then handed them to the woman with the baby. The woman looked gratefully into my mom's eyes. Mom looked tearful. The woman got up and moved on to another stranger.

I made another attempt to go into a store, but a storekeeper came out and poked a cane at a homeless dog that was lying across the front of the doorway. All around us were dogs, laying on the cold stone of the ground, there were a dozen of them that migrated inside from the sweltering heat, and they waited for scraps of pastry to fall so they could claim them.

I took a long breath, and felt my tummy grumble.

"Maybe we should try this later, I am so hungry, let's just go get some food now". I knew mom wouldn't argue, her irritability was worse than mine when it came to being hungry. I had seen her many times get snappy when dinner wasn't done by six. If she had to wait at all, her body would start to sag, her eyes looked sorrowful, and before long she would start opening the refrigerator door, or ask my dad every minute when the meat would be done, or if anybody minded if she ate the salad first.

We walked away from Galleria Umberto searching for someplace to eat. Most restaurants we found were not opening until four, and it was almost two. By the time we reached the bay front, I was biting on my necklace, threatening to eat it if we didn't find something soon. I wished I could just go back to the hotel and eat the buffalo mozzarella with basil and tomato I had eaten the first night we arrived. A part of me wished I could have stayed at the hotel all day just reading my copy of Don Quixote. I was tired of trying to keep up. It seemed that we had not stopped since we landed in Italy. We finally found a restaurant, and by the time we made it back to the trolley, my feet were swollen and I was exhausted.

{6} - A CHANCE MEETING

The Sea water was already warm from the previous day's heat when the sun peaked its glowing face up to look out over the Mediterranean. In a cavern on a small Island, a streak of cerulean blue touched the calm pool within the cave and stretched out upon the walls, filling the cave with bright blue light. The glowing grotto soaked in the morning.

I awoke in our cool hotel room, unsure of the time, the room was still black as the night. The windows were covered with mechanical blinds that sealed all the light out. I went to the wall and pushed a button, which lifted the blinds like a garage door.

Sun beamed into our room, the day already looked hot. Outside the window hung rows and rows of clean laundry stretched between our hotel and an apartment across the way. The colorful laundry filled the whole corridor. In the windows across from mine, women were hanging laundry, talking to their children, cooking on the stove; life was happening right in front of me, and just a minute before I was in total darkness.

I perked up with the light that flooded our room, it was the day we were going to take the ferry from Naples to Capri to explore the Blue Grotto and go see the cave where the walls were lit in a magnificent blue. From the moment I saw the pictures of the Grotto online, it became the one thing that I wanted to see when we went to Italy. I was certain that it held some mysterious treasure, and I couldn't wait to have some of the magic revealed to me.

Mom and I sifted through our luggage and picked out comfortable walking clothes. I chose a sleeveless linen shirt, with rainbow stripes that darted into a v down the center. On the bottom I wore my favorite brown J crew skirt that went just past my knees, it had an elastic top with two layers of thin cotton that hung loose around me.

Mom put on a classy black tank top with lace and a fitted black cotton skirt that went just above her knees.

We packed up our map and travel book, along with a couple of extra water bottles, and headed out to the trolley that took us down the steep hill into the city. We scooted in and squeezed our way through to find that there were two seats empty for us. Right as we sat down the trolley began its descent. It reminded me of the rides in Disneyland. They both had the same damp smells and cool tunnels. It was attached to a long cable, and click clacked into the dark center of the tunnel; it wasn't long before the light from the bottom entrance filled up the tunnel again.

Mom bought an iced tea for both of us and we set off in what we guessed was the right direction. We walked enthusiastically for some time, noticing little quirky things, like a basket covered in burlap full of live snails for sale sitting out in front of a little market. The air was rich with the scent of fish and sea.

We made up a game to see how many stores were closed in the middle of the day. Many of them opened between 7 a.m. and 9 a.m., then shut midday around noon or two, then reopened again in the late afternoon. Others were closed for the rest of the day, and wouldn't open again until the next day. Some of the stores were shut already, we had slept in till well past ten. If we lived there and slept in everyday, we would miss a lot.

Our game came to an end when we entered a part of town that seemed abandoned. We were walking aimlessly. The initial thrill of new things started waning and I began to get the impression that we were lost.

Where was the ferry that took us to Capri? I was getting anxious to get to the Grotta Azurra. The heat was close to unbearable, and I started wondering to myself why I was even in Italy with my mom. Our connection was hardly different than our relating back home; shopping, movies, gossip, analyzing the injustice of love and relationships. Italy had some beautiful things, but I thought I would feel something more, and I couldn't help but miss Ahron, he seemed so far away.

I stopped for a moment to pull out the map of Naples then looked around to see the name of the street we were on. There wasn't anybody around to ask for help. It seemed that we had wandered into a deserted part of town. Unlike Rome, we didn't have a walking map showing us each turn to take to get where we wanted to go, so we wound through the streets, working our way to the sea, where we hoped to find the ferry that would take us to the Island of Capri. I noticed a high stone arch up ahead on the right and we walked toward it to see if it might give us a clue about where we were.

"Wrenna, I think this is the name of the hotel we wanted to stay at, remember I tried to call a bunch of times, but I could never get through to make a reservation." Mom pointed to the name etched into the stone archway above us: Il Mare Fontane. We peered curiously through into the courtyard, which turned out to be a circular driveway, where guests could be delivered by car or taxi.

In the middle of the round drive was a Fountain all dried up and spotted with moss. We climbed the stairs that led to the hotel doors. At the top I tugged at the door. It opened. I looked back at my mom checking to see if she approved of me exploring, and she was already moving her head in to see.

The lobby was empty, musty, and dark, and smelled like a dungeon. Mom and I lingered for a moment waiting to see if there was any kind of clue as to why the hotel had shut down.

"Should we go in and check it out?" mom asked hesitating.

"Uhh," I gazed around the totally empty hotel. "I think we should go." I had a sudden urge to turn and leave, I did not want to have a run in with the Godfather and his minions. We hurried out of the hotel that at one time might have been magical but now seemed haunted and untrustworthy. Both of us walked with our eyes focused on getting through the archway. I was relieved to get back out on the street.

Our eyes readjusted to the light and we started up a short hill in the direction toward what we figured was the ocean. At the top of the hill we stopped short, the horizon spread out around us, the hot noon sun beamed across the water. I had to shade my eyes from the sunlight above. To our left, a sidewalk wound down to the seaside and into the city. We started down the hill and suddenly, out of nowhere a man was walking a few feet in front of us. After a moment he turned around.

"Hello!" said the man in a cheerful voice. He tilted slightly, suspended by whimsy, floating on his toes toward us. His grin was alight with joy and wonder, he smiled at me with sparkling blue eyes. I laughed inside, giddy and curious. Smiling at him, I flirtatiously asked,

"Did you say hello?" I had not heard English spoken for days, at least not in this friendly manner; was this an ally? Was this someone who could show us something about what I was supposed to be experiencing in Italy?

"Yhess, I say hello". His voice was gravelly and his eyes spoke playfully, so much was said through his deep blue eyes. It was as if I had met him before, already I felt I knew him, and I was smitten.

"Oh, how refreshing to hear English," I commented, then I became aware of my naïveté. Is this guy authentic, or is he just trying to schmooze two American women in order to steal something or lure us in to some kind of vulnerable trap? Is this guy a sexual predator? I felt panic in my stomach, and then took a breath.

"What is your name?" I began acting cool, so that he wouldn't sense that I was hesitant to trust him.

"I am Pietro." He answered as the three of us

walked side by side down the sidewalk. I was drawn through the sound of his voice into his eyes where I found sincerity and longing and began to let down my guard, my intuition told me that I could trust that this guy had good enough intentions. I looked over at my mom though just to make sure she was feeling the same thing. She walked alongside me quietly but I could tell she was intrigued.

"Di dove se?" I asked where he lived in Italian. He guffawed and gestured with his hand in amusement.

"Yhoo speek Eetaliaan!"

"Si, un po'", I held my fingers out to show him I only knew 'a little'.

"Di Dove se?"

"Ah! I am of dis place, here een Napoli. I am ouwt whakking forrh mi holeeday. I see yhoo and I heer Amereecan accent and I say Hallo." We all walked down the sidewalk along a tall cement wall that created a shade of relief.

"How do you know English?" I asked Pietro.

"I work een Lowndon for-uh tree yheers, I have learn speak Eengleesh so fast.
Ahnd, what yhou here for, fohr holeeday?"

"My mom and I have been planning this trip for five years. She came to Italy once and then wanted to bring me back to see what it is like."

"So, you come here to Napoli? I don't see many Amereecan here. They go to Rome, no?"

"Yeah, I know. We were already in Rome first, but we thought it would be fun to experience the difference in the food and the culture as we go more south."

"Ah, dis is good idea."

"Right now we are on our way to see the Grotta

Azzurra. Have you been there?" I asked him, thinking he might know where to find the dock with the ferry.

"Ah, yhes, is okay. Is place for tourist, I go there wit my friends many tiame."

"Oh really? Do you know where the ferry is? We tried to find it yesterday but we had no luck."

"Ah si, is this way, down here. Yhoo see Castol del'ovo? Es dee castol a sorcerer, he uh, put un ovo een dis castol?" Pietro inflected a question as if asking if we understood him. "He say, dis castol wheel foll into the sea eef dis ovo, how do you say een eenglish?" he paused his story and looked questioningly at us.

"Ovo," I said, thinking of the translation for ovo in English, "is that an egg?".

"Ah si, egg. Eef dis egg break, the castel wheel foll".

We walked silently for a moment taking in his story and looking out at the bay to our right. The neighborhood was quiet and it seemed for a moment that we were alone in the city, just the three of us. The Bay had so many stories to offer the imagination. It brought images of Knights and Pirates, Vikings and Princesses, War and Lost Love. Naples had so much history living in the stones of the structures.

Pietro finished his explanation of the egg castle as we rounded a corner that took us up close to the castle he spoke of. It was oval shaped and long, and much less ornate than the castles of Great Britain. It filled its own small peninsula, darting out into the sea, where waves crashed upon the foundation walls. Of course the castle did not harbor inhabitants anymore, in fact it seemed totally deserted, aside from the occasional tourist walking up through the un-gated corridors.

We could traverse the courtyards and outside paths to get to see the view from the top, but all the metal doors into the castle were heavy and locked.

I imagined myself living in a castle like that one. I had always been in love with castles, especially the ones that hang over cliffs with mist rising like dragons breath out of deep canyons. Mom and I followed Pietro around the wide curve to the top courtyard of the castle. I crossed the open court and looked over the edge. Waves were lashing at the stone far below. I thought of Ahron, wishing he was there with me.

"I'm doing it, I'm growing up," I thought. "I'll come back a woman with experience and Ahron will see that I'm not just a young pizza girl anymore, making pizzas and living with my parents". I sighed and turned to see where mom had gone. For a moment I forgot about the stranger we picked up. There he was, chatting it up with my mom. She was telling him about her ancestors living in Trieste, on the border of Northern Italy and about her Grandparents coming through Ellis Island as many other immigrants did.

"I came to Italy when I was in my mid-thirties with my dad, we traveled for a month together," my mother explained to him as the wind gusted through the top courtyard of the castle.

"What?!" Pietro asked loudly over the wind. "I-came-to-Italy-when-I-was-in-my   mid-thirties-with-my-dad," my mother slowed down her speech and articulated loudly so that Pietro could understand what she said.

"What?!" Pietro still couldn't understand her over the wind, so we started to walk back down in to the corridor and mom repeated herself again.

"...we-went-to-Slovenia-and-Italy-together".

"Yhou and yhour fadther, you go on holee-day?" Pietro finally heard her.

"Yes".

"Si? Yhou leefe yhour cheeldren ahnd yhour husbhand for sahm time?

"Yes".

"Yhour husbhand no care, he no mind yhou leeve? He no mind yhou go adther cuontree, weerth many good-looking men?" Pietro looked surprised.

"No, he didn't mind," mom bit her lip as she confidently announced her free ability as a woman to do as she pleased.

"Een Eetalee, dee wife stay home, she go, thee husbhand not know how to cook, he not know how to clean, he is in trobul no?" I laughed at Pietro's portrayal of Italian men and their dependence upon women to keep them fed and clean and in order. I thought about my dad during the time when mom had gone on her long trip with my grandpa. Dad had done his best, certainly we ate plenty of frozen pot pies, T.V. dinners, and other convenient mom's gone kinds of snacks. Our laundry piled up and it wasn't until the day before mom came home that dad spent a day cleaning all of it, I was actually crying because I didn't have any room left in my dresser for the clothes.

"I know some men in America that can't live without their wives cooking and doing everything for them all the time," she subtly rolled her eyes to herself thinking of some of my dad's friends. "I can't do that, I have to be free to do what I want to do."

I had heard my mother say this before whenever

she talked about her affair with Reign. Anytime I asked her what dad thought about her having another lover, she'd say, "well, I am going to do what I am going to do and that's it. I got so tired of just being home all the time, I didn't have a life of my own. I was entertaining all the time! It was the pits. Some of it was fun, we traveled a lot and did fun things with you and the boys, and Carver and I had fun going to the city and eating out. Carver is romantic, and cares about me, but when we had kids I just never got enough sleep, and Carver was out partying a lot in the beginning with business partners. He'd come home drunk or he'd be studying all the time and we didn't have any money. I finally just burned out".

"What did dad think when he found out about your affair?"

"Well, he was not happy. We fought about it all night long, but that didn't stop me from seeing Reign, and dad knew it. I was invested in both of them and it wasn't something I just wanted to end abruptly on either end. I finally told him that I couldn't be with one man, if he wanted to be with me, he had to accept that I wanted to have other relationships. I didn't want to be limited to love just one person. I loved them both in different ways, they both served different things in me".

I looked over at my mom, a woman who held so many mysteries, and watched the sea wind blow through her hair as she chatted away with a man we hardly knew. There was something about her I never realized before, a part of her that I never knew existed. For a moment she wasn't my mom, she was just this woman finding herself; she was just this woman writing her own story.

Laura Marie Parker

{7} - RED MARTINI'S AND THE ORIGINAL PIZZA

At the base of the Castel dell'ovo was the Santa Lucia port, a harbor full of small fishing boats and a little bar with tables outside, to sit and enjoy the gentle sea breeze and watch fisherman working and tinkering with gear.

The midday sun beat down on us. I looked out at the sea wondering where the Grotto was out there and when I would get there, our new guide seemed more interested in showing us the history of his hometown. Instead of walking further, the heat drug us into a decision to stop and have a drink.

A barmaid came and served us menus and little bowls of olives and salty nuts. Her skin was darkened by the sun, and her long hair was tied up into a wild pony tail. She quickly looked Pietro up and down raising an eyebrow at him. He spoke to her in Italian. I could make out a few words like Americana, aqua minerale gassata, vacanza; I even thought I heard the word cugina, which means cousin. She looked at

Pietro skeptically, then smiled in amusement at us and went to tend to other patrons.

"Does this say Red Martini? *Martini Rosso*. What is that? Have you ever had that before Pietro?" I pointed at the words on the menu.

"No. We try dis?" Pietro asked.

"Si. Let's try it." I said decidedly.

"What is it you're looking at?" my mother leaned over to glance at the menu, lifting her sunglasses up so that she could read the print.

"This," I showed her, "It's called a Red Martini, do you know what that is?"

"No. It sounds good though, I want to try it." All three of us ordered the Red Martini and a couple of appetizers to share.

During the wait for our drinks I observed the waiters across the dock at a fancy restaurant get ready for their night. I took in the smells of cooking food and wafts of fish in the sea breeze. It was quiet for once, we caught the city in an in between moment.

I swirled the water in my glass watching the bubbles release off the side and float to the top. Above me, a seagull called. Looking up I saw the large brown rock of Castel dell'ovo, I had just been at the top looking down at all the movement, and now I was looking up at the still, cloudless ocean sky. I wanted to cry. I did not know why I was sitting here with this man we didn't know. Mom seemed so happy to be sharing her heritage with him, she indulged stories of her father and his struggles and triumphs of moving to the U.S., going to school for his PHD and becoming a doctor.

Pietro listened, and I could see him occasionally look at me, though he was attractive, a restless feeling settled into me, I didn't want to have to entertain him. I hoped that he would have somewhere to be after our drinks, so that mom and I could go find the ferry to the Blue Grotto. Also, I still wanted to go back to the shopping center we'd been to the day before to find a money clip for Ahron.

With the thought of Ahron I was comforted, in spite of my culture shock and the chaos that danced around me, at least I had Ahron. I daydreamed about my return from Italy and how I would drive to Ahron's little po-dunk town and surprise him. I thought about him smiling and seeing a new woman in me, a world traveler, a woman who had traveled farther than him, I would be so mysterious, he'd want to marry me. "Will you marry me? Will you marry me?" I just kept hearing those words in my mind, wishing and hopeful that Ahron would be ready for me when I got home.

Our barmaid roused me out of my dreaming, setting down three glasses full of dull crimson liquid and round ice cubes that brightened the drink. I took a sip. It was refreshing, the sweetness was not sugary, instead it had a smoothness with hints of Bing cherry and citrus; it was thick and light at the same time. Yum. I was thirsty and drank it quickly.

I forgot about my day dream of Ahron all together and became present and intoxicated anew with the air and the breeze, with the vibration of taxis and the stern nature of rough fisherman, the aroma of fish and fruit, salt and rust.

The castle rock softened in the hot sun, like a stiff and proper king, who finally takes his wine and fish feast in the private royal courtyard, thickset, browned, naked, hefty, unburdened for brief moments, but still so important even in a time of dormancy.

And there in the shade of the castle's wall, Pietro courted like a Prince in a dream of so many women, yet, he also danced a dervish, whimsy dance of a Jester in Court foolishly prancing without forethought of the end.

I traced the lines of him with my eyes. He wasn't quite pretty or rugged, but something in between. His arms and chest were tanned and strong, and his soul could not hide, just as the musk of a Manzanita bush in bloom cannot mask its scent. I enjoyed the way he looked at me, like he knew something, maybe about a dream he once had of me.

"Maybe I could love this man", I thought dreamily as I looked at his soft eyes beaming with childlike innocence. Our eyes met and we held each other's gaze intensely for a moment. Again, I felt that I knew him already somehow, he was so familiar.

"Oh, Rhaina," he sighed.

My mother silently observed, trying to make herself invisible, but out of the corner of my eye I was aware of her watching.

I directed my gaze to the bay, where a fisherman was tidying his boat, putting ropes and nets away.

On second thought, I didn't want to get involved with Pietro. There was something about him that was too sure of himself. I felt a neediness in him that made me want more space. I wanted to leave him there all of a sudden, with his empty martini glass. I wanted to tell him it was nice to meet him, and that I was ready to continue on the way with only my mom, but I didn't. My mother looked so pleased, she seemed so intrigued,

I kept my mouth shut. I figured I'd give her this little thrill then we'd get back to our trip, just the two of us.

***

As the bay breeze picked up mid-afternoon, it gently pushed the three of us away from the water and toward the city. Pietro wanted us to see a Pizzeria he claimed was the oldest in the world, "The place where pizza began," he told us.

We walked a couple of blocks up from the perimeter of the bay for a bit. I told Pietro about the man we saw the first day in Naples, who stepped out of his car in a Gold suit, "Do you think he might have been connected with the mafia?" I asked.

"Ah, si, Probolee. Whhat he do?"

"We were sitting at a table waiting for our food, and a town car pulled up. Two bigger guys got out dressed in nice suits, then a guy in a gold suit got out and they went into the restaurant all together. When they came out the guy in the gold suit was carrying a bag that almost seemed like a towel tied up with a bundle in it, it was about the size of a soccar ball."

"You tink it monee? It was proboblee mafioso. They jhus thake and thake tings frome peepole." Pietro nodded. Thee uh, uh mafioso is much trubbal no? They haf much powhere heer, like a whaat you call in America?"

"A gang?" my mother filled in.

"A gang. What iz dis gang you say?" He looked questioningly at my mother.

"A gang is a group of people that are powerful together. Sometimes they get violent." mom answered simply.

"Oh, dis iz like mafioso. I tell you about timme I haf friend heer in Napoli, he get trubbal wit this Mafioso, they no like heem, they...how yhou say?" he paused holding out his hand as if reaching for the word.

"Oh um," my mother assisted, "oh um, like threaten?"

"Waht?"

"Threaten?"

"Waht?"

"Threaten. Um, let's see...," my mother slowed her pace and rolled her eyeballs upward as if searching her brain for the right words. "Threaten is when someone tells you they are going to do something to you if you don't do what they want".

"Jhess, waht dis word yhou say?"

"ThreaTen," my mother answered enunciating the word for him.

"Treatan. Si, dis Mafioso treatan my friend, he gonn haf trubble? Then they haf angry at me? I worry. No? They say to me they angry, they tell me, treatan me to uhgh, break my legs. I am scary no? I go, I tell my frend, I mast go naw to Lowndon, I no wan trubble wit Mafioso. So. I go. I haf to pack. Pack. Dis right no? To pack?" he asked about the correctness of his word use.

"Si, to pack," I assured him.

"I haf paak my tings so fast, I tell my mama' I muss go naw, my frend does not haf money for somesing, ahnd Mafioso treatan me and my frend. He come affter me I say sahm tings to dis Mafioso ahnd I do not know he is mafia ahnd he say I mhast go or he keehl me, no?"

"I am so scary, he whas no happy, my mama' was no happy, baht I muss go, so I go to Lowndon. I buy ticket, I go trauvle, I get wherk. I am wherking, wherking ahnd I make enough monie to send famalie in Eetalee e I find dis guy and I giv him monie. Ahnd he say he no khill me, so I caam back. I make mach morr monie een Lowndon. I save saam monie and I caam back to my home. In Lowndon I live for almhost tree yhears, I work in the city wit stones".

"With Stones?" my mother gave him an inquisitive look.

"I lay them into the grawnd"

"Like a brick layer? My grandfather did that, he was a mason". I could tell my mom was fascinated by Pietro's character.

Pietro and my mother walked ahead of me talking. Mom asked more questions about the kind of work Pietro did, and told him about her Grandfather's masonry work. It seemed from where I walked behind them that every other word was 'what?' My mind was spinning. I stared jealously at Pietro, I felt so alone trudging behind them in the heat of the city. "Why was my mother so interested in this guy?" I wondered.

I tried to speak some Italian with Pietro, but he kept trying to teach me more words, as if he were committed to having me learn the entire language. I had not learned the language to know it forever, I learned it to get credit in school, and to know some when I came to travel so we wouldn't be entirely lost, but like most other things in my life, I was not committed to learning it well, I had other things I was trying to conquer, like marrying Ahron.

Pietro finally turned to me, "We are caaming to dis pizzeria, iz whare pizza beghin. You haf Pizza?"

I didn't want to tell him how much I hated pizza

after working for five years in a pizza place. I had spent the last couple of those years slapping pepperoni slices onto mountains of cheese and thinking to myself that I would show those bosses of mine when I went to Europe and became a world traveler, I would grow up right out of that pizza place and never look back.

I didn't tell Pietro about that because it would take too much energy to try to translate my thoughts between our languages. Instead I just surrendered and said, "I have Pizza".

I looked up and around at the street we were walking on. We were on a hill that gradually climbed through the city to an area that was a bit like a Piazza in Rome. Branches spread out, like standing on the trunk of a tree as a squirrel, looking at the many directions. Where I was from, most of the streets were on a grid, they might not be perfectly straight, but they didn't take the form of life on a tree.

On one branch, a man stood on scaffolding dressed in a white paint suit handpainting the window trim on a five story apartment building. Maybe he was only responsible for his section, but he was the only one, and it seemed like he had only painted a few windows so far. The rest of the building was mottled with patches of bare stone where the paint had chipped away.

It was amazing how time was slower in Italy. In the city in America, people just hire a crew to come and power-blast a building with paint, and then they move on to the next thing, without even having really experienced the first thing. From where I stood, the painter seemed to be interacting with the building, like it had a spirit.   The tree branches of this part of Napoli were quieter up and away from the bay and the afternoon was suddenly peaceful. We split off to the left down one of the branches, where the street was much narrower, walking a little way down the cobbled road to find a sign hanging above us, sticking out of the wall on the stone building. The door was locked and the window where we would have ordered was also shut and locked.

"AAohh, it is close." Pietro announced. We stood and looked at it for a moment. I wasn't convinced that this really was the oldest pizza place in the world, but Pietro insisted.

"Are you sure this is the first pizza place ever? How can you know that?" I asked skeptically.

"It jhus is. I know. Pizza ees eetalian, ahnd dis is the place where it was first made." He talked very matter-of-factly, almost lecturing me, like a teacher who was not open to what the student might know. I started to pipe in my thought that something like pizza couldn't just BE invented at one little place, but I held my breath, knowing that it would take an hour to argue about one little thing.

I felt tired and hungry, and I wanted to go back to our hotel. I was relieved when mom said she was ready too, but I had mixed feelings when she asked Pietro to help us find our way back. I worried that he would know where we were staying and he might just stalk us and then want to spend the whole next day with us again. On the other hand, I had no idea where we were and didn't have the energy to be the guide, or to get lost again. So, I followed the two of them up through the winding streets. I heard parts of the conversation be-tween Pietro and my mother, Pietro would say something about the history of Naples, my mother would talk about her heritage, and much of the conversation was filled with one or the other saying, "WHAT?"

I finally tuned them out and gazed into the store windows or studied the cobblestones. The cobbled roads filled the whole city. I wondered about when the first cobble was placed, and if some roads were left as dusty alleys for a long time until the city grew larger. I had no doubt that someone like Pietro had been down on their knees, placing each one in the ground. No machine could have done such work. Machines do things that are cut and straight and linear and flat, hands make things unique, humans make things that have soul and connection and chaotic beauty. That was what it felt like in Napoli, like it had a kind of chaotic beauty. It showed itself with the veil ripped off the bedchamber of two lovers, the mystery just revealed itself in its raw state, there was no need to give it makeup or pretty silk clothing like Rome; this place said it with an honest tongue.

"You are beuootiful," Pietro said. He rode the trolley up the hill with us, all the way to the door of the hotel. Now he stood looking at me, standing so close. I felt embarrassed. I was afraid that the hotel staff were going to see me and know that we had been had by some con artist. I was still waiting for Pietro to reveal his big secret, that he had something to sell me, that he really was mafia, or most likely, that he was just a player, who seduced American women with his accent and his charisma, promising them the chance to be swept away from their banal existence into a world of magic and excitement. But, there was something very sincere, that came from the core of Pietro, it was something that even a con artist couldn't emulate, beyond charisma. Pietro was a Fool, and I liked that part about him. He had so much enthusiasm for discovery that I had to give him credit for having an ounce of authenticity in him. It was that enthusiasm that both my mom and I appreciated, because culturally it was hard to find in America. None-the-less, I was happy to say goodbye to Pietro, because his enthusiasm would sometimes shift into neediness. The second he crossed that line, I was turned off.

I stood outside the hotel pleased that I was beautiful to him. Pietro gave us kisses on the cheeks, then looked at me, "Rhaina," he stood unmoving, waiting for something...an invitation? Then without any thread to cling to, I switched off my emotions and let him go.

Laura Marie Parker

{8} - AIRPORT STRIKE

I would have sat staring at the screen, waiting for flight 112 to have a new scheduled time, I would have waited for the word canceled to disappear.

Lines of travelers made their way to the ticket attendants, some held their carryon bags trying to find out where the luggage that they already checked had gone. Sitting in the middle of the perturbed foreign tourists, I felt a twinge of anxiety winding up from my center into my mind, the kind you feel when you're lost and you don't have the faintest idea of how to get back. My mind was frozen. It was as if Fate canceled the part of my life that was planned and threw me into the dark alley where it was my turn to choose my own destiny.

We were stuck in a foreign city, I couldn't remember my Italian at all or think of any way out.

Flight 112 didn't seem to be changing status, so I joined the throngs of confused travelers at the back of the line—I would have sat there as long as I could, but then my mother said,

"Let's call Pietro, he offered to take us there".

"I don't know mom, I think the strike will be over soon, I mean by the time we get a hold of him, and he drives us down, the flight will be open".

"I'm not so sure Wrenna, this could go on for days." I slumped down in my chair. Why did it feel like I had to make the decision? She knew how I felt about Pietro. I stewed over the thought of him, how persistent he was. He had found the one secret passage way into our lives, and my mom was going to let him use it.

***

He didn't even know our last names, but somehow he had said the right thing to the concierge when he called and was transferred to our room number. I couldn't believe it when I picked up the phone to hear his voice on the other line.

"Ciao Rhaina, you good? Dis Pietro." My heart started beating and I was annoyed that he had taken it upon himself to call. I didn't tell him to call or keep in touch, I expected that I had seen the last of him.

"Ciao, umm, si, bene." I sat on my bed and looked over at the other bed where my mom sat whispering, "who is it?" I cupped my hand over the receiver, and responded childishly, "its Pietro mom". Her eyes lit in surprise. "Here, you talk to him." Without saying anything more to Pietro I handed the phone to my mom. After a minute of talking she reached for my Don Quixote book and the pen I used for my journal, then jotted something down on the inside cover of the book. She then said thank you to Pietro and hung up the phone.

"What was that all about? How did he even get our room number?"

"Oh, well, he told the concierge our first names, and said that he was calling to tell us that the airport is going on strike tomorrow, which is true. I think he figured that Pietro was our friend. Maybe things are different in Italy with hotel privacy."

"Well that doesn't make me feel very safe." I said

sarcastically.

"Anyway, he said that in the case that our flight gets cancelled, he would be happy to take us."

"Oh." I didn't know what to say, I hoped that everything would go well, and our flight would go as planned. I hoped.

I was exhausted and fell immediately to sleep, putting the phone call out of my head, and happy that the next day we would be on the move to a quieter country setting where I wouldn't have to walk miles and miles through the city.

***

My mother was frantic in the airport, thinking we might have to stay overnight. It was one of those things; choose door one or two and either one will determine the rest of your life. Everything is like that in a sense, but some things set you on a path which you can never turn around or change your mind; once the decision is made, it's made.

"Okay, let's call him."

I tried the complicated telephones with my credit card, but I couldn't get any of them to work. With each pay phone I failed to understand how to make it work and my mom's panic level rose. Her panic seeped into me like the energy of a battery being touched to my tongue; it was acidic and electric. After I tried the last phone without success, I was relieved for a moment thinking we were back to square one, waiting for the strike to be over. But then, mom pointed out a girl a few years younger than I, walking with her mother and carrying a cell phone. I walked over to where she stood. I tried at first to sign and talk in English to get my idea across, but neither of them spoke a word of English, so I pulled out the most broken Italian I knew, and finally her mother caught on to what I was asking. I tried to offer them money to use their phone, but they wouldn't accept it. Finally I got through to Pietro's cell phone, after the third ring I almost gave up, because in the back of my head I still didn't know if I wanted to set myself up for that kind of escapade. But, right as I was about to give up I heard,

"Pronto?" come through from the other side.

"Ciao, Pietro?" My chest tightened, acid rose up into my throat, excitement and dread coursed through me; there was no turning back now.

"Hey, uh, the airport strike made our flight canceled and we don't know when we're going to be able to fly. Does your offer still stand for taking us to Sicilia?"

I knew he would say yes, and then we would be stuck wondering if we'd ever make it home. Then, it struck me, isn't that what life is supposed to be about? Taking risks from time to time, jumping off cliffs into an exhilarating splash of a deep pool, just for the thrill of it? Looking for treasure, experiencing pleasure, that's what life is about. It is always scary looking over the edge at the river rushing downstream and wondering if your feet are going to hit the bottom, or if your head will hit a rock if you don't jump out far enough. But most of the time you do jump far enough and the water is deep enough, and the rush is incredible. So, I surrendered, because I didn't want to sit and wait for the flight to change. Because I couldn't change it, I couldn't control it. Maybe I could have made a wiser decision, but I didn't have any better ideas.

I hung up the phone.

"Is he coming?" Mom looked inquisitively at me.

I nodded and laughed a little, then sat down with a feeling that the wind had been swept out of me. My trip was *not* going as planned.

"Oh, this is great, it's an adventure," mom announced, suddenly full of glee,

"Can you imagine how long we would have to wait if Pietro wasn't able to come get us? It feels like we were meant to meet him for some reason." I wasn't so sure Pietro was anything special.

"I think Pietro likes you Wrenna, he just looks at you that way."

"Yeah, I think maybe you're right," I tried to not sound too grumpy about it. I was at least a little flattered that an Italian man was enamored by me, though I still wasn't thrilled we were going to drive through the southern part of the country with him.

"I just think it's nice that he pays attention to you. Most of the guys you date usually leave you guessing and you're always just waiting around for them to show up.

Sometimes they don't. It's nice to have someone around who's dependable."

"Mom, we hung out with Pietro for, like, a few hours."

"I know, but I can tell he is persistent. I like men who don't give up.

Persistence is good."

She did make a point, it's not like Ahron ever actually called me, I was always the one to call him, and when I did we laughed and joked about stuff, and I would hope that he would hint something about loving me, but he never really did. One time I was lying in bed with him, before he moved away and I asked him if he loved me, he answered, "not the way you want me to". I couldn't help but think though that he just wasn't ready to be in love with me that I scared him, we had this chemistry was so strong. I guess I figured if I was persistent Ahron would eventually get more comfortable with the energy that pulsed between *us*.

***

A half an hour later, we stood outside the airport. The air was thick and buzzing like a swarm of bees. I watched the circle of tiny foreign cars swoop in and out of lanes, muster speed, parallel-park, as if they were all part of a child's train and automobile set. Behind us the building was still full of stinging cancellations as people zipped in and out of portals trying to make new arrangements.

Pietro pulled up in a small white hatchback with two doors. He was intensely watching the cars move with him in the swift action of the airport shuttle area. Despite his focus on the traffic, he was looking with wonder, his eyes full of excitement and his movements enthusiastic like a young boy playing with his flashy new sword.

As soon as he saw us, an opening in the chaos of cars appeared and he eased up to the curb. For a moment, time stopped, the busy airport and the dramas of the travelers disappeared. Pietro peered out of the window and we looked at each other, I was grateful... For a moment I saw in his eyes, he was a friend, and I couldn't help but laugh.

He hopped out of the car and opened the back hatch.

"Dis is yhours?" He stood with our suitcases at

his feet, looking at the bags in disbelief, then he burst out laughing. Before he could load our luggage into the back, he had to move his tools out and put them in the small space of the back seat. There was a triangle wooden box full of simple hand tools that reminded me of something I'd find in my Grandfather's workshop. He moved the box along with a car jack onto the floor behind his seat, (Later my mom told me how enamored she became at the moment with the little boy that peeked out of Pietro's soul. The way he took care to move his things gently was like that of a small boy who took pride in his possessions. He crammed one of our huge bags into the very back, filling the entire space of his little car, the other one that belonged to me got stuffed into the back seat, leaving barely enough room for one person to sit. Mom insisted that I sit in the front.

The airport sank away into the Napoli shoreline just as a wave slides back into the mass of the ocean. Heat rippled up from the pavement in front of us, but we were graced with a velvety breeze through the windows. Though my senses were filled with the smell of summer, flowers, salty air, sunscreen and gasoline, coconut oils and fruit juices, I was grieving. The afternoon sun knocked at my door and asked me to come out. My heart told it to come back another day; all of my expectations for the trip had changed. The trip I'd planned for five years with my mother was over, this was something entirely new and different.

Pietro turned on the radio. Italian music came popping out. I turned to look out the window at the beaches. The Amalfi coast was dotted with beach combers; babies and mothers rested under striped umbrellas, tents were set up selling sopas and Italian snacks, and it reminded me of the circus. In spite of my subtle resentment, I couldn't help but appreciate the beauty of the place. I sat back into my seat a little more and looked into the rear view window at my mother, graceful, relaxed, lovely and smiling letting the wind blow the hair into her face.

"So smitten." I thought, she thinks I'll just sit here and chat with Pietro.   Pietro glanced at me. I was tired from the stress of the airport and the heat, and looked away. He glanced at me again. This time I cracked a smile.

"Ah, Rhaina", he sighed.

***

We stopped for lunch and gas about forty minutes past departure. I was nauseous, I hadn't eaten in a while and felt somehow that I was holding back some truth, afraid to express the parts of me that were so uncomfortable. I expected for everything to be as I had planned, and there was just something about Pietro and about the whole situation that I just couldn't accept.

Pietro went inside a tiny market at the gas station. Mom followed him with the intention to stock up on water bottles. I sat at the foot of the stairs, getting some fresh air.

"Eghem, Ahh, Rhaina, what you want? I buy you lunch." I turned to see Pietro poking his head out of the door.

"I, um, I don't know, what are my choices?"

"Ahh," he ducked back in and came out with a paper menu. I looked over the menu which was written all in Italian; luckily I knew the words for chicken and ham.

"Um, this one," I pointed to a description of a sandwich that included some cheese and meat, I really didn't know what I was getting, but I figured any food would be good.

I got up and went inside with Pietro, he veered off to order sandwiches. Mom had gone to find a rest-room, so I sat down at the counter and Pietro finally joined me. I was nervous being left alone with him. He perched with his hand hooked under his head, twisted toward me, like he was posing for a photo. He looked at me so intensely. I just looked around the little station, not really taking in much, but pretending to be occupied so that I didn't have to respond to Pietro's longing energy. I was happy when mom returned and Pietro took his turn in the bathroom. While he was gone the sandwiches were served.

I took one giant bite delighting in the flavors. I loved how real the sandwich was, it was made with care, melted cheese, a handmade olive tapenade, some roasted vegetables that dripped olive oil over my fingers. I was a quarter of the way through the sandwich when Pietro sat down again beside me.

"Ohh, this sandwich is so good," I said chewing the baguette.

"I know, this why I order it for myself," I stopped chewing for a moment, not sure what to do. Embarrassed I tried to tell him that I didn't know, how foolish I felt, trying to pretend I knew what I was ordering, then eating his sandwich which was totally different than mine.

"Oh, I'm so sorry, I didn't realize this was your

sandwich."

"Is ok, I eat," he held up my sandwich, which looked like a dry chicken sandwich and certainly not as appetizing. I secretly celebrated as I ate, but then I took pity on Pietro, and offered him a bite of mine.

"No." he put his hand up gesturing that he was over it.

"Are you sure?" I asked again, giving him my cutest smile. He looked at the sandwich, and leaned over taking a big bite.

"Is much better than dis one." I laughed at his honesty, then reached over and took the sandwich out of his hand, ripping it in half and exchanging it for half of the good one. We gobbled both of them down. I took my turn with the restroom, then went back outside to find Pietro without my mom, he told me she went back inside to freshen up. We sat down on the stairs to wait. Again he turned to me with a look of passion in his eyes, passion and need. I started to feel guilty, like I was leading him on somehow.

"Ohhh Rhaina." I squirmed around a bit. He looked at me desperately, "Jus one kees, Rhaina." Somehow I felt I had to kiss him, like if I didn't he might get mad enough to leave, and we would be there stranded between point A and point B. So, I kissed him, on the lips, for a few seconds then pulled away. I felt a little guilty that I was acting. He looked stunned, as if he'd been shot by cupid's arrow. He batted his eyes at me, and I knew that he really wasn't mafia, he wasn't trying to con us, he was in pursuit for nothing more than a pining, a sweet romance, he had fallen for me.

Mom pushed her way out of the door, her hair was brushed, her lipstick freshly applied. I resented her, I resented Pietro. I was a pawn, using myself, for the security and assurance that we would have a place to sleep that night. I picked up my little plastic cup of water and walked to the car. I wanted to cry, I wanted to talk and vent with my mom like we did the first night in Rome, but I didn't know how, I didn't think she would listen. She was just like Pietro, so in love that she just couldn't see outside of that. I held my tongue, again.

Pietro and my mother walked to the car together, both with smitten looks, and both in a world of their own. We all climbed back into the car and started cruising again.

As I caught little tides of sea breeze, I began to calm down. The city was far behind us, and in a simple transition of scenery I saw Italy fully for the first time. The Amalfi coast took my breath away. For miles and miles we drove along a Cliffside, where ocean beach was all I could see. Sometimes I saw families picnicking, or drops of color speckling the sands, when we drove by some popular place to sunbathe and swim. Warm muggy wind blew upon my face, everything smelled wonderful, like summer. Mom's eyes were closed, she looked so peaceful in the back seat, resting her head, and letting the wind blow over her. Pietro focused on the road; he seemed to have no thought about anything but driving, but there was something else. He wasn't thinking about his next move. He wasn't thinking about me kissing him. He wasn't even thinking about me. He was feeling, he was being in the feeling of experience. I watched him for a while, but he didn't notice, then I turned my attention back to the ocean. This isn't so bad, it'll make a great story, I thought, and

I started to see something magical about all of it.

The drive took us six or seven hours and we finally reached the boot of Italy, Reggio de Cambria. Pietro pulled into an abandoned dirt lot and parked, as if he had planned it. The lot looked over a small valley, and across the gap was an apartment building. An older Italian woman appeared out on the balcony of her apartment across from the landing where we were. She looked at us and Pietro started conversing with her. They yelled back and forth at each other for a minute. I threw my mother a smile and raised my eyes back at her. We both laughed and then Pietro turned and said, "She is watch the caar for me ountil I git bachk."

"Do you know her Pietro?" my mother asked.

"No, she is nice lady yeh?" Pietro began reaching for our luggage from the back of his tiny car.

We unpacked everything, our comically oversized luggage, Pietro's extra shirt and hat, and our back packs. We had to make our way from the landing down a partially cobbled dirt road to where the ferry would take us across to Sicily. Pietro carried my large suitcase, my mother carried hers and I carried the extra bags. Mom's bag kept dragging and flopping over. Over time she got the wheels straight again, she would get going in a straight line and it would flop again. By the time we made it to the bottom of the cobbled hill, our stomach's hurt from laughing at ourselves.

"I think we are supposed to go down there," mom pointed out.

"How are we supposed to get there?" I asked. "There isn't a road,"

"We can just go down this hill," mom pointed

over a railing at a steep dirt hill.

At the bottom was a station for the ferry.

"Okaaiiy," I was skeptical, but also, ready to keep up with the twists in the adventure. I lifted up my bag and held it so it wouldn't fall, while trying to make it over the rail. Once over, I pressed my heels into the ground and wondered how I would get the bag down without crashing or sliding. Then I had an idea. I pushed the luggage to give it momentum, and it tumbled all the way down to the bottom. The black leather was now a dirty brown color, the same as my butt after I slid down the hill to catch the bag. Mom followed my example, she fell down a couple of times, but made it to the bottom. Our legs were scratched up, but we made it to the landing. I grabbed my bag and started up the small hill to get to the other railing where the building was, lugging my heavy bag one pull at a time to the top.

Pietro went inside the building and inquired about the ferry.

"We go..." he pointed across the pavement, another 500 feet away, "over there".

We got our luggage on rollers and walked across the hot pavement. Pietro disappeared to get us tickets and when he reappeared he said the ferry left in ten minutes.

Mom and I both got the impression that the men on the ferry at the boot of Italy didn't see American women riding very often. When the moment came to figure out where to put our luggage, there was a duel of testosterone between the men on the boat and Pietro. We were on the lower floor and Pietro had already gone up to the second floor. Mom and I stood confused trying to ask where we should put our other luggage. The men kept pointing at the front of the boat.

Pietro yelled at us to bring it up to the upper deck, but the stairs were way too steep and windy and the bags were far too heavy to haul them up ourselves. We argued with Pietro that the men wanted us to put our bags up front and finally we just ignored Pietro and the men and left them right at the bottom of the stairs. The ferry shoved off from the shore, and there were very few people aboard, we figured our bags would be okay for the fifteen minute ferry ride.

The setting sun and the light from the sky turned pink-orange and dusky purple, and my tension slipped away with the sunlight below the horizon. Mom and Pietro sat on a bench looking out over the water with a look of exhaustion and disbelief on their faces.

We docked at a little fishing town called Messina, hoping to catch a train to Palermo, but the last train had already departed, the next one would arrive at seven in the morning.

I looked in our travel books and found a couple of cheap hostels within walking distance. None of us had the energy to find dinner but we figured that going to bed on an empty stomach might leave us restless, so we journeyed out at ten o'clock to find anything that was open. My guide book warned about the streets in Messina at night, that we were at risk of being mugged and all sorts of things, but having Pietro made it feel safer.

On our walk the streets were very quiet, and actually peaceful. We approached a little corner restaurant at the end of a street, where the lights were still on and the windows were steamy. Inside, it was humid, filled with smells of garlic, noodles, tomato sauce, and onions, and pots of water steaming behind the counter. Coming out of the cool night, it felt comforting to be warmed by steam and delicious scents. We looked over the menus, and were pleasantly surprised to see that everything was inexpensive. A liter of wine was only three Euros.

One young man waited on us. Another young man and an older man worked behind the counter. They looked like father and sons.

When our food arrived we sat like old friends, laughing about our luggage rolling down the big hill to get to the ferry. I had a growing gratitude for Pietro being along for the adventure, there were moments of spontaneity that my mother and I may not have experienced without him.

I started to relax and accept Pietro traveling with us. I appreciated that he ate with gusto, the way my family did at the holidays. He reminded me of my brother, always hungry and wanting the most quality food. The meal in that little restaurant was the best food I had during the whole trip, maybe it was the reward of having traveled all day without knowing our destination that made it feel like home there. The fish was perfect, the pasta was delicious and the wine made everything feel fine. I was a bit tipsy on the way back to our hostel, tipsy enough to play at flirting with Pietro and it warmed me up to the idea of having a little fling.

{9} - A LITTLE JOURNEY

Thick navy blue fog settled into the spaces between the buildings of the little fishing village. Faint glowing lights speckled the ocean. The night was filled with a sense of unknown.

Our hostel had two full sized beds and one single bed. There was a little bathroom with a shower, but the shower had not curtain, and the drain was not very effective, so most of the water was left to be mopped up with towels. Mom went to wash up. Meanwhile I slipped on my sheer beige nightgown and made my way out to the balcony to take in the ocean air. The cool fog was a relief after the hot nights in the city.

I leaned on the railing and observed the mysterious place we had arrived at. The only sound other than the lapping of water by the docks was the shower running inside.

Without any warning or sound, I felt a gentle brush of a hand come across my waist, and before I knew what was happening Pietro pressed softly into my body with his. I surrendered into him. He brushed his face along my neck, I could feel his breath on the back of my ear, breathing breathing. He kissed my neck, my legs gave way, and he caught me, turning me around toward him, kissing me. I received his and kissed him back.

Inside, the shower turned off. I pulled away and pushed Pietro from me.

"I need to go to sleep Pietro." I said, walking back inside and sliding into bed. I tucked into a ball and lay silent. It was awkward feeling turned on with my mother in the next room.

Mom came out oblivious to our intimacy on the balcony. Her face was soft without makeup on, her hair dripped over her shoulders into the towel wrapped around her. She applied some lotion to her face, and while Pietro used the bathroom, she took the opportunity to change into a nightgown, then laid down in bed and put two orange plugs into her ears to block out the sound so she could sleep. The lights were out when Pietro lay down in his bed.

I faded into a dream and was interrupted by the sound of forced breathing. It sounded like a saw cutting, like the croup I had had as a child. Pietro was breathing in and out trying to catch his breath. I turned my back to him and pulled my pillow over my head gritting my teeth. I was so mad, wishing again that our trip to Italy was still just mom and I. I pressed my arms tighter against my ears; if I could have I would have squeezed my head right off, just for the night so my body could rest. I was already exhausted from all of the unexpected emotions playing in my body, and now the sound of his breathing made me irritable, I wished I could have just slept until Pietro disappeared.

I stood up, and stomped through the room.

"Wha argh yhou doee'?" Came his scratchy stuffed up voice. I ignored him, but in the corner of my eye I could see him, tucked into his tiny single bed. He lay under a sheet and his head, which seemed large in proportion to his body under the covers, poked out. His eyes were wide, like a little boy. Maybe scared, maybe curious, but definitely tired and full of wonder.

"Hey," I almost wanted to chuckle he sounded so funny, but I remembered that I was tired and annoyed and put out.

"Hey, wha argh yhou doeen?" he spoke quickly, raspy. I ignored him, he was hoping I would give in again, I was hoping he would suddenly be cured and sleep; so I could sleep. But, he softened me when he looked over at me in the doorway of the bathroom, sounding sad as if he'd rarely been away from his mother when he's sick, "I halvf loose my, my speaking."

I turned away again into the bathroom and turned on the shower as hot as it would go. Steam filled the room. I shut the door to keep it in.

"Come here" I said.

"What yhou want?" he asked.

"Just come here," he got up and came into the small bathroom where the hot shower was billowing steam, and water was going everywhere, "Go in there and take deep breaths, then come out in a minute, it will help your voice."

"Yeah?" He started doing as I said, and I left him in there to breath. In a moment he came back out, I told him to take a big breath and go back in, he did this a couple of times, then I shut off the shower, and mopped up as much water as I could with the towels that were already so wet from mom's shower.

"It help, I speak bettar now, no?" His voice did sound better.

"When I live wit mi mama', she give me warm milk and honey, dis helps." I thought for a moment about where I could get warm milk and honey, but I was sure everything was closed. I hoped that my effort would help enough that I could get some sleep without having to hear his cough all night.

"Okay, Pietro, I have to get to sleep."

"I sleep wit you?"

"No Pietro, I need to sleep by myself. Goodnight." I shut off my lamp and lay back down. I lay in bed listening to Pietro's breath get rhythmical as he slept. I thought about his kiss and his hand on my belly.

I still resented my mom's smitten ideas of me falling for Pietro, but I felt something stir in me that I was curious to follow, I figured, why not? This is Italy.

***

"You want I read yhour palm? I learned dis from a gypsy laydee one time." Pietro leaned over from his seat on the train, we were heading to Palermo, Sicily.

"Sure."

He picked up my hand and studied it.

"This here, it is yhour life line. See this? This line goes arhound, you haf very long life, but right here you haf truuhble, it does not brheak, so you not die, but here there are three ways, somesing gets broken no? Yhour path change." He drew his finger down the line on my right hand that wrapped around my palm. Then he turned my wrist a little and looked on the side of my hand under my pinky finger.

"Yhou see dis? It say how many cheeldren you haf. Yhou look on both hands, here these are your miscarry, ahnd, dis is how many baby you haf. Yhou haf tree baby and one miscarry."

"Wait, I want to see yours Pietro." I held up his hand and looked at the side of it. "You are going to have two babies, wait, what about your other hand, does it count if you're a man to have a miscarriage? Do these represent the physical body of the baby or the spirit of the baby?

"I don understand."

"Well, you know, you're a man, you are not the one that actually has the baby, so I just wonder...oh never mind, I don't think it matters anyway, you don't have any lines over here." I thought about his prediction. I never totally trusted the idea of palm reading, was he right that I would have three kids? And if I had three and he only had two, was there really any future for us?

"Let's try it on my mom, she's already had all the kids she's gonna have, we can test it on her."

"Sylvie, geev me yhour hand." My mom had been watching our exchange with delight. I was sure the thought of Pietro and I talking about babies made her giddy. She put her hand into Pietro's and giggled a little, like it tickled to have him swiping his fingers over her lifeline. "Yhou haf three babies, but one miscarry, did yhou haf miscarry Sylvie?"

"You know right before I had my first baby, I really thought I did have a miscarriage, I was pretty sure. My period was so late and then it finally came on."

"Dis right, Ha!" Pietro was amazed at himself. Mom and I laughed together, both entertained by Pietro's playfulness.

"Oooh," my mom sighed. "I am so tired, driving all that way yesterday was a lot, I think I may take a little nap." She lay back, and closed her eyes. Soon she was breathing peacefully, with her earplugs in, and her face mask on.

"Rhaina,"

"Si?"

"Rhaina, you mean it when you kiss me? I make you angree?" I took a deep breath, I didn't know exactly how to answer.

"Um, I like you Pietro, it's just hard because we are with my mom, and, I don't know, I...it's just weird that's all."

"You like dis kiss we have? This kiss last night? Oh Rhaina, oh oh Rhaina." He looked at me with longing, I could sense that he wanted to kiss me again.

"Yes, Pietro, it was nice," I paused, sure I didn't want to kiss him there on the train. "Pietro, I am going to take a little rest too," I pretended not to notice that he was blatantly wanting to get very close with me. I just shut my eyes and pressed my head against the window. When I heard him settle in and start breathing longer breaths, I opened my eyes and peered out at the Southern Italian landscape. Heat waves rose up from the rooftops, the trees looked parched, but used to the heat...I slipped into a daydream.

I delivered a baby and Pietro was smiling at me, receiving it into his arms. It was a boy, a little blonde boy like him. Then, suddenly my mom and Pietro and I were together walking, the baby was with me, and we were all shopping together, spending time together, talking and laughing. The next daydream was Pietro asking me to marry him, he kept asking me, and each time I came to answer, he would ask again. I stopped for a moment, and asked myself, what about his family? Did I really want to live in Italy, away from my family? And I don't know if I could take him away from this, this is where he belonged, and I don't belong here. I lay back and fell asleep. When I woke, my mother rustled me and told me we'd arrived.

In the train station Pietro helped us call a taxi to go to the airport where we would pick up our rental car. We were assigned us a green fiat and loaded all our things into the back. Mom sat next to her suitcase, which took up most of the back seat. Pietro asked directions to Scopello, the little town where we had booked a stay in a quaint bed and breakfast. We called ahead to inform them that we were bringing another guest, a man. She commented that she was certain the householders were not thrilled about our spontaneous tag along.

***

The warm colored road bent and stretched into the country ahead of us. Rich green trees held their branches out like mimes in Rome, beckoning to be looked at, to be sat under, to be tested for their strength.

We drove out of the city again and aimed for the small country village of Scopello; this time I insisted on sitting in the back, so mom took her blissed out state with her to the front seat where she put in a dance CD which she turned up to let the beats bump out of the open window. She was like a teenager, she reminded me of me, when I used to skip school with my friend Lauren, she looked like nothing could shake her from her state of happiness and freedom.

Up ahead we spotted a few rock buildings to the left of us and pulled over to pee. Inside a little store we found a pair of goggles and a snorkel for Pietro to use.

Mom peeked into a stone archway and disappeared behind it. She poked her head back out with a giddy girl smile and eyes wide.

"Let's eat here! Isn't it cute? And look, there's a little garden out back!"

The place seemed closed to me, at least the people were not particularity enthusiastic to serve us, but there was plenty of food in metal containers behind a glass shield and an Italian man who waited for us to order, so I asked for a plate of pasta with sauce and a bit of fish.

"Oh this is great! I just love this kind of food!" my mother chirped enthusiastically.

I found a shaded swinging summer couch that was the only shade underneath a shimmering olive tree. I felt peaceful for a moment. Pietro ordered his food while I surveyed the scene.

The eating area was tucked back in a garden away from the road. An old wood burning pizza oven in a wall of the building told of history and friendship, though presently it seemed abandoned and drab.

Mom brought my food to me.

"Are you okay?" she asked as she handed me my food.

"Eh." I looked down at my noodles not feeling very hungry. The sun had eased its way into my shade and I felt the pressure of the heat beating down on me. "It's just...I'm just really hot."

Pietro came over by us and we all shifted to sit in the grass behind the swing, squeezing into the last shade in the yard. I picked around at my food, having a hard time filling my belly in such heat. I nibbled while Pietro chowed his down. Once he was finished we de-

---

cided to continue on to Scopello.

With my plate still half full, and mom's still with some food left, we bussed our plates back to the people who owned the establishment. We had not yet paid for our food, so my mother shuffled through her wallet to find some cash.   Pietro was speaking gruffly with the men behind the counter.

"Non ti piace il cibo?" the man said to Pietro. [You do not like the food?]

"Queste donne sono American," Pietro answered. [These women are American.] "Sono calde e non molto affanati." [They are hot and not very hungry.]

"Basta! Via con te!" [Away with you!] "Non voglio i vostri, non vi piace il cibo, non prendere i soldi," [I do not want your money, you do not like the food, I will not take your money.]

"Ci faremo carico, il cibo era buono." [We will pay the food was good.] "No, no pay." The man behind the counter stopped looking at Pietro and continued to work.

"No?"

"No."

"What did he say Pietro?" My mother looked at him quizzically.

"He said he will no achept ouhr monee, per uh, he had insult, because he think we no like heez food?"

"Oh no, tell him we are full". Mom understood the cultural insult that when we did not eat all of the food, the Italian man believed his food was not good enough for us to want to eat it all. She used to tell me that my great-grandmother was a big food pusher, always trying to fatten my dad up, offering him way more food than he could eat, and it was a compliment to the chef if you could eat and eat.

"I told him that, he does non whant thee monee."

"Ok." Mom looked a bit crest fallen, though she perked up fairly quickly when we took our places back in the fiat, rolled down the windows and turned on a dance song called First Kiss. It was hot summer breeze and back country roads from there to the edge of...

{10} - SCOPELLO, SICILIA.

Pietro drove slowly into the village; it was very small with a population of only 400 people. It seemed like we were driving down a driveway rather than the entrance to a town.

There were thick bushes harboring the road. We crept along and at once our heads were drawn to the right into a cemetery where a gathering of people stood listening to a church service.

Beyond the cemetery was a strip of rock buildings, all very old and quaint. It was late in the afternoon and the village itself seemed to be listening to a sermon.

We pulled up to a three story building, set back from the street. It had potted trees out front, and reminded me a bit of the stucco buildings in Mexico. Our Pensione offered dinner and breakfast with our room. I looked forward to not having to find food at any random restaurant, this would be our home for a few days.

Mom hopped out of the fiat and went inside to announce our arrival. The hostess of Pensione S informed mom that our room was ready, dinner would be served at six in the dining room. Mom reappeared outside as Pietro and I were unloading our luggage and laughing.

"We are on the third floor, and I don't think there is an elevator," mom filled us in. We took one look at our hefty bags and burst out laughing again.

"Well, at least once we get them up there, we aren't going anywhere for a few days," she pointed out.

Just then, a man with dark tan skin, and no expression on his face, appeared at the door, and walked toward us. He looked right past Pietro and spoke to my mother. "I help yhou," he said in a dry tone. He took my mother's big bag and began wheeling it along into the lobby/dining area and back toward a set of stairs. He was limping, and slightly dragging one leg, having to stop with each step to drag it up to meet the other. We followed politely and slow. The man started up the stairs, dragging his foot, then dragging the bag. Mom kept looking back at me with a worried look on her face, like she felt awful having him take the bags all the way up with a leg that didn't function very well.

At every landing the man's working leg thudded into the stone floor followed by a long scuff of his dragging leg. Finally he reached the top and unlocked the heavy wooden door for the three of us. He spoke in Italian to Pietro, as he did not seem to speak much English.

"Prego." The man grunted as a here you go.

"Grazie." Pietro answered in a male way of meeting his gruffness.

The door shut and we busied ourselves around the room. A small square window opened up overlooking a dry landscape of Scopello. In the corner, a cot had been set up for Pietro and a large folding screen divided the cot from the rest of the room. "Mom look, they put a screen up next to the cot."

"Oh hoo ho hahaha!" my mother's giant laugh flowed out of her, "they are suspicious of us, when I talked to the woman on the phone, she didn't sound pleased at all that we were bringing Pietro."

Pietro chuckled, "This they call a jiggle yeah? In Lowndon I learn this word. A man who takes many women, no?"

"Si," I smiled at the way he pronounced jiggalo.

"They tink I ham tryink to uh...seduction?"

"Seduce"

"Si, seduce, a mother and a daughter. Ha! This, this is very fanny!"

"That guy was strange wasn't he? He was sort of Prude", mom commented. "I think that was the woman's husband, he is the other owner."

"No, it wasn't, was it? I couldn't imagine the two of them together at all", I scoffed.

"Yeah, I wonder what happened to him, maybe it was a neurological condition," mom wondered. "I don't know, they are a strange couple though, I'm curious about how they are with each other." She lay her head back against a pillow on the double bed that we were sharing. We'd moved the divider screen out of the way and Pietro lay back with his head propped up by his arms. He wore a pair of jean shorts and his soft curly leg hair relaxed with the rest of him. He was so comfortable in his body, and he seemed to take joy in every moment.

"They are unhappy people, they make so manny

faces like dis." He frowned and then he laughed, "Why so unhappy?" he shrugged.

"I go to these travel place, Sardenia, Lowndon, other place, sometimes I meet people who are not with money, they live, uh on the streets you know, and they ask al the time. I need maanee, I need maanee, my children, my home, I am hungry, they say. These people, sometime they are sad, sometime they are happy, when they have food. These people that live here, they have a house, and food, a fancy place and they still make face like this," he frowned again. "Dis is Paradiso".

"You never know with people though, it seems like something happened to the husband, maybe it was traumatic for them," my mother chimed in sympathetically. "Sometimes those things can be hard for people. I keep thinking of the woman we saw in Naples with her baby. She came right up to my feet and was touching me so sensually—and holding her baby out, she patted my feet and touched my calf. I couldn't understand anything she said, but the way she touched me was so..." my mom's nostrils opened wide and she took in a small breath, "It was just so vulnerable, I felt her, her sadness, she was so desperate, it made me feel desperate", she blinked out soft tears that floated down her cheeks, then she sighed and fiddled with a string dangling from the quilt on the bed. She looked distant as if she was staring into a portal of memory.

"Anyway" she continued," I just think some people have more difficult lives".

We all worked in silence for a few minutes, putting away our things.

"I'm hungry, is it time for dinner yet?" I asked. My mother looked at a small watch she carried with her in her purse.

"Oh! Dinner started half an hour ago, we should go, I'm excited to see what she cooks," she pulled out a tiny box and took two gold earrings out. Looking into the mirror and tilting her head she took out two smaller simple golden hoops and filled the holes again with the more ornate ones. She then applied a fresh layer of Neon Pink to her lips, and announced she was ready.

Pietro gave me his arm to steady me on our way down the stairs, where I saw some things I hadn't noticed on our way up. On the third floor landing there was a mirror; we all looked at each other through it as we took our careful steps down. My mother observed Pietro and me, especially him. I could see her eyes tracing his figure, taking in his very broad shoulders, I saw the way she feasted on his swagger, like it was a fresh kill of meat in the cold of winter.

Pietro reminded me of someone. His cocky confidence and goofy little boy gestures and the way he liked to be looked at; he was a version of a man who used to come by my house as a small child, a man that my mother had loved. His broad shoulders made him swagger, like a boat on the ocean tipping at each dip of the tide. The look in his eyes was the same; soft, a bit mischievous, knowing, it was like looking into the eyes of a dream I used to have—something familiar. He reminded me of Reign Castleman, the man my mother had had an affair with years before. I shook the image of him away and refocused on the stairs.

As we approached the second floor landing I caught a glimpse of my mom in another mirror, looking back and forth at Pietro and I, and I couldn't help but wonder if she wasn't reliving an experience from her past through the two of us, it occurred to me that maybe our spirits were intertwined and somehow they were coming together to remember something.

As we entered the lower level, we saw that the open room was now full of guests; tables were set and carafes of red wine adorned the tables.

We sat down where the Hostess directed us. Pietro poured himself a glass of wine.

"Rhaina, would you like?"

I looked at him blankly then beyond him at the other people in the dining room. They were stiff. It was as if our entrance stopped time. I reached out to pour myself some water, but my hands were shaking and I thought I might vomit.   I left the table mumbling that I had to go to the bathroom, and when I hit the second story, my stomach churned, I ran to the top floor and jiggled the lock, my hands were shaking so much it made me even more nervous. I flung the door open and fell down on the bed, dry heaving, holding my stomach. As soon as I was laying down a flood of tears ran down my face and I began to sob. I was filled with a wanting. Wanting what I didn't know. I just wanted what I wanted. Ahron and my summer romance two years before, my mom and I to have the vacation that we had planned for five years. I didn't want to be in Italy with my mom *and* Pietro, feeling guilty and lost. It was all so overwhelming. I knew I had to collect myself, but I couldn't. I had to perform, but I had no will to play a part anymore. I put the spotlight on myself, it was my fault I felt that way. I heard a knock on the door. Mom came in.

"What's wrong?" She looked at my swollen eyes,

and dirty river cheeks. I took a deep breath and blamed it on the first night in a new place. She saw right through me.

"Are you thinking of Ahron?" She asked.

I nodded, even though it was much more than Ahron—how could I explain what I saw, that Pietro was reminiscent of this man that haunted my childhood, or that I thought mom was putting something on me, wanting something to happen between him and me. My lips began to tremble.

"Is anything else going on?" mom asked after a minute.

"Mmm, I just don't understand why we had to bring Pietro along," I whined.

"Well, we wouldn't be here if it wasn't for him helping us," she lectured.

"I guess, but he could have just driven us and then left us to get on the train."

"I don't know Wrenna, he helped a lot with the translating and getting through some of Sicily."

"Yeah, that's true. Well, I..." I paused, "do you think he kinda walks like Reign?" Mom pulled back for a second, surprised.

"Yeah, he's built a lot like him. He's impulsive and charismatic like Reign too."

"Is that why you like him?"

"Maybe," she tilted her head contemplating my observation.

I looked out the window at the tree bending in the gentle breeze.

"Why don't you want him here?" Mom asked.

"He's kinda of suffocating. He just stares at me and looks at me, and..." "Oh, he's just arduous, he's passionate, and I think he really likes you. I don't get why you go for guys like Ahron who don't seem into you. I think Ahron's a game player. He doesn't call you back, you're always sitting around waiting for him. Does he even make you happy?"

"Well yeah, I really like him."

"Whenever I hear you talking about him, you seem sad or heartbroken over him."

"Yeah..." I trailed off. "But, if I am persistent Ahron will finally realize that he wants to be with me. Maybe he just isn't ready yet to settle down, after all I am only 20 and he's 29. Maybe he's just waiting until I am a little more mature. He wants me to see the world, and I am. Maybe I'm just not ready for him totally either."

"Hmmm, maybe. I've just never seen anybody look at you like Pietro does, it just seems like there is something there."

"Yeah, that's true, he does *really* look at me."

"Well, I am still hungry and I left Pietro down there all alone with all of our food." Mom announced.

At the thought of Pietro sitting alone with a room full of awkward people, I started laughing. He was probably gobbling down his meal, totally unaware of how uncomfortable everyone else was. Mom left and told me she would make up some excuse for my sudden exit, and promised she'd bring up my food.

I lay alone with the window open. The crickets were chirping, the air came soft and warm through the window.

After all my anxiety, I started to relax. I looked out the window at the little courtyard below, lit with only a couple of tiny lights. "This is summer in Italy," I thought, "Romantic, good food, hot, vibrant…how am I so confused in the middle of this beautiful place? I am supposed to be in love, I am supposed to be having the time of my life!" I sat back down.

"Maybe I need to have my own experience with Pietro, and forget about mom and her past, maybe it isn't fair to Pietro to make him into something he isn't. Maybe I should just get to know him a little". It was in that thought that I decided I would enjoy myself, embrace Pietro and stop resisting the experience.

Pietro came in then, wearing his light blue cotton cutoff shirt and jeans. He was older than me by twelve years. Despite our age difference, I did find him attractive. I loved how his arms looked strong from working, rather than working out, he was beautiful, masculine, sexy, confident in his body, funny, and utterly naive; so, when he asked me to take a walk with him for 'digestion', I agreed. Mom stayed back, claiming she wanted to get to bed early. Pietro waited with my mom on the other side of the screen while I changed out of my dinner clothes and into a pair of jeans and a comfy shirt.

"WWeeOOOhh, kooonk, klonk, konk, zeeeepo, zeeepo, zeeeepo," a few soapy bubbles floated up and over to the bed where I lay and popped on my hair. Pietro had found our light-up bubble gun. Mom and I got caught up in the festivities of Rome one night and she bought a toy gun from a vendor that blew bubbles, lit up and made strings of galactic sounds. She purchased it as a gift for my nephews, but Pietro thought it was the funniest thing he'd ever seen. I looked at Pietro and he pretended to shoot me. Bubbles came out of the gun and I reached out and popped one. We all let out a symphony of laughter.

"Who is this mysterious man?" I wondered.

"We go for a walk Rhaina?" I wasn't sure if Pietro was asking or stating the idea to me.

"Oh. Uh." I glanced at mom, she was pretending to not pay attention. Would I be safe with him along? I supposed so, Pietro didn't seem to be going anywhere, and a walk seemed innocent enough. I did enjoy adventure, and somehow it seemed Pietro and I were already embarking on one together.

{11} - SOMEONE ELSE'S DREAM

The tiled front room of the pensione had a cool welcome when we arrived back from our walk. I had a sense that the room was watching us, and we had disturbed it in its moment of solitude. The hallway leading to the kitchen was dark, all the candles had been snuffed out. Pietro and I glided through the foyer to the stairs.

I was subtly aware of my act, an act that came and went on its own accord. I liked to play with seduction, I liked to tease. A part of me feared Pietro, but another part craved the wild natured serendipity of meeting him. There was a certain power pulsing through our experience, a spirit of a story that was stalking us.

I took each step carefully up the stairs, feeling my pelvis turn liquid. I felt the lines up the back of my pantyhose pulling him in from behind, innocently leading his eyes to the jackpot, like a yellow brick road, sending him home. Every click of my heel ignited our imaginations.

At the top of the first flight of stairs I was met face to face with my own image reflecting back at me from a full length mirror. I looked through it and straight at Pietro's reflection, where he met my eyes with his. I rounded the first staircase and approached the second set, starting up faster, a part of me held back from my game, or maybe I was simply playing the game more competitively now. At the edge of this stairwell rested a bookcase where I stopped and looked over the books uncaringly. I ached somewhat for him to reach up and touch me, pull the small of my back into him, let our energies swirl. I wanted him, and yet, where could I go from there really? I wanted to fall in love, but how could I fall in love with him? I would let myself go, then in just a few days, we would fly off in a plane, homeward bound, and he would go back to laying bricks, to his mama', to Napoli.

I randomly lifted a book off one of the shelves, pretended to be interested then replaced it. As I turned to face the third flight of stairs, I released the energy that had risen between us. It fell away from me and down into the cold stony tile beneath our feet. But, just as a wave in the tide shifts, I let go, I was flushed again, turned on by the tension between us and by the fantasy. The forbidden fruit is always so desirable.   I turned around in mid step, and Pietro stepped right into my path. Without hesitation, he slipped his hand past the fabric of my skirt and along my thigh. Instead of sloppy impatience, our movements were quick and perfectly smooth, the rise and fall of tension between us built a strong base of precision and accuracy. I had no trouble unbuttoning his jeans. I locked into the swiveling of hot molten ore in the V of my volcano. My head dove down between his legs, and we became one energy moving so quickly and swiftly together that we stood still, unleashing thoughts of future and past. We gracefully fell into each other and leaned into the stairs, being careful not to make a sound, and I caught a glimpse of our bodies and our embrace in the mirror on the next landing.

As he kissed me I pictured my mother peacefully sleeping in a bed, through the door right above us, with a light breeze blowing over her white cotton sheets. It struck me that we had traded places. What she lived through years ago with Reign lay under the surface unfinished. That part of her life was buried and yet the ghosts still remained and came out to haunt us the day we met Pietro. There was something about Pietro, something that my mother felt in him that reminded her of a time. I couldn't understand it, I felt taken in by Pietro's energy, and yet, at the same time, I felt I was living someone else's life. I couldn't tell if I was doing this for me, or for her.

I pulled myself from Pietro, acting cool, acting like I was purposely teasing him, because I had gone far enough. I didn't know what would happen if I let myself go completely.

The door was locked when I reached it, and I fumbled with the key, my fingers shook, from adrenaline, from knowing that he frightened me but not knowing why. When I entered, I heard mom stir. I knew she would ask, what happened, did you have fun, where did you go? I knew she would hear an incomplete answer in my voice and inquire later for more. But, when I lay down she mumbled, "Are you okay?" through her groggy, ear-plugged sleep, and when I answered, "I'm okay," She responded simply, "good", then pulled the covers a little tighter and went back to sleep. Pietro lingered behind me a flight down the stairs, probably wondering what happened, and why I had suddenly turned off and turned away. I left the door open a bit so that he could come in his own time.

I didn't know what happened either, It was as if Pietro had come into my life as a mirror; a mirror into my soul. He showed me my desire to be free and wild; he showed about experiencing life as it comes, but there was more, Pietro carried a key to a door that had been shut and locked for a long time; the key I needed to walk down into the roots of my beginning.

***

In the morning we woke up to the smell of coffee wafting past the cracks of the door. I rolled over, drained of energy. Too much emotion welled up in me and I had no place to put it. I felt this incredible need to talk to my mom about everything that was going on inside of me, but I assumed that she had just as much if not more happening in her. Before I opened my eyes, I heard the sounds of the toy gun. Noises like bombs dropping, and sirens, machine guns and arcade sounds came darting out. I buried my head, trying to go back to sleep and trying to ignore it. The gun kept whirring and popping. I boiled in defeat; I could not compete with that ridiculous gun. What had brought smiles to my face the night before was now tormenting me and my confusion over Pietro. I had to wake up and face him...and my mother. They spewed child-like excitement that filled me with enough guilt to throw in the towel and toss the covers away. I sat up, squinting my eyes at the sunlight, wanting to laugh at how pissed I was, but I didn't smile.

I showered, dressed and made my way downstairs with my mom and Pietro to the tables that were cheerfully clad, with tiny perky flowers that looked as if they'd already had a few cups of coffee. As we took our seats we were served cookie-crackers with slices of bread and marmalade along with coffee and orange juice. I looked around me and could see our welcome was wearing thinner as the various couples throughout the pensione became aware that the three of us shared a room at the top of the stairs. We were risqué. Pietro didn't seem to take any offense or even notice, he filled himself with what he could, then announced he would go pull up the car.

Mom and I joined Pietro in the fiat, after we packed our snorkels and swimsuits, then embarked on a venture to the sea, intending to hike two miles into the hills to a cove for swimming and relaxation. With our large umbrella, hats, sun block and water in possession, we were set for a day trek.

The tension I carried about Pietro eased by the afternoon when we arrived in the parking lot at the beginning of a trail. The area was preserved well. Like any national forest, people could only hike in and out, and there were no motor vehicles or pets allowed. The only sign of animals in the area were wild animals and occasional horse droppings from the park rangers that tidied up after the tourists had gone home. We paid the small park fee and started out, at first a bit awkwardly, trying to set a pace. Pietro started humming a tune under his breath and I recognized it, but couldn't put any words to it.

"What are you singing?" It drove me crazy how familiar it was. I thought I had heard the tune sometime when I was younger. Song files in my brain started unloading but I just couldn't connect the tune he hummed with any words.

Then he suddenly burst out with lyrics.

"Ohhhhh, sooloohhh mio...la luh, lay law," he only knew the beginning of the chorus then sang the rest of the tune the best he could.

I had heard Oh Solo Mio before, but I still had a nagging feeling about the tune.

As we walked along the cliffs of the ocean, I hummed the song under my breath. The ocean radiated green and blue, mimicking the eyes of my past lovers. It was reminiscent of every magazine advertisement for tropical getaways that I had never explored. The rich green airbrushed trees bounced out of the cliffs at us. Way down below, I could see through the water. The waves gently lapped up on the beach, unlike the crashing waves of the coast we used to visit when I was a child. The color of the water was the same as the pictures of the Blue Grotto. I allowed as much of my resentment as I could float away into the pristine scenery, and that's when it hit me. The song. It was an Elvis song, Now or Never. I smiled and turned to Pietro with a giggle.

"It's NOoow or neeevver, come hold me tight, kiss me my darlin', be mine tonight, tom..."He cut me off.

"Tommoorough, will be too late, it's now or never..."and we finished together, 'My love won't wait!" In the elation of finding a song we could sing together we boisterously sang louder and continued the verses with mom watching and joyously laughing behind us.

"I've spent a lifetime, waiting for the right time...La la la la la....la la la la la".
We were both belly laughing at not knowing the rest of the words.

"That was Great!" mom said as she wound down along the dirt path and rock steps to where Pietro and I had stopped to look out over the wood railing at the sea. We leaned together with our shoulders pressed together. Had my mother not been there, I might have kissed him, I might have gone as far as kissing him right there for as long as I wanted, but I couldn't leave my mother out, I thought it would be too uncomfortable.

We finally reached a cove after two hours of hiking and sweating, ready to swim and refresh ourselves. The landscape was a child's painting splashed randomly with inky color. Triumph of reaching our destination reenergized the drag that had slowed our pace during the last small stretch before we reached our paradise. And the paradise was ours. The few other people that populated the sand were mere props, we paid no attention to their presence, and made our way carefully down the last inches of the path. Gritty sand, made of tiny rocks scratched the surface of my feet, and when warmed by the sun they filled me with a kind of torturous thrill.

We found a small cavern, shaded by a large rock on the far end of the beach, just a quick jog to the water, and shady enough to cool us. We hadn't anticipated how strenuous of a hike we'd set out on, so when we sat down our stomachs called out, summoning an unexpected appetite. We were unprepared with only left over slices of bread and a can of sour cream onion Pringles that I threw into my back pack that morning.

Kindly enough we rationed out the tiny amount of food and rested quietly in our cave, dazed and taking in the scenery.

Mom headed to the edge of the water and slipped in to explore the shoreline. I watched her snorkel drift away like the fin of a shark. I remembered summer's as a child when mom and dad took my brothers and me to the lake. While I captured tadpoles with my brother, my dad would sit in the shade and skim through John Grisham novels, and mom would swim from one end of the lake to the other and back. There was never a need to worry that she might get lost or that she might drown because the florescent orange of her snorkel poked out of the water outlining her route. The stiff tube would glide our direction and as soon as we saw mom's white skin emerge, we knew it was time to go home. Somehow the innocence of those lake memories seemed ironic when I looked out at her moving farther away then turned my head to see the empty rocks and my fathers' absence, but in his place sat Pietro.

Mom came back up on the shore looking tired and laid down on her towel to warm up and take a rest. I had never known my mom to sun bathe, it was too slow for her. Typically, she just sat on a towel and watched us kids, or headed out to find iced tea, so I was surprised to see her just flop down on the towel and close her eyes, I even thought I detected a tiny smile across her lips.

After resting, I licked the salt off my lips and my craving for the water motivated me to get up and dig my face mask out from my back pack. I handed a cheap pair of plastic goggles and snorkel to Pietro that we had bought at a little store before we left. He smiled sweetly at me, with excitement swimming in his eyes. I felt protective and tender toward him maybe because we were in a paradise of our own.

The ocean, the sand, the enormous blue sky stretched with rainbows of water and fish darting below, it belonged to us, it was ours.

Pietro and I jumped into the deep pool shocking the tiny hairs on our bodies. The goose bumps on his arms and legs were magnified through my mask. I shivered and he reached for my hand. We laughed at how goofy we looked, big eyes, faces stretched and noses squished. As we kicked along he would point at the tiny schools of fish, and we'd point our bodies down, take a breath and kick hard to scare them and break up their meetings. It surprised me how easy moving through the water and staying afloat was in comparison to swimming back and forth in the public pool back home. The water felt like air, it was clear and my body could breathe under there. Pietro swam contentedly with my small hand fit into his. When we reached the peninsula that divided our cove from the vastness of the ocean, we stopped and examined the seaweeds and coral on the rocks.

Pietro gave a gentle tug and spun me around, kissing me while he kicked to balance us in the water. There was nothing to hang onto but each other. As I kissed him, movies swam into my mind; memories that weren't mine. It was like a flashback, in black and white, but the people in the flashback weren't Pietro and I. They were Reign and my mother, in the water in Tahiti. She told me of the extreme chemistry that brought them together, she was out of control; she couldn't help but follow her obsessive draw to him. I heard her story echoing in my head:

"There were people up on the beach, families, couples..."She and Reign swam out far into the ocean, far enough out to have privacy, then separated.

"I was looking at everything under the water, and it was beautiful, the coral had the most unique colors. The whole trip was like a dream, we had sex all the time, everywhere, but just as soon as we were done, I craved him again. It was so draining, but I was addicted to him."

Her voice rang in my ears as Pietro slid his foot upon a rock to balance himself. I closed my eyes using only my body and hands to stay connected with the waves and the touch of Pietro. His square hand rested at my waist helping me stay afloat.   My mother's distant hollow voice continued,

"He swam up behind me and pulled me into him. Then he put his fingers behind my thigh and started to mess around with me." She shyly unraveled her memory to me, wanting me to know but at the same time holding back a certain eagerness to tell it how it was.

"I would hold my breath and dunk under water to go down on him. When I started to climax, I moaned through the snorkel and it made this really loud noise that carried through the water, but I didn't care about people hearing me, I just kept getting louder."

I drifted back in consciousness, and my hand had slipped into Pietro's red swim briefs. We bobbed and swayed with the rippling water. Every motion was rhythmical, keeping in time with the ocean. Such an innocent moment of discovery for me and yet I was already wrapped up by someone else's moment of desire. How could I mold my own story when she had already one-upped every future move of mine? It had been that way since the day I learned of her affair with Reign. My ears burned with the sounds fluttering from my mother's memory, and then the lapping waves on the cliff beside me broke the far off sound of her voice and my concentration.

The water around me was milky with Pietro's satisfaction. I liked the power I had, to give him pleasure like that. What a strange Deja vu', how could I be replaying my mother's story with this man I hardly knew? I couldn't stay in the water with Pietro any longer, I was afraid of being too vulnerable. I swam away. Somehow I felt more than just my own vulnerability though, I also felt an anger that wasn't mine, some war that I was fighting, as if my mother had unfinished business with Reign, and Pietro had shown up in his place, only this time my mother wasn't fighting the war, it was me.

When we returned to the pensione, our bodies were sunburned and we were tired and hungry.

"Let's skip dinner tonight at the pensione and go have dinner at that little restaurant around the corner. The one we saw when we were driving in." Mom was enthusiastic about having dinner out of the dining room where everyone just stared at us like we were being inappropriate.

We were seated at an outdoor table and immediately discovered that the bar had red martinis. When the drinks arrived I happily drank mine down. The red vermouth in the drink had a perfectly sweet, dry and refreshing taste to it. The three of us were hooting and laughing together, making jokes, and telling stories when our waitress brought out plates of pasta for Pietro and me, and a beautiful Sicilian Salad for my mother.

"How do you know each other?" the waitress asked Pietro with a strong Italian accent?

"I meet dem in Napoli. They go down dis street ahnd we walk, we make frend. Dis not the end, the plane they are going to fly on does not fly for dem, so I bring dem here." Pietro summed up our journey so quickly I had to laugh, which made red martini go into my nose. I started coughing and laughing at the same time. The waitress laughed at me, as if she had gotten the joke.

"What eez fanny Rhaina? Yhou choke?" I took a drink of water and took a breath, thinking about all the things in between the story he had not mentioned about the three of us. How could any of us possibly explain it? How could anyone understand what we could hardly even see ourselves? Pietro reminded me more and more of my mother's lover, even though he was also so different from Reign, I could see how my mom longed for something in him. He was impulsive and adventurous. He didn't need to know what was next. He appreciated our raw and unpredictable female spirits, as if he was all the more turned on by the changing of our minds, or a sudden outburst of emotion. We both felt it, it was freeing to feel like we were in charge, like we were the ones leading this trip. And, at the very same time, I didn't want to take responsibility for breaking someone's heart, it felt so complicated. Yet, when Pietro shared with the waitress that he was just helping us out because we were all friends, I had to laugh. I was so concerned about how we looked to people, but Pietro was our friend, he had swooped us up and taken us on a great journey, all the while enjoying himself.

{12} - SPIRIT LIVES
IN THE BONES

We took a day trip in the Fiat to Palermo.

Mom sat in the back seat letting the wind blow through her hair.

After a few days with Pietro I was beginning to build a myth around him, he was not a strange character from the streets of a foreign country, instead he was just him, and the deeper we got into the world away from our worlds the more we were able to create our own story.

Into Palermo, the vibration changed from the soft green and winding country road to a harsh hotness. The ease of trees and countryside slipped away and was replaced with the edge of one of the most famous centers of mafia in Europe.

"Wherth are you taking me?" Pietro asked again. "I don understan dis you talk about."

"We are going to a crypt Pietro. It's a place called the Capuchin Crypt where the bones of past priests have been preserved."

"What? Why we go here?"

"It's interesting. Mom and I went to one in Rome. This one actually has a lot of the bones that came from the Volcano erupting on Mt. Vesuvius."

Pietro looked contemplative. He didn't say anything, but leaned in toward the front window, letting his arm relax onto the steering wheel. The silhouette of his nose had a line, like a cliff that jetted out toward the ocean then became a steep grade the rest of the way down. The line, the way he leaned, the way he bobbed so easily, like a small boat on a gentle lake, was like a young boy.

We pulled into the parking lot of the Crypt only a few minutes after it opened, so there weren't very many cars parked yet. Not far from our parking place were a couple of intimidating serious men. I didn't think much of them, they spoke another language, lived in another culture, and I had no need to communicate or interact with them. To Pietro, they represented something very different. I could tell Pietro was holding his ground, but underneath he seemed quieter, his laughter and joyful whimsy disappeared. He had to shape shift in order to protect himself. We stayed in the car fumbling through our stuff, looking busy, acting like we didn't notice the men. Pietro finally got out and started speaking to them in Italian. They sounded threatening in a different way than I had ever heard, they did not yell, at all. They had the power of Sicilian Mafia backing them up, they didn't need to yell. They spoke quietly and minced little words, and their voices carried a certainty like death.

Pietro returned to us, and the men moved on. Once we reached the entrance of the crypt my mother expressed that she had been hesitant to leave the car. Pietro assured her that he had taken care of it. He paid the men off and told them that we were his cousins from America and he was showing us around.

We entered the Crypt down a ramp that took us into a cooler cave. Around us were dim lights and the skeletons of former priests and the people of Mt. Vesuvius (after it erupted, they were collected from the ashes and reassembled into the Crypt).

"Why we cam here?" Pietro asked, looking around with an expression on his face like we were playing a joke on him.

"My sister-in-law said this place was really fascinating," I told him. "It's not something you see every day."

"Si, but this is jiok." Pietro gestured at the figures hanging on the walls.   "These guys are real Pietro, they are preserved; they have been preserved for a really long time." I looked at the line of some Priests in brown robes all hanging on the wall. The structures of each face looked different. Some cheek bones were high, some were low, the eye sockets were round or oval or almond shaped. The jaw bones were particularly variant in the skeleton faces.

"No, this no real" Pietro looked at me wondering why I would lie to him.

"It is,"

"Si? I no believe dis. Why no barry dem?"
"They are supposed to symbolize that we shouldn't be afraid of death, they are supposed to remind us that everything dies, it is just a natural process of life." Mom chimed in.

"I don understan, why no let dees peepol go to eart. They go in groun, eh they go bak to eart. How dis plase say deth a naturalle? Pietro looked at me confused.

"Hmm, I don't know, I guess in a sense we are inside the earth." I shrugged my shoulders.

The crypt remained cooler, a nice relief from the hard heat of the city out of the cave. We walked all the way to the back, the coolest part of the crypt, where a glass case took up a corner of a hollowed out rock room. A plaque on the outside read, Rosalia Lombardo, la Bella Addormentata, meaning sleeping beauty. The plaque explained that she was the last person to be placed in the crypt in 1920. She was perfectly preserved.

"Ughk," Pietro had a horrified expression as he looked at her on the alter. "Dis realle!?" He was in total disbelief. I could tell he'd never seen anything like it before. It made me laugh that he was so innocent in that way, I liked that he was sensitive to the macabre, it made me feel real. I was so used to everyone back home always acting like they knew everything because they watched it on T.V. or read it in a book, but I could tell that Pietro was really experiencing this for the first time, just as a child might feel chilled by a ghost in a haunted house on Halloween.

"I wan get out of here, I no wan see anymore." Pietro actually looked a little pale.

We hiked back out, and felt warmer as we closed in on the entrance. Outside the heat took us into its grip and would not relent. We got into our car and instead of turning on the air conditioning we rolled down the windows and fanned ourselves.

Just around the corner, Pietro parked again in front of a little Gelateria. The three of us were thrilled to find something to cool us off again.

Mom went to the bathroom and Pietro and I

went outside to sit on the hot curb, licking our cones together. There was nothing to say, because saying things in different languages sometimes felt like way too much effort, so we just licked at the ice-cream and looked at the pavement sending heatwaves off the stones in the ground. I tasted the pistachio gelato, it was like no other ice cream I had ever had before. The consistency was more smooth and creamy, not as icy or hard as ice creams I remembered. The nuts weren't stale or freezer burned, but truly nutty and flavorful; it was the most real and delicious treat.

"I taste yhours?" Pietro raised his eyebrows at me.

"Si," I held out my cone for him to take a lick, then he held his hand out with his cone that had strawberry gelato. It tasted just like the strawberries from my grandma's garden. She used to pick the little berries and put them in a small colander, then rinse them and sprinkle sugar on top, adding heavy cream to finish it off.

Mom came back out licking her lemon sorbetto.

"OH, I just love tart things, taste this Wrenna, isn't it sooo good?" I licked the sorbet, and again was amazed at the real flavor it had. The lemon's tartness tasted like honey made by bees that licked the nectar from a lemon blossom. Mom devoured hers.

By the time we sunk back into the hot leather seats of the fiat, we were overflowing like twitter-pated birds splashing their wings in a fountain. I buckled my seat belt and had to slip a piece of my skirt underneath the buckle, it was so hot on my skin.

The day didn't feel like it could get any hotter.

We drove for a bit and followed signs toward the beach. When we arrived mom and I found our swim suits in our swim bag and looked around to find a changing room, but the only thing we could see was a bathroom with a line at least ten people long; they looked hot and uncomfortable. We agreed to hold towels around each other and change underneath, so that we could get to the ocean as soon as possible.

Every inch of the beach had families and lovers, machismo bodybuilders and babies stretched out on blankets, under umbrellas, listening to boom boxes. All the men wore speedos, and their chests were covered with swarthy patches of hair, and buried with a gold chain or two hanging around their necks. Babies' butts were bare or barely covered, and they happily cooed and tossed sand with their shovels or their hands this way and that.

We immediately jumped in the ocean and swam out a ways. Pietro and I took to each other like boyfriend and girlfriend, kissing and bobbing together. The water felt so refreshing. Not many feet away some young girls and boys played joyfully in the water, running and splashing one another.

We came out of the ocean and found our little patch of towels. Mom sat lathered up in sun screen, white as a slippery albino lizard, ready to take on the UV rays. She watched all the people around us, in constant movement and play. A man came by holding a stick six or seven feet long over his shoulder. The stick was bulging with items for sale, goggles, blowup beach balls, snorkels, flip-flops, cheap hats, squirt guns, buckets, shovels, and sunscreen. He was a walking store on the beach, just in case anyone forgot something.

We swam a few more times and watched more people, most of the younger women wore bikinis that hiked so high up their butt and thigh, it was a wonder they weren't actually naked, and the same women had breasts that looked like something out of Baywatch with David Hasselhoff in the early 90's.

Pietro leaned back into the shade of an umbrella, posed with his hands under his head he rested his eyes. Soon, the beach emptied; I enjoyed watching how the families packed all of their belongings together and walked slowly back to their cars.
We made our way too, as the sun came lower into the sky.

The drive home was quiet. We left the radio off and listened to the ocean and the soft wind, it was the last night we would spend in Sicily, the next day we would fly home.

***

We decided to have one more round of Red Martinis before our meal at the pensione. It seemed that after a few days of being there, the looks we had gotten before finally toned down, we were old news already. The night seemed quiet compared to our adventure to Palermo and the Oceanside full of beachcombers. Each of us ate up every last bite of our meal, and looked around the table for more to eat. Mom and I were always delighted by food, and Pietro loved to eat. We chowed through the bread wrapped in a towel in a basket, and lathered butter on. We emptied the basket. When everything on the table had been consumed we made our way back to the room to decompress.

The night softened.

I sat down on the bed, and the warm breeze blew over me from the window.

Pietro, mom and I were all tipsy.

"Rhaina, you art beautiful," Pietro sighed as I slipped off my sandals.

Mom lay grinning next to me relaxing on the bed, her arms rested above her head exposing her hairy armpits.

"Thank you Pietro." I giggled and stood up, grabbed my digital camera and walked over to the end of the cot where he lay relaxing. I snapped a photo. From the foot of the bed, I could see a hole in the crotch of his pants. His legs were spread open and his arms tucked under his head. He just stared at me as I took pictures, I crawled up on him sitting on his chest and pointed the camera at his face. Click. One more, Click.

Through the lens I saw him differently. He was gentle. He was passive for a moment, and I wanted to sink into him. I wanted to fall in love with him, for me *and* for my mother.

"Ciao, Pietro". I said looking into his blue eyes; eyes that seemed bottomless, full of sunken treasure and shipwrecks. I blinked my eyes. I smiled because I couldn't help myself. I leaned down anchoring myself with my knees pressed around his broad chest bones, and touched my lips to his. He kissed me back as if nothing else existed in the world. My heart came pouring out into him, joy filled me for a moment. He kissed me deeper and I felt my body tingle, I felt a yearning in my breasts to press into him, a swelling in my sex to take him and love him, and suddenly I opened my eyes to see him so fully passionate, I remembered my mother laying on the bed, remaining quiet, not wanting to disrupt our intimate game.

I sat up, a flood of confusion filled my mind, and how can I be attempting to make love to this man, while my mom is sitting in the room? I sat for a moment on the edge of the bed. The breeze beckoned me from the window.

"Do you want to go for a walk Pietro?" I asked, knowing he would.

"Si, Rhaina, I go anywhere wit yhou." Pietro answered.

"Mom do you want to come?" She lay with her eyes closed, I could tell she was daydreaming. I could always tell when she was far away in her thoughts, but not actually paying much attention to what was going on around her.

"Noo," she sighed out of her dreaming, "I'm tired, I am going to rest, but enjoy your walk, the air outside is so nice right now." She sat up looking out the window, where the trees swayed gently in an evening breeze.

"Ok." I said as I searched for my long sleeved blouse in my luggage. I slipped on my white tie around shirt for the evening walk, and Pietro and I made our way down the four flights of stairs and out into the evening of Scopello.

***

Stepping out of the cool pensione, we walked right into the humid evening, where I could feel the thick balmy night pressing up to my skin, and the immense sensuality of hot wind was almost haunting. There was an electricity in the air that intrigued and frightened me. The dark evening sky wanted to trick our senses, trying to persuade us that the night should be cooler than the day, but the passion in the air steamed up the outdoors and set everything boiling and free. The crickets felt it. Instead of their usual chirping, they were screaming, making love; it was surround sound of nature's heated, passion filled music. We walked along amidst the corn fields and farm houses, on cobblestone roads under the full moon. Maybe the moon had everything to do with the crazed vibrations in the air, maybe Italy was shot years ago by cupid and the pure essence of it acted love, sang zealously, and spilled intimate secrets with everyone to remind us that we are all connected somehow.

My heart fluttered and I felt a little nervous. It was like some other force laid their own special effects on a one mile radius around Pietro and me. It seemed as if our sexual energy wound up nature and set it loose.

The closer I came to the end of the journey with Pietro, the closer that I felt to the center of what Italy is about; I felt a passion that moved from my soul. No matter who you are in Italy, an old woman in a bank who needs new shoes, the Mafioso, a pasta chef, an owner of a bed and breakfast, or a wanderer on holiday, it is impossible to be dull and asleep, passion sings through you like the crickets on that summer night, it blows over you and keeps you holding your breath for more, like an oscillating fan coming back again and again to ease the heat. No one holds back their need. Pietro certainly did not when it came to needing me.

The trees rustled in the steamy wind and rows of corn stalks danced like gypsies. We walked for the last time through the back roads of Scopello, saying ciao to the couples and happy families passing by. Pietro held my hand inside of his while we strolled slowly down the dirt road. As we passed a field of corn we heard the donkey that had been a reoccurring piece of entertainment since the day we arrived. I was frightened at first because we would never see the donkey, only hear it in the field below us, but that night the Donkey couldn't fool me, that night I was only afraid of one thing.

I thought the only way to get over my fear of losing myself to Pietro was to seduce him, maybe then I would hold the power.

We sat down on the rock wall of a bridge. Below us there was a small cliff and a dry river bed, above us the biggest moon I had ever seen. My legs opened so that each one rested on either side of the wall, he sat like a mirror in front of me. I had never reacted to a person before the way that I reacted to him. I saw things in him that reminded me of myself, things that reminded me of my mother's former lover.

We kissed. The force of energy that poured out of Pietro could not make up its mind whether or not to give into me. He was afraid of it too. Eager and anxious, like he wanted to devour me. He came at me all at once, I became defensive and hesitated.

He reached his construction muscled hands around my waist and slid his thumbs underneath my bellybutton. That was convincing. I closed my eyes, and lifted my hips to slide his fingers under my panties. It took only his right thumb to make my hips writhe back and forth. He stirred me like the shooting light above us darting into the milky-way. A few seconds later I stood up, zipped up and walked away.

I couldn't understand how I felt in love and

turned on one moment, and the next angry and scared.

Pietro caught up with me, convinced I still wanted to play the game. He wrapped his arms around me from behind and turned me into him. When he held me, I stayed there because I felt a need in him, like I might tear him apart if I pulled away.

"Abbraccia me. Abbraccia me. Oh Rhaina," I held on, curious about his desperation. I felt I had been there before, letting someone hold me to please them, to be polite. Instead of turning away this time, my anger pushed me over the edge, I wanted to understand. I wanted to know why he came, why my mother persisted like she did in the airport. How had we come together like this?

I held his hand as he pulled me in the direction of a yard blocked off by another rock wall. We hopped over the water and my stomach fluttered, nervous excitement fueled me.

"Are you sure this is okay? No one is going to shoot us are they? Isn't this private property?" I kept imagining some Mafioso with a shotgun blasting us away for invading his space. A muffle of voices and music floated through the air like the smell of a Barbecue through a neighborhood. There was a round of concrete that lay out of place under a leafy maple tree; we sat down on it. Both of us knew what we were doing there, already aroused we waited almost awkwardly for a sign or a gesture from each other to make a move. Without knowing how it started, I found myself like an ocean wrapping around him as he dove hands first into me, his eyes glazed over, in a world clouded by desire. We held onto one another; life vests holding each other afloat. It would be a shame to be drowned before we reached the island where the secret treasure of our reason together was buried. We were thieves, stealing the clock, slipping away again into no-time.

Somewhere in that presence, I was lifted out of my body, and a memory snagged me, like the changing of direction in a dream, where one part of a room fades away and you enter into another.

I remembered his embrace, the one that needed me like Pietro needed. It held me like I belonged to it, it possessed me but I didn't understand how.

They both had those broad shoulders, and the same swagger.

I remembered Reign standing outside our front door,

I looked up at him through the rectangle window panes of the door. He stood back almost hiding in the hinges, his barrel chest silhouetted; framed by the pillars of the porch. He held his head proud, curious like a child, mischievous, as if he was waiting for me to give him a boundary.

"My dad isn't home," I told him. I was three, as high as his thigh. He was curious, the way he looked at me, what was he doing at my house?

"Is your mom here?" He looked at me with tenderness. I did not understand.

"Yeah," I stared, studying him.

My mother appeared behind me, taking the door in her hand and opening it wider to let him in.

"Oh, hi Reign," she said flipping her hair back. She raised her eyebrows innocently with a flirtatious smile, the way she did when she ran into attractive men in the store. He took the opportunity to come in without hesitation, stepping over the threshold into the living room. We were the only ones home, mom and I, my brothers were at school, and my father was working at his office not many blocks

away. I thought of him, wishing he was there to make this man go.

I could tell Reign wanted to be there alone with my mother, though he was also curious —about me. The two of them sat down on our velvet mauve couch. She sat in her usual place with her legs crossed, wearing a classy skirt that came just above her knee line. Her breasts were beautifully outlined in a blouse with a layer of lacy brazier peeking out. The pink lipstick freshly applied to her lips and framed within her short-bangs-identity gave her a mysterious confidence. She was fabulous, a model, a lady of the town. And he knew it.

I sat coloring a picture at our glass coffee table, watching my mom and this man, who was sprawled with his legs posed open, his crotch proudly relaxed, his arm rested confidently, directed toward my mother, as if welcoming her energy to meet with his. She was playfully smiling and laughing with him.

They seemed not to notice me watching them. I blinked.

A tiny prickling irritated my eye. Something was in it. I rubbed at it, trying to get it out.

I went to my mom crying, leaning into her and whispering, "I have something in my eye." I stuffed my head into her lap where it was warm, where I wanted to be. She pushed me up and quickly examined my face.

"Have Reign take a look. Reign can you see if she has anything in her eye?"

I stayed where I was.

"Come here baby," he waved his hand for me to come to his side, so I walked over and stood with my head stretched over for him to examine my eye.

He pulled the eyelid down a bit and looked.
"I don't see anything,"
"But it still hurts," I cried.
"Come here baby," he gestured to climb up into his

lap, I hesitated but worried I would be rude if I did not, so I lay down upon him, a tiny body floating on top of his round belly and broad shoulders. My chest pressed up against him, and he pulled me in. He was hugging me. And somewhere in that hug there was a yearning, but what kind of yearning? Something familiar, but uncomfortable, like the lover's you find and do not trust. I remember feeling numb to him, clenching my teeth together, trying to push off of him.

"Sshh, just lay here for a minute, it'll feel better."

I laid there a little limp body, listening to my instincts, how long do I have to lay here to be polite? I didn't stay long before I shoved my little arms into his chest and pushed myself off of him. As we separated it felt like the snap of a magnet.

"I should probably go," he said getting up. Mom walked him to the door. They stood together.

"Wrenna, go get me a glass of water in the kitchen," mom said with a flirtatious smirk on her face. Reign smiled at her, she tossed her head and giggled lightly. I didn't move.

"Will you go check and see what time it is? Young and the Restless is almost on." I took her second prompt, and went to the kitchen, I wanted to please her; all children want to please their parents. I could hear my mother whispering and giggling softly. They were the same sounds she made when she kissed my father in the kitchen at night, while they were cooking dinner.

She appeared next to me. Reign had gone.

She was drifting, as if her head were bobbing on top of her body; she drifted back to her task of pulling out the laundry from the machine.

***

Back in our room, my mother lay quietly next to me in the bed, breathing softly.

Pietro lay in his own cot.

"Rhaina, he called over to me. May I sleep wit you?"

"What?" I thought about how once again I had dodged out of my own game with Pietro no letting things go too far with him.

"No. I want to sleep," I said, happy to have space from him.

"Please Rhaina, I wheel jhus lay wit you, I no touch you." I didn't answer him, so my mother answered for me.

"You can have my side," she said, sliding out from under the sheet to switch places with Pietro.

At that I tightened myself into a ball and closed my eyes. Pietro came dancing over. My mother glided softly and sleepily onto Pietro's cot, falling back to sleep.

"I jhus wan to sleep next yhou, Ahh Rhaina, yhou art bewtiful." Pietro lay on his back, his hands folded in his lap. He wore briefs and his broad bare chest opened to the ceiling. A part of me yearned to touch him, to be felt and caressed again by him, to surrender like I had by the field, but I couldn't stop thinking of all the reasons not to. What about Ahron? The man I love? What about my mother? What about two different continents; a relationship would never work for us, I couldn't live in Italy, so far away from my family. And what about that man in my memory? Why did I feel so much the same with Pietro as I did with that man seventeen years before? I didn't want to hurt Pietro, but I choose to be cold. No warmth from me or I would just be leading him on.

"Rhaina, why you not speak wit me?"

I didn't know what to say to him, I had no idea

how to express my reasons for not loving him, aside from the obvious that my mother was right there in the room, and how could I possibly explore him if she was right there? It felt like the wrong time. I remained quiet.

"Are yhou made at me?" He asked with sadness in his voice.

"I just want to go to sleep," I responded coldly.

"Fine." he said curtly.

I felt something land on the blanket next to me. I opened an eye.

A small golden box with a curled ribbon lay by my hand.

"What is this?" I asked as I placed my hand over it.

"It is forhh you," he rolled over to face me with his hand propping his head up. I turned with my head resting still on the pillow, and rolled my eyes to look at him, then rolled them back to look at the box I held up in front of me. The box was very light, I lifted a flap on one side and then another, and poured out its contents. They were beautiful, a pair of earrings the color of the sky.

"They remine me of your eyz." he said. I softened. I felt defeated.

"Thank you." I paused. "Pietro?"

"Yhes?"

"Can we go to sleep now?"

"Yhes."

I rolled as far to one side as I could.

Pietro lay with his head cradled in his arms.

At some point we fell asleep.

{13} - FLYING HOME

We didn't talk much while we packed, nobody even made a crack about how full our suitcases had gotten, and I could barely zip mine. Mom and Pietro were particularly somber. I was relieved to be heading home.

The car ride was quiet, we were saving our words for goodbye. I extracted our dance CD from the player and replaced it in my carry on. In the rear view mirror I saw mom's tight face. She was never one to hold back tears, I suppose she wasn't ready to let them flow yet, she was holding on as long as she could.

We were making our way down the city streets of Palermo, looking for the exit to the airport when suddenly Pietro pulled off to a parking spot.

"I be right bach!" He jumped out of the car and disappeared into a stone building. The city was awake and locals chatted away over morning expressos and pastries, some were shopping at the little market area that we had come upon. I waited in the car, but mom took the opportunity to get out and look over a rack of clothing, just one last look before we left.

Pietro emerged from the building into a pack of bustling people, and as he made his way through, he held up a bouquet that filled his arms. He approached the car, where I sat against the warm hood.

"Dis eez for yhou and yhou Sylvie," he said, handing me a huge bouquet of oregano. "Dis eez Italian spice, so yhou never forget Italia. My mama' no like Sicilian oregano, she say, Napoli oregano bettar, but dis ok, I whan yhou have dis memory of Italy at America." The bundle permeated the entire space around me, and it was lovely. "I take dis one for mi mama', she say she no like it, but I know she like it." I reached up and touched the earrings that Pietro had given me the night before. They were tiny tear drops, little moon stones, the color of my eyes. He was thoughtful and romantic. It made me smile. I smiled up at him.

"Hey Pietro. Grazie. Grazie, for the earrings. They were a very thoughtful gift. When did you get them?"

"I go, dis time you thake shower," he chuckled at his cleverness. "I see them when I go into dis shop, and I think, deez are like Rhaina's eyez. Yhou haf beautiful eyes Rhaina, I gone miss yhou."

"Thank you Pietro."

Inside the car, we were buried in the aroma of Oregano, but we all laughed and enjoyed the uplifting spice. Mom perked up and made a joke about the people at the bed and breakfast being relieved that we were gone. It was almost as if we had returned to our normal little family of Mom and Pietro and I, chuckling and making jokes. Our joyful moods faded away again as soon as we arrived at the airport. We returned the car keys to the rental counter. Our flight would leave in only thirty minutes, we had five more to wait until it began boarding. It seemed like a lot of goodbye to fit into such a small window of time.

I stood watching mom hold back her tears, patting Pietro on the shoulder, the way her mother used to do to us as a way of saying the things she never knew how to say. I felt that this was not the end of Pietro. We had created a bond with him, and even more than being bunk mates at summer camp for a week, he came to us, as an angel, he came to guide our souls on their path, to reassure that my mother and I found something different than our same old routine.

Mom gave him one last hug, sinking deeply into him, giving way to her feelings for him for the first time since we met. It was odd seeing my mother like that, I was used to knowing her as mom, as the woman married to my father. I was used to only seeing her lean into my father in the way she did with him, soft and comforted, sometimes playful or flirtatious, but this was nothing like that. It was as if she had found a sacred pool that reflected to her the secrets of herself she had hidden away for a long time, in his embrace her ancestors were able to fly back from where they were left, and bring back to her all that was lost of her culture.

As she turned away, she let the tears come down.

It was my turn to say goodbye.

I held onto the straps of my luggage, standing in the boarding corridor. Pietro came to me, he looked out of breath, like he had fallen and gotten the wind knocked out of him.

"Oh Rhaina," he cried. Tears beaded up in his eyes. "How I gone loose yhou? Come bach to me, my Rhaina.

I not gone loose yhou now." I put my bags down softly, unsure of what to do. I knew I didn't feel the way he did, I didn't feel I needed to be sad, my heart wasn't breaking. There went my mother, a ball of emotions, and here I stood in front of a man who was enamored with me, and I felt unriveted. I was afraid that if I let myself feel anything, I would be hurt, and be helpless to do anything about it. So, I held Pietro in my arms, hoping that would satiate him, hoping it would soothe his heart. He picked me up into him, lifted me off the ground and held me close to him. It was his sureness that made me embrace him. We kissed deeply, and though a part of me loved it, another part clung to the life I had left at home.

"Ciao Pietro, arrivederci, ci vediamo." He reached for my hand and kissed it.

"Ciao my princess, my fragolina. You my fragolina. Ciao Bella, my Rhaina." I held my bouquet of oregano up to my chest, picked up my suitcase, and leaned over to kiss him on the cheek. He held his hand up to his face, and I saw the expression of awe come across him again.

I turned and walked down the corridor, then looked back once more before I turned the corner. Pietro was watching me, his face was twisted up and crying. I felt tears stream down my face as well, but not because I missed him, because I didn't understand why I didn't long for him, or why I couldn't love him the way he loved me, or why my mother was so determined for me to love him. I knew I still had a long journey ahead of me.

Goodbye Pietro. I turned and wheeled my over-stuffed suitcase around the corner and he was gone.

With the bouquet secured alongside my carryon in the compartments above us, I sunk down into my seat. Mom sat stiffly, averting her eyes from everyone, while I waited next to her ready for the plane to lift off. It was relieving that the pressure of Pietro's pursuit was no longer pressing at me, though a new weight pulled at me that I was vaguely conscious of.

The engine's sound and vibration intensified filling with pressure as the plane pushed itself into the air, pulling up, up and leveling out. The fasten seatbelt light went off. I observed that my body felt less tense once we floated safely among the clouds. Mom also let her tense body release, and it came out as a deep sob, a sob and moan that carried loudly over the seated passengers. For a moment I thought someone might come and say she needed to be quiet because she was causing people to worry.

I was anxious for her and didn't know what to do. For a moment I relaxed knowing Pietro was out of the way and we could go home and go back to normal. Mom could have her secret life and I could go find Ahron and figure out how to get him to realize he loved me, then let Italy be a story of the past; but even as we lifted off, leaving the country behind us, Italy had left its imprint, and so had Pietro.

I reached out and hugged mom's body into mine; she buried her face into my lap. Sobbing, she let out what seemed to be years of grief; grief for her father, grief for the separation of her ancestor's from their family; grief for things unknown to me. It all came out. I held her head, brushing my fingers through her hair, trying to soothe her. Her hair was beginning to have grey strands, it blended well with the light brown color and was hard to notice; its fine texture made it soft and easy to comb through.

My eyes went out of focus, I did not want to notice anyone looking at us.

I wanted so much to have deep compassion for my mother's disappointment. I wanted to tell her I'd marry Pietro, just so....just so she would be happy, but I couldn't, I could hardly bring myself to feel any loss or grief over leaving him, much less make promises I couldn't keep. Her sobbing quieted into a softer cry, and I felt again another release of pressure and a bit more calm.

I was relieved and my previous resentment toward her began to transform. I saw that despite what others might think about her, she was not crazy, she was homesick for her culture in the Old Country.

And there was something even more complicated than leaving her ancestors behind. Our trip was a timeless adventure, one where she was unbound by commitments or the conditions of being a woman in a time of demanding patriarchal expectations. In Italy she was able to follow her heart. In Italy she was able to be the Goddess that she is and not second guess herself for a second.

I saw clearly that she wasn't just my mother, but a woman who wanted to live by the sea and swim in the ocean with all the wild creatures, wear no bathing suit and be wild too. She wanted to be unbound by time, unbound by her sexuality, be her male part and her female part—and not have either of those parts oppressed or abused. She wanted to dance, and change with the wind, and to sing with the choir even though the nuns told her to not use her voice.

I looked up for a moment, refocusing my eyes and noticed that no one was looking at us at all. In fact, I could see that the deep weeping sounds had no effect at all on the people, they accepted her type of grief. Maybe that was she chose that moment to cry like she did, because Italy was her mother's lap. It was safe and welcoming, it understood her spirit.

The scent of oregano filled the air, and suddenly I missed that place we had just left. I was glad I had that aromatic herb, happy to have something to carry with me in my life as a memory to that wild adventure. Even so, I was certain, I would never go back again.

{14} - LETTERS

Mom was glum and her eyes were puffy from crying. Luckily, we planned to stay an extra night in Portland before returning home. Going directly back may have been too much culture shock for our tender hearts.

We went for dinner at the Ramada restaurant, but we didn't eat much. I ordered waffles with strawberries and whipped cream in an attempt to fill myself after being with my mother during her small death.

When my food came I took only a couple bites; before realizing I was feeling the letdown of our trip. Now that I was back in America, what did I have to look forward to?

"Ahron. Yes, Ahron. I should call him tonight!" I thought, "No, maybe I'll just write him another letter. No, maybe I'll just go drive to his house once I've re-situated myself back home again. Hmmm". I started to think about Pietro. I thought about how he looked at me and how he was so sad to see me leave, I had never experienced anyone with that kind of passion for me, the kind that made him want to come out of his life and follow me for five days.

I spread the whipped cream over the dips in the waffle with my fork.

"Mom? Why do you like Pietro so much?" Her

eyes suddenly sprang to life and perked up, as if she felt a bit of hope that Pietro was not all lost.

"Oh." she started with a sigh. "I just love how he...how arduous he is. And he had a funny sense of humor, he was always laughing and having a good time, he had a lot of passion for life, he appreciated all the food we ate, and he was spontaneous and up for anything...

"I loved his voice, how gravelly it was. Ullmmm," she paused and drew her eyes back as a lover might, suddenly escaping into another reality.

"He was just romantic...and innocent...like a little boy." At that, she stopped and quieted her voice realizing that she had started talking louder. We sat across from each other in a booth with green vinyl-lined benches and wooden head boards dividing us from other eaters. Mom was always so protective of the secret life she lived alongside the seemingly ordinary role of housewife.

***

We arrived in Bend the next afternoon and my father was waiting for us. I stepped off the shuttle and he stood there holding flowers, dressed in a clean outfit, he looked handsome, and much thinner than when we left him. He was healthy looking though, and his skin was dark from the sun. I couldn't believe how much he transformed in just three weeks. I felt so much about him, so curious about his experience while we were gone. Somehow, I felt for the first time a distance from him, but I wasn't sure why. He was my dad, and I was happy to see him. I sensed a nervousness in him, an edge that I felt deep but never spoke of, a fear that he would be abandoned, but he showed up, ready to meet us.

I thought I would be happy to be home, away from Italy, away from the pressing feeling I felt about pleasing my mother, but as I stepped off the shuttle, I was aware that I was still trapped, I had nowhere to go but back home with my parents, a place that suddenly felt artificially safe.

I was much quieter in the days following our return and I half avoided my mother. I didn't know how to support her, I just felt responsible for making her happy. I felt I was the only person that could bring back her happiness; she was so distant since our return. I assumed she was still mourning something from Italy. I wanted to find a reason for her sadness, something other than the truth, so that I could fix it, but I knew it would never be the same. We had died, a piece of our lives was dead, we could not bring it back, as much as we tried looking for the pieces to put back together, they were not there.

***

The next few weeks I went out with my friends as if nothing had changed. Mom was quiet, she hardly spoke, and my father was good at filling the silence with stories, it was one of his gifts, to alchemize the un-comfortable awkward silence with a story, and often a funny one. There was no one way of changing mom's depressed state, at some point she would find a way out, but it seemed impenetrable, like something be-yond my control, so I let it be.

I was lost without her companionship, I had al-ways bounced my ideas off of her and we talked about everything, but I wasn't sure how much I could trust her opinions, and anytime I tried to connect, she just wanted to talk about Pietro and the Old Country, I needed to talk to someone else, someone who would listen to me.

"Hi Ahron." my voice sounded like a six-year-old.

A small silence on the other end and, "hi." his voice was quiet.

"I just wanted to call and say hello. Mom and I just got back from Italy".

"Yeah! I got your postcard,"

"You did? Already? I thought they took forever to show up. I guess my dad got one too actually. Anyway, I sent you a few," I laughed, happy to be talking to him. Anytime I heard his voice I felt like sighing over and over, and remembered the cool evenings I spent with him cuddled up on his mattress when we first met.

"How was it?"

"What? Italy?"

"Yeah, Italy," I could tell he was smiling, he had this tone of voice that changed when he was flirting, which went along with a part of his sense of humor that had an edge of sarcasm in it. Usually sarcasm in my family came out with a pack of energy that always seemed to be covering up deeper feelings, and I was often hurt by it, but when Ahron did it, it made me laugh, and it kept our conversation light.

"Well," I stopped for a moment, sorting through the memories of my trip.
Suddenly I felt like crying. I felt that I had messed something up. I didn't want to lie to Ahron and not tell him about Pietro. But, at the same time I realized that

I *had* called him because I was confused about all of it. I wasn't sure what was right or wrong. I took a breath and pushed away the sensation to cry.

"Well..," my voice changed to one of a gossipy nature, one that would allow me to not claim any accountability in the least for my part in the Pietro scandal.

"Oh my God Ahron, it was really weird. The first part was cool, we went to Rome, and did a lot of shopping. We went and saw this crazy place underground with a whole bunch of bones made into different arrangements that was interesting. I don't know, there was a lot, I had a hard time when I arrived, and it was pretty crazy culture shock. Anyway, um, well...we met this guy." I stopped. Ahron was always up for an entertaining story.

"Or he met us. At first I thought he was mafia, but it turned out he just had a crush on me," was I telling him this to make him jealous?

"Ugh, anyway he followed us through Naples one day. My mom really liked him, but I wasn't interested in him, it was really mom that wanted me to go for him... anyway, it was kinda weird." I trailed off for a minute, not sure why I had called him in the first place. Was it to confess myself that I had cheated on our ethereal girlboyfriend relationship? I did feel guilty that I claimed to be in love with Ahron, but that I just couldn't seem to keep my focus on him, though I couldn't deny that I always just wanted to be with him, it was like an addiction. Although, if he actually showed more interest, maybe I would be more loyal. Yeah, why was I being so hard on myself about Pietro, it's not like Ahron had ever even told me he loved me.

My gossip voice came back, but this time, I jumped into story telling mode.

"Anyway, there was this airport strike, and we were stuck in Naples, so mom insisted we call Pietro, because he had offered to drive us. And so we did, and he came and picked us up and drove us down to the boot of Italy, and THEN, he came with us all the way to Sicily!" I stopped because I didn't really have more to say. I wondered if he would judge me, or if he would know my innocence in the whole situation. Somehow I blamed him for the whole thing happening in the first place. He was the one that told me I should travel the world after all. The other end of the line was quiet.

"Are you still there?" I asked.

"Uh, oh. Yeah." he sounded sad, or serious maybe. My heart sunk. I shouldn't have told him. What was I even grasping at anyway with this guy?

"Sounds like quite the trip, like your mom was kind of crazy!" He laughed. I laughed.
"It was kind of crazy, I am still processing it, and it definitely wasn't as fun as I wanted it to be."

Ahron and I talked for a little while longer, I asked him about his fishing camp that he went to for the summer, and I wished him a belated birthday.. He listened mostly, but chimed in with a funny story here and there and any time I started to interrupt him, he would catch me with this funny sound he made, like, "hey, I'm telling the story now".

Finally we said goodnight and I hung up the phone. As usual I was left wondering why it had to be only that phone call. Why hadn't he invited me to see him? Didn't he want to make love to me? Didn't he want to see me?

As I went over the conversation in my mind, I wondered if I had betrayed my mom, I made it sound like she was setting me up and like the trip was a total bust, but she was really just there being hopeful, I was the one who was trying Pietro on. I was the one that went and kissed him and strung him along. I sat down on my sofa. I was so confused, and I worried that somehow now Ahron was going to think I was as crazy as my mom. He definitely listened to me, the thing I always loved most about him, but he still didn't say he loved me. And what about Pietro? Why did he have to come into our lives in the first place? Where did he even come from? After talking to Ahron, I realized that I couldn't even begin to explain the thing that my mother and I had experienced in Italy together. There was something mystical about it, something that spoke like a dream through it all, as if we had called Pietro, but neither of us knew why.

***

A few days after I talked to Ahron, I was still feeling like an idiot, but then I received a letter from Pietro, and remembered his humour, and I couldn't help but laugh and get over myself a little. He wrote a hello to mom also, and when I showed it to her, she brightened up. A series of postcards and letters and finally emails went back and forth between Pietro and me, like we were old chums. For the time being I put Ahron aside from my thoughts, after all, he hadn't even tried to call me since our last talk, and he probably never would.

With each letter mom perked up a bit, and I began to wonder if she was right, maybe I was miss-

ing something from my heritage, maybe Pietro held the
key to some mystery that had yet to be discovered.

***

[Letter]

31, July 2002

Hello Renna or Hello Princess,
I hope your return whit your family is great for the
rest of them and whit your friends too, I miss you my
princess but don't care too math I bee OK The time
sometimes is fast and sometime is slowly it is de-
pends what you doing, and depends how you feel in-
side; anyway if is fast or slooly I tray too be always
happy, I think I be happy beeches Im happy inside just
when I was whit you I feel more happy, so now Im less
happy and if you feel the same we most stay near very
close do you think so or not? Tell me yes o just don't
live me alone forever bee my now or let just bee my if
you do Im the most happy men in the Whorld. Ciao
princess. Ciao Sylvie. da Pietro com affetto a big kiss

[Postcard]

3 Aug, 2002

Hello Renna, I just went in the bar next Zi Teresa res-
taurant and drink 2 martini. Naw Im apstairs the cas-
tle and I se all panoramic that I se whit you in the port
of Napoli there is the biggest boat of the world it's the
golden princess; so she have you name. I send to you
this post card because you don't wont tolk about pizza
but almost you can se the best pizza! I love you
A kiss return to you

Pietro.

[Postcard]

7 Aug, 2002

Ciao, Renna I hope you don't be hungry because I gone again in Holiday, whitaut you my princess! Are you gone forghive me? If you do, next Holiday I be your cavaliere agein. The water it's more cold here and The food is very good you and your mam will be liked too much here, like Sicilia, "I feel like you are here"

Bye Bye Fragolina, ciao Sylvie.

[Email]

1.8.2002

hello sweet fragolina,
how are you Im fine and I hope you to, I think this is good way to write whit you but I didn't ear you voice, so for sometimes it's ok.

I just call you yesterday and may your borders and after your father ansvering to me, I say to them that I call you bach but I go to sleep, naw I no you work more I would like to help you for don't meeting you be tired and becouse you are to precise for me so I would you stay at home and rest, not becouse I whont think like at old italian mentality but just becuouse you don't be consumed from work.

bye bye my preterite actrice

big kiss fragolina by Pietro.

[Email]

3.8.2002

Dear Renna,
My sweet fragolina I receive the pictures, I vrely like tham and naw I can remember better that you and your mam are so fanny I laug so much when I seen you face agein its more reason that I whont see you, any place that we find for me it's right because whit you I stay everywhere, but if you want a place whit wally I have a wally for you it's inside me, and this wally it's gone be always full of love, you don't have to bay it's your and I never thank bach this from you.

My love for you it's true andI gone believe in everything good in this world because you come to me and I know hoo send you to me, so naw what I have to do it is just be happy in this best party whit you and meeaking sure that we are invited next party to whit all good people thanks for the shirt they are good size I just want know where is this banana city I would like by something for you and you mam from there too so ones we go there, oh I just call you a fragolina and you whant call me banana men. thake care beautiful princess

Infinity kiss for you, and one for your mam for

meeaking a wanderfull princess whit lots of love

Pietro

[Email]

10.8.2002

Ciao fragolina
Im ride your email and when I ride that you love me, I start flying I don't no where Im going or arrival, now I be flying forever if you want stop me you mast go in the sky, find me and put me on the earth again, do you think it's a giok, no it's no a giok you love me and Im full full full full very creasy naw so this it's the best surprise for me in my life naw deny surprise from you to it's the best because I love you and you love me so you are my special think in life, if before I lose I don't care too much but naw I winn because Im whit you and I be never lose I be love you because you are my angel.

ciao ciao fragolina just be happy a great kiss for you from the sky.

[Letter]

14th, Aug 2002
Ciao Sweet fragolina,
Im This Time I gone be alone I gone Treating you like a fragola, it is finish The season of fragola {strawberries} I gone bay last one end put in the fridge, so I can have you always like frech and beautiful, and when is The season
of fragola I gone bay everyday a fresh fragola, so it's like I never be alone naw; it's like a Drag; because some body saying the love it's like a Drag, and if is vrily I want be all the Thime very Stont. So you are my preferit fruit and my preferit Drag, so I gone be the

most eater of This Things in The Whorld, I was before The most one ho eat a fragola for This I very feel you inside to me because also if I don't you from long Time; and if is nobady ho making a fragola I gone have all receive of you in myself. Werner, I love you, and I don't want be very possessive, but you seat that you love me so when I see you again I gone very eat you, so you most be seare Ok, just be cute, what frees lemon and saw Martini "she I bring Marini"

Bye Bye my sweet fragolina
Ciao Ciao Sylvie,

[Postcard]

21.8.2002 Sardegna

My Renna,
Seriusli or not meaby I luuk like sometaims too you but, it is very fanny all the time that I have in Sicilia and Sardegna but I prefer more the time when I meet you. Naw it's Finisch my holiday and the all Fanny thincks be just a remember and if the remember thinks it's seriusli or not! I live you, but I don't gone lose you my fragolina ciao
Ciao Renna and Sylvie,
This is The Queen Park in Caserta; Renna I don't won't treating yo like a Princess; you are The Princess; "My Princess".

{15} - AN INVITATION

"WHEN YOU WALK IN A DREAM AND YOU KNOW YOUR NOT DREAMING SENORE', SCUZA ME CAN'T YOU SEE YOU'RE BACK IN OL' NAPOLI, THAT'S AMORE!" DEAN MARTIN

I found the 011* number written on the inside cover of Don Quixote, and dialed. It was late by then, almost midnight, so it would be around 9 a.m. in Italy.

Kch kch xch xch—

"Pronto?"

"Ciao Pietro"

"Rhaina?"

"Si,"

"Ah—oh—Rhaina. Is you?"

"Si. It's me." *Lonely, wondering.*

"How art yhou?"

"Molto bene, grazie, y tu, I mean e tu?"

"Bettar, now I talk wit yhou."

It is late, I am feeling lonely and lost, yearning for something different.

"Rhaina, ciao ciao mi fragolina, Oh, Rhaina, Rhaina."

*I'm breathing into a portal, a dusty portal, and when
I hold my breath I feel his, touching just below my ribcage,
tugging at a memory of where I came from.*

"I miss you Pietro."

"I miss you Rhaina. Oh Rhaina. I am thinking still
this. That you lhove me."

I sighed. How could I not love this guy? He
was funny, and he wrote me letters, he was passionate.

"I do," I whispered. Hadn't I told him that the
other night? I did love him, or I would fall more in love
with him, when he came. What if I just passed him up
and he was the guy I was supposed to be with? What if I
was sitting around waiting for Ahron and I let go of this
opportunity, then Ahron just never came around?

"I go morh on holeeday, to dees place where I
go to thee sea. Oh fragolina, I hope forth yhou to be
here wit me. I want to kees you my sweet fragolina."

I sat on the cold cement floor of the T.V.
room that used to be a garage. My parents slept on
the other end of the house. It was just him and me in
that moment.

"Pietro, I want to see you again, I want you
to come to America."

"Si?!, For real? You see me again? I come?
You really want me come?" I stopped for a moment,
considering what just came out of me. I couldn't
turn back now, if I changed my mind the movie
would stop here, there would be no happy ending,
there would be no movie.

"Si, Pietro, you told me you want to come, I
want you to come."

"I buy my ticket tomorrow, I go and I buy my
ticket, I come to Amerika to see my Rhaina. Oh, I love

you Rhaina."

"I love you too Pietro." I loved saying those words, they made me feel special and important, to be in love with someone who loved me.

"Ah, Rhaina, you love me, I am so happy."

I suddenly felt tired, the long day had caught up with me.

"Pietro, I am so tired, I need to go to sleep. I will talk to you soon."

"Okay my fragolina, I talk wit you soon. I come to Amerika. I talk wit you tomorrow." His gravelly voice went quiet, but he continued to breath, holding on, waiting for me to hang up the phone.

"Goodnight Pietro," I sighed.

"Ciao...Rhaina." I hung up.

The next day, Pietro called and told me he had bought a ticket. I felt a tightening in the center of my body, but had no explanation for it. I was going to love Pietro, I knew it. I put my thoughts to work on remembering the fantasy of him in Sicily, the erotic couple of moments we had on the stairs and out on the rock wall and about how he followed me from Naples to Sicily. I felt so important being the center of his universe. I suddenly felt excited, I couldn't wait to tell my mother when I saw her.

Immediately, when the news reached her, her entire demeanor changed, she became in love with life again. Every day she moved with tremendous purpose through the house, readying everything for Pietro's arrival. It was decided that he would stay down in a little house that she usually used for her private practice. It was only a short walk from our house.

For a short season mom and I became best friends again, talking everyday about Italy, and Pietro.

The closer it got to him coming the more invested I became in keeping him. In my mind I was giving him a chance to get away from the mafia, and the culture of Italy that was economically hard on the people. I felt I was saving Pietro from having to work as a mason six days a week, twelve hours a day, because that seemed like far too much. I wanted to save him, to bring him to America and give him the chance to live the American dream, whatever that was. So, with my mother and me fantasizing together, we began to dream up a plan to get Pietro a Visa.

I stood looking at myself in my mother's mirror. She fluffed her bangs and applied new lipstick while I picked up curvy bottles of perfume from the golden trays on her dresser.

"I could marry him mom, you know to get him citizenship, and I mean I could always divorce him if it didn't work out, I only need to be married to him long enough for him to be able to live in America." I saw my mother's eyes spark.

"Mom. You know what we should do? We should go to a wedding store and I could try on dresses. We'll tell the people in there that I am engaged!"

"That's a great idea," I could see the gears turning in her head. "But, you need a ring, you could wear my engagement ring". She reached over to a small gold music box and opened it, pulling out her diamond engagement ring, and holding it out to me. I slipped it on my right ring finger, and the diamond rolled down, hanging inside my hand.

"I don't know if this is gonna work, the ring is too big, it's falling off my finger."
I turned it around and squinched my fingers together to hold the ring in place. "There, I'll just hold my hand tight so it doesn't fall off. If they ask any questions I'll tell them it was the groom's grandmothers and that I still have to have it refitted." The story was growing in my mind. And my mother's excitement was growing too.

An hour later we drove out South of town along the highway strip. When we pulled up to the little shop with wedding gowns posing in the windows, I felt a nervous twinge in my stomach. The gowns never made a lot of sense to me. I couldn't understand a dress that could only be worn for one day, just to look pretty, it seemed like a waste of time and a waste of money. But, here I was looking into the window tracing the stiff curves of silk and lace, fabrics of white, the one color I could never wear, because I inevitably would spill something down the front. I felt most comfortable sitting on the floor or the ground, and white never survived those tendencies of mine.

We pushed open the heavy door and tiny bells above us announced our arrival.
A coy woman sat with an air of boredom behind a counter.

"Can I help you?" the woman raised her eyebrows, sizing us up, and deciding we weren't worth working too hard to please.

"Yes." I piped up putting on my act, "I just got engaged and we're looking for wedding dresses".

"Alright," she hesitated for a moment, and I gripped my mother's ring in place. She stood up and led us to a raised platform, where she touched my elbow and guided me up. She took her measuring tape and wrapped it around my breasts, my waist and my hips. She measured my height.

"Do you have anything in particular in mind?" I froze. I had friends that obsessed over magazines, looking at wedding dresses and clothes, but I never understood style like that, I just liked comfort.

"No, I am really just trying to get an idea of what I want."

"Go ahead and take a look around, this area over here is what we have that is close to your size." She left us to look.

Mom looked over the modern satin dresses. We both excused them, they were simple, but reminded me of a Disney Cinderella dress for a three-year-old. Most of the other dresses were conservative, made for a first lady, or a business woman. I started to imagine something romantic because I was marrying an Italian man, and Italy is Romantic. Just then, mom and I saw a dress at the same time. It had the shape of Snow White's humble country dress, with a bell curve on the bottom and rounded shoulders. It was off white, making it look antique, reminding me of my ancestors and their culture in the old world. There were tiny beads embroidered into intricate designs across the chest. We both agreed I should try it on, so we found the lady at the front again and asked her for her help. She came over and told me it would be a few minutes, it was the only one and she would have to take it off the mannequin. She finally returned to us, holding up the dress as if carrying it over a threshold.

"Here you are." She handed it to my mother, and drew a curtain around the stage turning it into our dressing room.

Mom helped me pull it over my head. The back was flayed open, and the dress did not have a zipper, it only had buttons all the way up the back. So, one at a time, mom buttoned each one, and the dress began to hug my hips, and my waist, and my bust. I could feel my mom delicately fitting the little buttons into each eye hole. She finally finished, and we pulled back the curtain.

We both stood looking at me in the mirror. The dress came up on my neck elegantly, with soft coils of lace, and there was a V of sheer lace that revealed a bit of my chest. My breasts were perfectly held in and hugged, but not too tight, and I looked like a woman. It was my dress, one I never thought I had ever dreamed of. I looked at my mom to see what she thought. The corner of her eyes were wet, and she looked as if she might cry.

"This reminds me of the women in Italy Wrenna, I love how romantic it is." We both knew I was stunning. I had never dressed up so fancy before. Even during prom, I looked pretty, but still looked like an adolescent, but in this dress, standing with my mother, I felt older and important and special.

Pietro suddenly came into my mind, and I imagined us. I thought about him standing at the alter seeing me in that dress, and I could almost see his heart beating outside his tuxedo. How in love he would be when he saw me. I sighed and thought about the day he threw the tiny golden box of earrings at me when I was being grumpy at him, and now here I stood wearing those beautiful blue gemstone earrings that he said matched the color of my eyes, "The coelor of the sea" he said.

As I stared at myself in the mirror, I had a flush of sureness that I would marry Pietro, I could feel it. My mother would be so happy.

Just then, the store lady came back and looked at me, a bit surprised.

"It fits you perfectly. What are the chances that the one dress in here that doesn't have another size, the only one you wanted to try on would fit you just right?" She looked baffled. I knew it was meant to be.

"I love it," I told her. "It kind of takes my breath away". I turned and looked at the back, at the long line of buttons intricately jetting up the back, and just as easily as I fell in love with myself as a bride, I was now unsure if I could commit to such a dress, after all it was only one day, and what would that day do to the rest of my life?

I reached back around my neck and began to unbutton the dress.

"Oh, are you taking it off?" asked my mother.

"Yeah, I am ready to go, I'm getting hungry." She helped me with the rest of the buttons and the curtain was drawn again as I pulled on my normal clothes.

We put the dress on hold and exited the shop jumping into mom's Ford Truck.

"That was a great dress! You looked so good in it," mom praised me.

"Yeah, it was really pretty, it fit me perfectly." I mused. But, in my mind I couldn't help but wonder if it wasn't just an illusion, just a fleeting illusion.

***

A few days before his arrival, Pietro called un-
expectedly. He was quiet at first, and I sensed that he
had something on his mind. I wondered if he felt something from me, if he questioned my integrity in asking
him to come.

"Rhaina, I haf tell yhou somesing, Yhou art my
Angel. But, I haf another Angel. She live in another
place. And I haf tell yhou." He paused, and I stood
listening, confused and suddenly nervous. I thought
Pietro was in love with me, does this mean that he's in
love with someone else too? I was right, he was a con
artist, and right when I was convinced that there was
a man out there that couldn't possibly break my heart
because he was so persistent, and so insistent that I was
the one, he tells me that there is someone else.

"I don't understand Pietro. What do you
mean?"

Pietro waited quietly on the other end of the
line.

"I have a dah-ter. She is my other Angel."

"Really?"

"Si, She is Fourrh, I haf her, but she not see me
anymorrh, she live in Mexico. I fall in love once, yeah?
And I haf baby with my love. My family takes her
in, but her fathher, he no happy, we werrh not marry,
Ahnd, he tink I ask beffore we haf love so we can marry,
but he no want his dagh-ter in other country, so he take
her and my Angel bach. I no see her for long time." I
could hear the sadness in his voice, and I wasn't sure
what to make of it. "I am afraid you no like me, if I haf

163

dah-ter."

"Oh, Pietro, it's okay, I don't mind, I mean, it makes sense, your 32, you've had a lot more time than I have to do things like that, it's not really that surprising. I mean I
have a lot of friends that come from divorced families, but then new families come together and there are step-sisters and brothers; I know people who have kids with people and then their relationship doesn't do well and so they end up going separate ways when the baby is still little. I am not jealous, if that's what you're worried about."

"Oh, I am happy you say dis. I was worry you no love me aghain Rhaina. I lhove you."

"I love you too Pietro."

"I com see yhou soon mi fragolina, kisses to yhou. I send email when I come on de plane. I see yhou soon, Good night Rhaina."

"Good night Pietro, see you in a few days." I hung up and sat down on my bed. Whoa, that was some news. I felt suddenly unsure about Pietro coming. I couldn't believe how this story of Pietro kept on getting more and more complicated, and here I was inviting him to my home. I began to cry, everything was so confusing. Just the day before I was trying on wedding dresses convincing myself that I was going to marry a man I hardly knew so that he could get a Visa, and then he calls me and tells me he has a daughter. I don't even know him and here I was willing to sacrifice myself to save him and my mother. I felt crushed. I couldn't understand why it seemed that everything I thought was right, everything I was doing to make my mother happy, to make Pietro happy, wasn't making me happy.

***

[Email]

18th September, 2002
Ciao Renna,

Im coming to Portland on 19 of September at 21;12 o clock so you can coming to Portland so see you there, I hope you don't cheing mind agein, but if you do enyway Im in Portland and will be easy for me to find you and take you in some hospital ha...ha... ha. ciao ciao Renna.

***

September 19, 2002
   Travel is raw. Lightning strikes, fuel runs out, food goes bad, sometimes our internal compass fails, and there are never enough bathrooms, but we do it anyway for the unknown, for the chance that we will come upon magic in the midst of pandemonium and away from the banal.
   We left for the airport early, mom wanted to make sure we were there for Pietro's arrival, she didn't want him to arrive and have nowhere to go. For my part, I was excited about the idea of sitting in the airport and watching couples meet after a long time apart, kissing, holding each other.
   There were shuttle stops in every section from A to Z to take us to the waiting areas. Some people were flying off to another business meeting, ready for two weeks of greasy fast food, steaks, mashed potatoes with salty margarine on

165

top, and too many thick amber drinks on the rocks. One person slept, curled up on a bench in a cloud of jet lag, catching up with time.

A few people held flowers and occasionally paced, or gazed out the window to stare at the sky. I stared with them, waiting to see the plane that Pietro was on, I imagined I would know it when I saw it; once I was connected with someone I could feel them getting close or far away. I could always find my friends, maybe I just knew their routines, but it was more than that, there was a thread, some kind of psychic connection that wove us together. Pietro was already woven into my life, the thread that connected us was bringing him closer to me.

My mother described our travel together as a constant premonition. It was like a dream coming to life. In dreams we have no need for self-control, there are no boundaries, and we don't have to be civilized. Dreams are free, they are our own projections without consequences. It is in the physical existence where we are conditioned to think we are limited. But, just like that plane on its way to bring Pietro, I was in-between, the dream and the reality. I couldn't help think about Ahron, what about him? He has been the one for me, so why am I doing this to him? But, on the other hand, he was the one who left, and he's the one who never calls, so why should I sit around and pine away, at least Pietro writes to me. I am free. I chose this experience for a reason, it won't hurt to meet it and face it. Who knows, maybe I will learn to love him.

I stared at a clean shaven boy of twenty, blue dress shirt, flowers held too tight in both hands, and he was barely breathing. I was barely breathing. I looked away from the boy and there, under the bright airport spotlight, shy and dressed in silk, was Pietro emerging from the humidity of bodies streaming out of the arrival gate.

My heart began to pound. He was swept this way and that by the flowing river of people, and suddenly I wanted to dive into him, sink into his chest and feel the energy of Italy, I wanted so badly to fall in love with him, to live life in the dream, to never wake up.

{16} - A CULTURAL DIVIDE

The ocean swelled and crashed onto the shore, and early autumn light shimmered on the wet sand. Up on the beach a woman in a wedding dress posed with her newlywed in his tux, for a photographer who made use of the sea breeze. Her hair waved like fronds of seaweed dancing in the current. They laughed and ran barefoot, the wedding dress had served its use as the perfect white and now she played for the camera.

"Look Wrenna, it's another wedding!" Mom tried to direct my attention to the lined up white chairs and flowers tied with ribbons flapping in the wind, the chairs were abandoned and a party of fancy people watched the couple from a distance.

My enthusiasm for marriage and weddings was already waning, after being in a hotel with Pietro and my mom again, all the mixed emotions I had left behind at the airport terminal in Italy came back; already I was unsure about being a traveling threesome again.

I noticed a difference in Pietro, maybe it was the jet lag, or the pressure on him to perform now that *he* was in a different country. I felt different too. In Italy I was able to play a part, and convince myself that Pietro could be my lover. Maybe it was that illusion that persuaded me to invite him. Whatever it was, I tried to be patient and remember the qualities of him that I liked when we walked along the cliffs overlooking the ocean in Sicily. I did my best, but it wasn't easy to ignore that Pietro stuck out like a colorful wood duck swimming among a flock of juvenile mallards.

"Is so windee, dis beach iz freddo, no like Eetalee, much more warm in ocean and spiaggia." I felt a little disappointed that he didn't like our coast, to me it had always been an emotional place, a place of fond memories with my family, and a place that I could hear my soul speaking through the wind. It always had a melancholy feeling with the storms, wind and grey waves; it stirred the soulful parts of me. In Italy the waves were softer, romantic, calming, but this sea could be ferocious and wild, dark and brooding, like that part of my female that came roaring just before my menses.   "Who wants to have wedding here, iz too cold, all di people have coats on." Pietro looked perplexed.

"It doesn't matter does it, isn't getting married about celebrating your love and friendship anyway?" I asked

"Husbhand and Whife can no be frends."

"What do you mean they can't be friends Pietro?" I didn't understand why Pietro seemed to be arguing with everything I said. "They live together, they do everything together. Why would you want to spend your life with someone that you're not friends with?" I challenged his belief.

"They haf house toghether, but no understan

each other." I began to feel my temper rising. I don't know why I got so angry with Pietro. It was as simple as flipping a switch sometimes to start me fuming.

"So, are you saying that when people get married, you're just married and there is no way of working together as friends? There is no equality?"

"I no mean equal, they are no equal, they different."

"Well, why can't they be equal? What if one person is unhappy with their role in their marriage?"

"Role? What you mean, this role, rolling, like boll?"

"No, I mean like, if the husband makes the money, and he is working all the time, and the wife stays home. What if he gets tired of working in his job and the wife gets tired of being home all the time? Then, they change and work out something new."

"But, this no happen, the woman stay home, and husband find other work." I was getting so frustrated, Pietro followed me, but I kept losing the point of what I was trying to get at, his accent was sometimes hard for me to understand. My patience grew thin.

"My brother is married, and he and his wife, they trade, they figure out what is best for each person and they support each other doing what they want to do," I said, hoping to present an example of friendship in a marriage that could help him understand me. "I just mean that supporting each other's dreams is what marriage is about."

"I don understand. Een eetalie, yhou get marry, you haf cheeldren, and the mama' stay home with cheeldren, she take care of howse, and the men make the monee."

"So, are you saying that a woman has no life other than taking care of her children and her husband?"

"When she is marry, yhes, before she marry, she go out, she dance, she work." I was furious, I couldn't believe that he was so old fashioned in his thinking, that a woman's life forever becomes about being a mother and taking care of everyone the second she gets married. If that was what marriage was about, then I didn't want anything to do with it.

"But wait, I still don't understand why men and women can't be friends?"

"Men and Women, they have love mhaking, they live together, but they no understand each other." I sank. I didn't get it. I wanted my lover to understand me, I wanted a partner who could have sympathy for me and listen to me when I needed help and guidance about the challenging things in life. I could hardly make it through a conversation with Pietro, we had such a hard time understanding each other. And the way Pietro made it sound, women were only good for having sex and child rearing. I was beginning to wonder why he was here, and why he even pursued me. I thought he was in love with me, but as I had suspected in Italy, I felt he was here to make me his, to possess me. I feared that if I married him, I would lose myself and serve only him. He would be the voice of our marriage, the decision maker. He might hear me, but the end decisions would be his.

After a few minutes of silence, Pietro announced he was hungry, and that we should seek out a restaurant to find some food. By the time we were seated in a booth at Mo's ready to get some clam chowder, I could tell that Pietro had completely moved on from our conversation, even though I was still confused. He was gazing at me with dreamy eyes.

"Oh Rhaina, eez so good to see yhou. I am een eetalie, and I think about yhour eyes all of time." I stared at him in disbelief. Hadn't we just determined that we completely disagreed about what marriage was about? Had he heard a single word I said? How could he be flirting with me and talking about my eyes? Didn't he get at all that I was angry at him? He didn't want to understand me, he just wanted to have me. I looked over at my mother, knowing she understood. She talked about this all the time, about always feeling misunderstood, about the double standard of men and women. This was her fight, to prove that women were more than just childbearing servants, to prove that we are creative beings, that we are free agents, that we have the power of choice! My mother was smiling. She looked high, she had heard our debate and had written it off as a young lover's spat. The moment that Pietro looked at me in the dreamy way, she could continue her fantasy of having some connection to Italy in her life forever.

I was right back to being alone and fighting the same war. I fought to make sure I didn't give myself away. It wasn't going to be easy. My mother had a strong hold on me.

***

"Well, Pietro," mom said, as we were barreling over the pass in her green ford pickup truck, "you will be staying in my little house."

"Little house? What eez dis?" Pietro asked

in wonder.

"I have a little house down the street from our main house, the front part of it is rented out, but I use the back house as my office. You get to stay in it until we figure something else out." Mom was speaking as if he were going to be in America permanently.

"Ah, I no stay wit Rhaina and you?" He looked disappointed.

"Oh, well, you can have your own space to come and go as you please there.
You can still come up and have meals with us if you like." Mom had it all planned out. She was clever, putting him in the little house, knowing that three weeks of my dad and Pietro in the house together would be more than a little awkward.

"Okay, I try this little house." I laughed, there were still parts of Pietro that I appreciated, despite my growing disillusionment with him.

We arrived home toward dinner time, the trip from the beach had taken almost six hours because we had to stop for lunch midway. Mom dropped Pietro off at the little house so he could shower and settle in a bit. She told him she would be back to pick him up for dinner, and at that time show him how to get up to our house six blocks up the road, so he could walk up any time.

We went home and showered. Dad hadn't arrived home from work yet. Mom was watching me. I could see her studying me, but I pretended not to notice. I was processing the experience of Pietro being in my home town.

I took a shower and shook any feelings I had that were unsure. As I dressed I took Pietro into consider-

ation, wanting to be beautiful for him. And with a costume on, one of my romantic casual skirts from Italy and a blouse, I felt convinced that I
could change Pietro's mind about men and women, it was really just a cultural difference of opinion. He probably didn't even really think that, I was just misunderstanding him. I pulled at my heart strings and loosened them, took a deep breath and met him at the door with my mom right behind.

"Hi Pietro," I said with a coy smile. He had shaved his face and showered, and he wore a clean silk shirt like the one he had on at the airport. He had a pair of jeans on that showed the strength of his leg muscles. I had never seen him so dressed up.

"Ciao Rhaina," he sighed, "you art beootiful." I felt special when he looked at me that way, like he was under a spell. I felt like I was a princess and he a prince.

Just then, my dad appeared behind me, standing patiently.

"Oh, this is my dad, Carver! Dad this is Pietro."

"Hi Pietro." He said looking into Pietro's eyes welcoming him. He reached over and shook his hand. Unlike a prom date, who often has underlying intentions of finding out what is hiding underneath that big puffy prom dress, Pietro had a genuine confidence, and he carried no shame for his love for me. After all he had traveled all the way here to see me, I suppose he saw no reason in hiding his affections, even in front of my dad.

Dinner was ready and we all sat down to eat. Pietro entertained us with stories of his travels, and enjoyed sharing a few pieces of history about where he grew up in Naples. Dad launched into some stories as well, unconcerned about whether Pietro understood him or not. My father was always a good story teller, and I imagine even if you didn't speak a word of English, you could appreciate the way he made impersonations with voice changes and hand gestures. Once he had a couple glasses of whiskey, he'd really start to make you laugh. The night went well, my mother had her zest for life back again. Her hysterical laughter rang through the house at our stories. I had fun chiming in and giving my version of one part or another, and this made her laugh even more. We drank wine and ate steak that my dad had BBQ'd on the grill. Pietro gave us a gift of roasted eggplant and peppers that his mother had sent along with him. He opened them up and ate them along with his BBQ.

After dinner, mom and Pietro and I took a walk in the brisk air, for digestion, and to deliver Pietro back to his little home-stay apartment. I was beginning to have another change of heart.

"Eez there a city? A center, wherth I might go?"

"Do you mean downtown?" I asked.

"A place wit shop, anhd a bar, orh wherth I go dance? Or I go get cafe' in morning?"

"Oh, well yeah, we can show you tomorrow. You can come up to the house and have breakfast with us, my dad will have plenty of coffee, and then I can show you where the town is."

"Okay, ciao ciao mi fragolina, you arth just as beautiful in America as Eetalie.
See you tomorrow."

I reached around him and gave him a hug, then

planted a kiss on his lips. He had come all the way here, and I felt that I wanted to make him feel welcome.

"Oh Rhaina," he had the same stunned look he had when I kissed him the first time. With an aloof turn, I swished my hair and caught up to my mom who was half way down the alley already making her way home. I was sure she had purposely given us some time alone.

After we returned from walking Pietro back, mom announced that she was going to bed. I was wired. I thought about going to find my best friend Corrine, but she and I were in a weird place with each other ever since I told her that Pietro was coming to visit. Dad was flipping through shows in the T.V. room. I went and sat down next to him, staring at the screen but not really watching. Occasionally, I would laugh or chime in. Dad was watching a building show. I liked the building shows too, they were pretty interesting and fun to see what the guys came up with in the end.
After a bit, I got up and went into the kitchen.

Feeling restless, I started doing dishes, and in the middle of them I was struck with inspiration to bake Pietro banana bread for breakfast. Oh! He would be so surprised! I loved to cook when I was feeling in love. I pulled out all the ingredients and got to work. As I mixed flour and smashed bananas, my dad came in to get more ice to make another drink.

"Whatcha doing?" He looked over my shoulder, inspecting my process. "I am making banana bread for Pietro for breakfast. He's coming over in the morning."

"I see." He raised his eyebrows and nodded. "Looks good".

The smell of bananas filled the house. I wondered if Pietro's intolerable idiosyncrasies were merely superficial and if his attractive attributes were enough for me to love him for a lifetime.

"Smells pretty good," dad announced as he came into the kitchen again. The lights behind him had been turned off. The clock on the oven read 11:01. "I'm heading to bed itty one," he said as he kissed me on the forehead.

"Good night dad, sleep well". After I pulled out the pans of bread, I turned out the remaining lights in the house and made my way to bed too. I was suddenly exhausted.

In the morning Pietro came over a little after nine. I offered him a seat at the end of the table, the opposite end from where my dad always sat. In the kitchen I prepared a little plate with two slices of banana bread and a square of butter on the side. I placed a little knife near it, and filled a tea cup of coffee, and a little cup with cream. I held the little dishes like a waitress and served Pietro.

"Prego," I said in a cute Italian accent. I had heard people say that in Italy as a way of saying 'here you go', or 'enjoy'.

Pietro took a slice of bread into his hand and took a bite. He spit it out, "iz so dry," he tossed the bread onto the plate, pausing and looking at the plate in a perplexed way. He then took a sip of the coffee I'd served and stared blankly at it. "Iz okay, I go to citi, I fand braakfast. No problem." He looked up at me with a proud look on his face, and scooted his chair back. "How you get to citi?"

I was mad. I had worked late making that bread

for him, I loved making banana bread and everyone always complimented me on how good it was, how could he be so ungrateful? I wanted to tell him how hard I was working to make him feel welcome, I wanted him to appreciate me and all the things I had to offer from my culture. I wanted him to hear me, but we spoke different languages. So, what could I say?

"I'll show you". I guided him out the front door and walked to the end of the driveway. "If you follow this street down to the second traffic light and turn left, you will find the citi."

"Ah grazie. You cam get braakfast wit me?"

"No, I have a lot of homework to do."

"Ok, I see you latar." I watched Pietro walk down the street, discovering the world around him. He swaggered casually in the late September sunlight. He wore flip-flops and a pair of short cut-off jeans with a cotton jersey cut right at the bottom of his waist line, where a half inch of bare waist caught the late summer breeze. On his head he wore a straw hat, to keep out the sun. His outfit was a bitter sweet reminder of the free spirit that danced with us through Italy, but somehow in this high desert American town, he was out of place. I couldn't help but relate to him. I admired that he was just him. He was certainly courageous and charismatic. And like him, I didn't always fit in either. I was still hurt by him not considering my feelings about the banana bread, but I let it go, if being comfortable in our town meant going out for breakfast so be it.

***

Leaning proudly against the doorsill of the kitchen, with his elbow cocked toward his head, Pietro posed, as if always ready for a Ralph Lauren photo shoot. It was dinnertime again.

He stood there in the kitchen; poised and pretty, with cutoff jeans stretched around his thick thighs. He was Italian, a man who adored mellanzane con Pork chop, and a fool, committed to what each moment brought his way.

Dad sat back in his chair, his arm curled, resting casually on the table. He held his glass of bourbon and water. He was rooted there, squinting an eye at Pietro.

"Why you beeild?" Pietro pointed toward the dollhouse in the living room.

"Sylvie wanted a replica of her ancestor's house." he explained.

"Haow long it take you?"

"About four weeks"

"By yourself?"

"Yeah by myself, I built it back there," Dad gestured toward his shop.

"Where you beild? In Bach yard!" Pietro said in disbelief.

"No, No" my father chastised," Sylvie just wanted me to make a *small* version of her grandparents old house in Illinois."

"Ah I think yhou beeild haus for Sylvie to live in. Pietro laughed, "we don understand each other...ehh how you beeild?"

"I cut out a lot of little tiny pieces," Carver held up his thumb and forefinger an inch apart to help Pietro understand, "then I nailed and glued them to scale".

"How you cut small?" Pietro was fascinated and bewildered. "You haf speciol tools?"

"Come on out and I'll show you." Dad opened the door, stepped out onto the porch and tugged at the breast pocket of his shirt. After hitting the pack of Marlboro lights just once on his square palm, he pinched out one cigarette and lit it. A tiny ember swung through the evening light as he led Pietro to show him his shop.

It was getting late and mom worked diligently in the kitchen fixing an anchovy pasta that was a favorite bon appétit recipe she was fond of making. I set the table and remained skeptical of my mom's motives. Even so I laughed with her at Pietro bouncing around my father's shop likely asking him questions that were like a young child who is dangerously curious in his exploration.

We saw the lights turn off in the shop. Dad walked out and locked up, returning the key to its place on top of the ceiling board at the carport. Pietro came in and washed his hands. He went over to where my mom stood, dressed elegantly in a shin length skirt with an apron and a blouse, with her gold hoop earrings and a fresh application of pink lipstick. She stood dreamily stirring the anchovies in the electric skillet. Pietro reached over and grabbed the spatula. He lifted it to his mouth, and stood for a moment.

"Dis is teribal!" he tossed his hand gesturing at the contents of the skillet. Mom paused, suddenly brought back to our kitchen from her dream. She stared only for a second with a furrowed brow and her mouth open. Her pride fell as she blankly looked at her day-long awaited meal. I watched her turn and walk toward the kitchen door; fuming, she steered toward the front door throwing her shoulders back and slamming it behind her.

I stood there, looking at Pietro. My father had exited to the back porch were he sucked down a cigarette. I wanted to turn and go to my room, or leave the house all together, but there I was, responsible for him. I was the one who invited him, I was the one that we were all acting out this silly play to please. I was supposed to be in love with Pietro, but at the moment I couldn't stand him. I couldn't believe how insulting he was to my mother, she had wanted to surprise him with Melanzane all Parmigiana, one of his favorite Italian dishes, and he couldn't even see that she was trying to make him feel at home.

I finally decided to go to my room, leaving him to talk to my father, whom I knew was clever enough to know what to do. But, as soon as I entered my room, he was there behind me.

"Rhaina, yhou made at me?" His eyes were sad, and he looked as if he knew he had done something wrong. I didn't want him to feel worse, so I shook my head, even though I was fuming. I couldn't say anything.

"Rhaina, you, say someting?"

I sighed and sat down on my bed.

"Actually Pietro, I am just really tired, I want to go to bed." I just wanted him to leave and go back to my mom's little house, so that I could be alone and process my world.

"Okay, I stay here."

"No, you can't stay here, there is a room for you down the road."

"I wan stay wit you. I love you Rhaina."

Ugh. I thought. What have I done?

"Will you please go down there? I need to get sleep, and I won't be able to sleep if you're here."

"I be very quiet. I won bodder yhou." His eyes softened with the look that I saw in him in Italy, the one that I knew meant he wasn't playing games. "Please Rhaina?"

"Fine. But, don't bug me." I immediately turned off the light, and went to my twin bed, crawled under my down comforter and lay there. I didn't even brush my teeth. I figured that it was the only way I was going to get the space I needed in order to ease the stress that was building inside of me.

Pietro lay down on the pull out couch. I rested and sleep started to take me in, when I became aware that Pietro was shifting around.

"What are you doing?" I asked in an irritated tone.

"I get comfortable." He answered innocently.

"Oh." I lay into my pillow again and again began to fall asleep, a dream image came into mind, and before I knew it I had drifted off to sleep. I awoke in the dark to a rank acidic smell permeating the entire space around me.

"Oah—agh! Pietro, your farts are so smelly." I ducked under the covers, but the smell seeped in, I couldn't get away from it, so I opened the window, and let the cold air flow into the room as I buried myself again in my down comforter. It didn't help, I was just colder and the smell was tangible, its tentacles assaulted my nostrils through the pores of the blanket. I started kicking my legs in frustration.

"Aaagh!" I mumbled a yell into my pillow. I

pushed my arms into the mattress, got up out of bed and left Pietro lying confused in my bedroom. He laughed at how smelly his farts were, but I was disgusted. I walked into the kitchen and looked at the thermostat; it was 37 degrees outside. "Ugh." I pouted to myself. I grabbed the cordless phone and went as far away from my bedroom as possible, sitting down in our T.V. room, I dialed Corrine's number, I needed my best friend's moral support.

"Hello...?"She answered with a tired grumble.

"Hi." I sighed. "Pietro is farting and I can't sleep."

"Ha ha ha ha!" Corrine burst out laughing. She often complained about my gas, especially when I slept over at her house and we had to fluff the blankets one hundred times through the night in order to avoid asphyxiation.

"I don't know what to do, I can't sleep, it's really rank Corrine, I opened the window but then it got too cold. I just want my bedroom back," I whined.

"Do you have anything nice smelly that you could put in your bed to distract you from his stench?" Her voice was sympathetic, but still had a hint of amusement in it.

"Hmmm," I got up and walked into the bathroom. Soap? No, too fragrant. I couldn't sleep with Lever 2000 or Old English. I tried the kitchen, the only thing I could find was a lemon sitting on the counter. "Oh, I found a lemon. I'm gonna try it, ugh, I just want to sleep. I'm just so tired, I'm so tired of all of this." I sighed again.

"Good luck honey, call me if you need me, and come over if you need to sleep here."

"Thanks Corrine, Goodnight"

"Goodnight, Bye." She hung up.

I made my way back to the bedroom where Pietro appeared to be sleeping. The room still reeked of sour milk and fermented eggplant. I crawled back under my covers and stuck the lemon next to my nostrils, finding that it was comforting enough to breath with my head buried under the covers and the window cracked a bit.

As I lay there I recalled the image of Pietro walking down the hill toward the city's center that morning. I was still fuming over his rejection of the banana bread I was excited to make for him. He had only been in town for a few days and we were learning that American food was not to his liking. He wanted things like hamburger with melanzane (eggplant) or Potatoes with lamb chop and asparagus, only traditional food from Naples was satisfactory to him. I must have been crazy to think that he would want to be in America. I fell asleep defeated.

***

I felt responsible for Pietro despite my mixed feelings for him, so I invited him to meet Corrine, she was curious about him, but also pretty skeptical after all the stories I had told her.

Pietro and I climbed into my Jeep Wagoneer and drove over to her house. The night had cooled down, but Pietro still sported his cut offs, and short shirt. When Corrine opened the door, she greeted Pietro and talked to him as if he didn't speak much English at all. The contrast of Italy vs. Beige walls and carpet made Pietro's accent sound even more thick and

Italian and out of place.

The three of us walked into the kitchen, where her dad and step brother were preparing sandwiches.

"Hi Dave, this is Pietro, he's visiting us from Italy."

"Hi Pietro, Nice to meet you," he reached out with a strong grip and shook Pietro's hand.

"Piacere," Pietro responded in Italian even though Corrine's family knew absolutely none of his language.

"Wat iz dis you make?" He stood directly over the pre sliced sandwich meat and a bag of sliced white bread. "It no look very good," he said matter-of-factly. I laughed to myself, amazed at how uncouth Pietro could be, he just said what he was thinking. Maybe it isn't his culture to be polite, it is his culture to be honest. I looked over at Corrine. She was grimacing and rolling her eyes. He wasn't making a very good first impression.

"It looks like plastik." Pietro leaned a little closer to inspect the bologna and then looked closely at the cheese. "You make dis? To eat? You eat dis?" He looked up at Corrine's dad, who had a puzzled but amused look on his face.

"Yep, we put that onto bread and make SAND-WICHES," Dave emphasized at the end as if Pietro didn't understand what a sandwich was.

"Ah, the sandwheech we eat in Italy, much bettar looking than dis. The bread, the meat, the melanzane, looks real." Every face in the kitchen was staring at Pietro in disbelief, and Pietro had no idea that he was being so rude. Quietly to myself, I admired his truthfulness and his standard of food but when Corrine piped in and directed us out the kitchen with a sour look on her face, I felt torn between Pietro's truth and my loyalty to my friend. As Pietro slipped his flip-flops back on, she shot me a horrified look, a look of pity that said, "Oh Wrenna, I can't believe you are thinking about marrying this guy, it may be the end of our friendship."

As we were ushered out the door, Corrine whispered, "I'm gonna let you take this one on your own tonight, I don't think I can hang with him," she opened her eyes wide, shaking her head and pursing her lips. "Good luck!" she said mockingly.

I went out under the evening sky, stuck with Pietro. My friend didn't even want to hang out with him because he thinks her turkey resembles a tupperware lid that's washed up out of the sea, and I still didn't really know why I invited him there in the first place.

We got in the car and I drove him out of the city limits, figuring I could at least show him one of my favorite things to do in town.

"Where art we goingk? He asked me as we made our way through the dark.

"Just driving,"

"Driving whereth?"

"Nowhere, sometimes we just drive to drive."

"Why you do dis?"

"Um I don't know, it's relaxing, it's fun."

"But where you drive to?"

"Nowhere in particu-lar."

"Ah, dis ah, I don't understand".

"Okay, well I guess we'll go back then." I found a side street and turned around, going back toward town again.

After a few minutes of driving quietly, Pietro spoke up, "I am hangree." "You're mad at me?"

"No, hangree, I am need food."

"Ah, si, there is a Mexican restaurant open with a drive through just a little way up the road." I drove him to the late night taco stand where Corrine and I liked to go after dancing in town.

We both ordered a taco combo. Once we got our food I drove home, it was only ten blocks away, and we ate in the dark driveway.

I gathered the wrappers and my purse and got out of the car. Pietro came up to me and scooped me into his arms. I looked down and rested my forehead on his chest. I didn't want to kiss him. I didn't feel attracted to him.

"Rhaina, you no kees me anymhore. Why no mhore?"

"Well, I am confused, I just don't know how it's going to work for us, you're only going to be here for a little while, and then you're gone", I answered.

"I no understand, you say you love me Rhaina."

"I know, it's just…my parents are inside, and I feel shy," which was part true, I didn't want my mom to see me. I didn't want to give her any satisfaction, I blamed her for my decision to invite Pietro. If she hadn't been so unhappy when she came home I wouldn't have considered asking Pietro to come.

"They sleeping, kees me Rhaina, just one time you kees me. I come to Amerika to kees you again." I had that feeling come back again, the feeling of being owned by someone who doesn't even know me. Again I felt like that little girl in Reign's arms, just wanting him to leave so I could go back to normal with my mother.

I didn't want to kiss him, but I remembered that he would only be here for another couple of weeks, and I felt responsible for leading him all the way here. I felt I should give him a prize. I looked up and brought my feelings of affection for him to the surface, I remembered being in Italy, and I became Rhaina in Italy. I turned to look into Pietro's eyes, and he puckered his lips to meet mine. "There," I thought, "that ought to keep him happy for a while."

"Pietro, I need to get ready for bed, do you want to walk back? I could drive you if you want." Pietro looked crestfallen,

"I don't understand you Rhaina, first you laak me, then you don't laak me, and I never know what you want."

I looked up at the clouds that were hovering in the dark sky.

"I know what you mean, I don't always know what I want either." I sighed. A part of me wanted to go inside with him and cuddle and make out. But, I was afraid to have sex with him, I just couldn't give him that power, and I couldn't put myself in that position, because I wasn't always the best at telling people no.

"I have to go to bed Pietro," I told him pulling away.

"Olready? It is early still," he was breathing heavy, I imagined I had left him swollen with lust, I could feel that he was frustrated with me. "Am I teasing him?" I wondered.

"Yes, I need to get up early to go to class in the morning".

Pietro was pouting. I pretended not to notice, because I didn't know what I felt or why. I felt manipulated, like I had no choice. Why couldn't I just let my mother be sad? Why couldn't I let her live her life and experience her sadness? I had to step in and try to make her happy by letting go of my own truth. I thought somehow that maybe she knew me better than I knew myself.

I felt nervous, almost like Pietro was going to get angry with me, I was afraid that I had teased him too much, but that wasn't my intention at all. I just wanted to give him a little something. Maybe I wanted to explore. But, why did I feel like, I had to continue? Why couldn't I just kiss him and stop there? I had some idea in my mind that once you start, it is cruel to stop until you've gotten someone off. I just couldn't do it.

"Do you want me to drive you back down to the little house?

"I go walking. Goodnight Rhaina. One more kees?" I sighed, and popped up on my toes meeting my lips to his."

"Good night Pietro." I turned and walked inside, leaving him standing out in the grass alone.

{17} - "NO GOOD DEED GOES UNPUNISHED"

While my mother kept busy looking for work for Pietro, I was busy getting all my classes in order. Pietro had already been visiting for a week. I had done well to include my mother in as many plans as possible, which wasn't hard, because she had taken it upon herself to help him get settled. The tables had turned. In Italy I only wanted to hang out with my mother, now back in America, I only wanted my mother to hang out with Pietro.

She seemed to have gotten over the night of culinary insult, just as I had with the banana bread. That part of Pietro I could accept, I admired that he didn't want to compromise his standards.

I stayed at school for as long as possible, and was pleased that I was assigned a short paper right away, to write an article for my journalism class. I had to have two resources, so I went to the downtown library to check out a couple of books. The article only needed to be a page long. I sat down at the computer station, to check my email, and noticed a guy on the other side of the table at another computer, looking at me. I smiled at him, he was attractive, and any time I looked up he would find a way to catch my eye. I finished up with my emails, printing off a few, and went to check out my books. As I made my way out to my car, I heard a voice from behind me,

"Hey." the voice was deep and nice. I turned around and saw a tall man, about my age, the man from the computer station.

"Hi."

"Hey, do you want to go on a date with me? I just moved here from Alaska, and when I saw you I just felt something about you." Excitement fluttered through my body, I felt so flattered; he seemed so sweet and genuine.

"Um, yeah, that would be fun".

"I'm James," he reached out his hand and I took it, we held onto to each other for moment.

"I'm Wrenna." I reached in my backpack and pulled out a pen, "here, do you want my number?" I wrote my phone number down on a little ripped piece of paper and handed it to him.

"Okay, I'll call you."

"Okay." We parted ways, and I wondered if I would actually hear from him. It was like that with dating, everywhere you go you're on the watch for someone who could be the one, and sometimes it's just a game you play with strangers, agreeing to go out to sushi or a movie, and ride in their car in trust that they'll treat you well.

Two days later, as if by dating rule, he called and asked me out for the next night. I told him where

I lived and he came to pick me up. When he walked up on the porch, I had not mentioned to anyone that he was coming. Mom and dad and Pietro were sitting at the table eating dinner. I had just finished my food when James stepped up to the French doors.

"Oh," I jumped up and went to open the door for him, grabbing my coat and purse, ready to make a quick exit. James was taller than my dad by a couple of inches.

I had never dated anybody that tall before, as I was typically courted by shorter men. In comparison to James, Pietro looked a lot older, I hadn't noticed how mature he looked before then.

"James, this is my mom, my dad, and our friend Pietro, he's visiting from Italy." James smiled politely at everyone, unaware of many questions in my family's minds.

Pietro nodded, sizing James up, then sat back down to the table. I opened up the French doors, kissed my dad on the cheek, and turned with an innocent smile to Pietro, acting as if I was doing nothing wrong, asserting that I was no woman to be claimed or owned.

***

"Wrenna, I think you hurt Pietro's feeling last night when you had James come over to pick you up," she said as we drove in the truck. She had asked me to come with her to check in with a restaurant about getting Pietro a job.

"Mom, you know I'm not in love with him, he's driving me nuts!"

"Well, he came all the way here, and you

haven't even given him a chance, you've hardly spent any time with him."

"I just don't want to, every time we hang out we argue about something, he's just too machismo for me. Besides, you are the one who wanted him to come mom." "Yeah...," she didn't say anything for a minute. "I don't know Wrenna, there is just something about him that I'm obsessed with. He just reminds me so much of my own culture, it's like there is something in him that makes me feel at home." She paused. "Wrenna?"

"Yeah?" I looked at my reflection in the side view mirror of the truck, watching myself speak as if I was in a movie with my mother.

"If you aren't going to go for him, would you mind if I tried?"

I turned to her and instead of feeling disgust or disapproval, like I imagined most girls in my position might, I felt validated. She had finally, in her way, admitted that she was the one who was swooning the whole time. The thing that she was trying to deny in herself, the thing that she had tried to pawn off on me was now a table turning.

"Go for it mom." I took a breath, and was happy to be off the Pietro hook.

    ***

I left James' house late, it was almost midnight. I had found a way to escape into his world, staying late into the night at his house. My relationship with Pietro was getting very complicated. I had confused him and myself, and I wanted to run away.

My tummy growled and I decided it might be a

nice gesture to bring Pietro some Mexican food, he had liked it so much the first time we got it. After spending time with James I was well aware that I just wanted to be friends with Pietro, I didn't want to marry him, or have a love affair with him, but he was a friend and there was something about him that reminded me of myself, so I at least wanted to see if I could make a friendship work. I ordered a taco combo and drove the few blocks to my mother's little office. I knocked, but it seemed like no one was around. Maybe Pietro had decided to go out. Oh well, it didn't matter that much. I drove toward home and pulled into the driveway. One of the dimmer lights in the kitchen glowed out onto the deck. I was surprised to see it on, usually only the blue light on the deck was left on for my late returns.

I entered into the living room and heard a shuffle coming from the family room.

Holding onto the Mexican food I rounded the corner into the T.V. room where I found Pietro sitting alone on the ground.

"Oh, Hi Pietro, what are you doing?"

"I have whait for you."

"Oh, great, alright. I brought you some Mexican food, do you want some?" I reached in the bag and pulled his out.

"Ah! Si, Si". I sat down next to him, and we gobbled away at our food. For a moment I felt happy that he was my friend. We sat and talked for quite a while. It felt nice to just talk and not feel like I needed to kiss him.

I heard a sound come from the other room, I wondered if my mom had gotten up to get some milk, but then I realized that the sound was coming from the other part of the house. I got up and walked into the living room.

"Hey mom,"

"Oh! Hi!" I looked at her and observed that she didn't look as if she'd been sleeping, she was much more awake than when I usually saw her in the middle of the night.

"What are you doing?"

"Oh...I. Just forgot to write something down for work." I could tell she was lying, but I didn't know why.

"What are you doing," she asked. "Did you just get home?"

"Yeah, I brought Pietro some food, we're just eating it in here". I stood for a moment, not sure what else to say. "Okay, goodnight."

"Good night". Mom walked back to her room, leaving me wondering what she could possibly be up to.

I returned to Pietro and fell silent. I couldn't help feeling like there was so much happening around me that I couldn't control, like some spirit was haunting me and trying to get my attention.

"You say you love me." Pietro looked up from his almost finished taco. He looked confused. I felt guilty. How did I drag him into all of this?

"I changed my mind Pietro, I was never in love with you. I said I loved you because I was confused. It's...my mom...I just thought that maybe because you loved me, I could finally have a good relationship with someone, but it turns out my mom is in love with you, not me." I had told him this already - I sounded like a scratched record repeating the same words over and over; each time I said them a little and each time they sounded more complicated and twisted.

"She thinks you remind her of her father and her childhood and I think there is a part of her that wants those things back. Does that make any sense?" I wanted it all to make sense and to have clear answers so he might understand, but the truth was, I didn't know any more than he did what was going on, and neither did my mother.

"But Rhaina, why you not love me?" I was beginning to get tired.

"It's just, Pietro, you're too...your always wanting to be in my space, it's suffocating."

"But, Rhaina you kiss me, you say you love me."

I didn't know how to tell him that his sexual energy was too intense, or that he reminded me of a lover my mother had 20 years ago. How could I tell him that he was critical and picky about what he ate, and that I didn't like how rude he could be. I couldn't answer his question because there was no *one* answer, and anyway none of those things really mattered. I just didn't love him. He didn't make my heart soar.

"I don understand. You say you love me. I cam here from Eetalee, I leave my familee, I leav my countri, and I spend my year of monie to come here." Pietro's face turned red. I watched him fuming. I wanted to be sympathetic, but I just couldn't. I was angry too. I felt I had been set up.

Pietro got up. "I go," he said.

"Back to Italy?" I asked.

"No, no bach to Italy! I haf ticket for five more days to fly bach. I am here, away from my home and there eez nothing for me here! I go away. Ciao Rhaina."

He walked out of the living room and out the front door.

I sat emotionless, I didn't want to feel anything. I had hurt him. But somehow I felt like a pawn. I felt that he needed me to be something I was not. I thought he was doing me a favor by loving me, that he was showing me what love could really be, two people who returned each other's appreciation and affection of one another. But, I had to learn in a difficult way, that I just couldn't force myself to love him, no matter how hard I tried.

***

In the morning I rolled out of bed, went to the kitchen and poured myself a cup of coffee. Dad was sitting at the dining room table, in his spot, reading the newspaper. I sat down and pulled at the comic section.

"Look at this dad, Bonnie's going on a date, and she has like 15 outfits piled up on the bed," I pointed to the picture.

"Ha! That looks familiar," and he mumbled a little quieter behind his newspaper, "your mother could put her to shame." I laughed. There was never enough room for my mom's clothes, she was a shopaholic and we all knew it, even her.

"How you hanging in there dad?" I said sarcastically, lightly prodding his shoulder with my finger. I had my dad on my side when it came to Pietro. When he first came I played off my excitement about Pietro, because I was convinced that I really wanted him to come, but after I had decided I didn't want to marry him, I began to make my father my ally. Anytime any boy would break my heart, he would say things to assure me that it was their loss, and in this case, I think my dad felt pretty alone too.

"Oh, it just keeps getting weirder and weirder. Last night I heard Pietro drive by. He must have met someone at the bar, because he sounded drunk and was riding on top of a car, yelling, "Rhaina! You fucking bitch!"

I hadn't expected that, and screwed my face up for a moment, processing the comment. I didn't actually care. I was surprised, but I laughed. My father shook his head. Nothing much seemed to phase him.

"Well, I guess Pietro is over me. I feel sorry for him, but dad, I just don't love him, and I don't want to marry him." I scrunched up my face. I held the comics in my hand, glancing at them, but I was deep in my own thoughts.

"Was it really Pietro on top of the car dad?"

"Yeah, he's pretty hard to miss."

I sipped my coffee and both of us went back to skimming over the newspaper. "You know dad, I invited Pietro here because I was tired of mom being so unhappy, and she just wants me to be in love with him. But, I don't…I don't know. I don't even like him half the time. He seems like he loves me, but then I don't feel like we really know each other." I sunk my cheek into my palm and pouted, staring at the wall across from me.

My dad shook the paper to straighten it.

"Well, you know what I say Wrenna, No good deed goes unpunished". I looked over at him as he reached for his cup of coffee. I sank. He was right. I did this to please my mother, I didn't invite Pietro here for me, I wanted him to come because I couldn't stand seeing my mother so unhappy. I wanted to fix it, but I couldn't. I couldn't love him for her.

Right then my mom walked in the front door, she had been out early in her search to find Pietro a job. I didn't think she had any idea about what my dad had witnessed the night before. Neither of us said anything right away. She went into the kitchen and filled up ice in her big plastic cup, along with some concentrated black tea and a little water. She came around the table and sat across from me; she looked chipper and we all made small talk. I was the one who brought up the event the previous night.

"Really, he did Carver?"

"Yep, it was him. Who else would it have been? Who else do we know that would crawl up on to the roof of a moving car and go down the road yelling?" My dad said all of this in a very matter-of-fact way. He stood up and turned slightly to open the door a crack, stepping out onto the deck, but leaving the door ajar so he could continue talking to us. He reached into his breast pocket and pulled out his pack of cigarettes, shaking one out, and sticking it in his mouth. His ritual of smoking was his signature, I had never known him to not smoke, and so I could never imagine him any other way.

My mother deflated. She seemed mad at my dad and me as if we were ganging up on her. I looked at him standing with his back against us now looking out at the yard, taking drags from his cigarette. Mom stared off in the distance, holding her hand around her cup with condensing droplets on the outside. A tension filled the room and I had nothing to say.

The day outside had patches of grey clouds and

patches of blue sky, making the light a striking yet melancholy day. The ground was wet from a light autumn rain in the early morning. Everything seemed fresh outside.

Inside the tobacco smoke made a trail and the coffee maker had drips of burnt coffee. I stood up and gathered my things, I needed to go somewhere, anywhere but there.

{18} - A MYSTERY UNFOLDS

"YOUR CHILDREN ARE NOT YOUR CHILDREN, THEY
ARE THE SONS AND DAUGHTERS OF LIFE'S LONGING
FOR ITSELF. THEY CAME THROUGH YOU BUT NOT
FROM YOU, AND THOUGH THEY ARE WITH YOU
THEY BELONG NOT TO YOU." KHALIL GHIBRAN, THE
PROPHET.

Time blurred after Pietro left. I would have just as well let Pietro go back to Italy and go on with his life, but mom couldn't let him go. We would go on walks and drives and process the experience; she continued to ask me what had happened and why I had such a change of heart?

"I thought you were in love with him Wrenna, I just don't understand, what happened?" She asked me as we were driving to the store.

"He's just so possessive, it's like he tries to own me. When we cook in the kitchen he takes over, tells me what to do, we blow up. Mom we can't stand each other, how is it that he can say he's in love with me and then be so controlling? When he hugs me, I feel the same energy I did when I was three and Reign came over. Remember? I got something in my eye, and I was crying because it hurt. I remember not wanting him there, and wanting dad because he was the one who always got slivers out of my fingers and lashes out of my eyes. Reign tried to hold me, to comfort me, but I was so uncomfortable. I wanted away from him, I wanted him to let go, but he didn't," I had exhausted all of my reasons to explain the simple fact that Pietro wasn't the one for me, but nothing quite satisfied mom.

"I don't know," I continued, "It's just Pietro, there's something about him, and he has the same intense energy that Reign had that makes me want to get away. It's like they both wanted to possess me, you know like I was this replacement for Pietro's daughter. He lost her, so somehow because he couldn't have her I became his angel. Reign was similar like he wanted to protect me and wanted me to be him, maybe because he always wanted a kid with you mom." The car rolled to a stop and I looked over at her in the passenger seat.

"I've even had the thought that Reign might be my father."

Mom's face puckered, and she said so simply without looking at me,

"That's because he is." With those simple words, tears streamed out of her eyes and dripped down onto her chest. I shook my head as if it might help to register the thought in my head, but I couldn't think. I felt a tear run down my neck, and my body went limp. Blank. That's what it was, Blank. What are you supposed to think after you hear something like that?

"Are you joking?" I chuckled a little and looked at her thinking that maybe she said it to throw in even more unneeded drama. But, she shook her head.

"I'm not joking." She could barely talk. She

looked like a guilty puppy waiting to get scolded for doing something wrong.

I searched for some sense in all of it.

"Are you sure?" The Pietro situation had been traumatic enough then she goes and tells me that who I am is not who I am. So, who am I?

I had to work in an hour, and I felt defeated.

"I need to drive, I need to talk for a minute; I can't go to work yet." I said as I turned the car the opposite direction from work. Tension filled the space between mom and me. We both cried as I headed for the country.

Connections, Coincidences, every memory and lie flooded through my head. It was a highway with too many exits, some of them leading nowhere, some leading to more and more roads of ways in which I understood my being, and my history. I am not who I think I am. My blood is different. A vision of the double helix appeared in my head and it twirled differently, the colors changed and flickered and I was lost. The freeway of me suddenly changed directions, I could never turn back again. My brothers; only half. My mother; full of lies. My father: all I could think was Oreo cookie moments and how much energy he put into me. I felt sad for him, I felt guilty for my brothers, because I was a lie, only half of what they thought I was. How could I have deceived so many people without ever knowing I was even lying? Only seconds ago I existed as a different person from the one I thought I was?

The Country outside of town was blotted with the oranges of changing trees, the grasses had all been plowed, and rested brown and matted, ready for winter to come and cover them with fresh layers of snow.

Crows glided down to the branches of a dead birch tree. The sky stretched open. Cool air coming from the crack in the car window had a chill to it, but the late fall sun beamed into the car and warmed us. I drove out to the countryside as far as I could go until I had to turn around to make it to work on time. I followed all the routes I took in high school, past the dairy farm, along the canal, reaching each back road turn off that led to another and another and finally looped back toward town. We drove quietly for the first fifteen minutes, then mom broke the silence.

"I met him when I was thirteen. He was seventeen. He would come over and do work for my dad and flirt with me. I was shy when I flirted back. He went away to college but he came back every summer. Reign and I continued our flirtation and started seeing each other, then he went away to school and I started dating Carver; we went to dances together and spent weekends hanging out. Then, the summer between my junior and senior year, Reign came back and I started seeing him again, but I was still with Carver too.

One day when Reign and I were hanging out at my house, Carver came by to see me and saw us together. He left and a few minutes later called me and told me he needed to talk to me. I told Reign he should go and Carver came back over and gave me an ultimatum.

"It's him or me," he said.

I went for a drive that night and I told Reign I couldn't see him anymore and why. He said he wanted to marry me when I was a little older and cried about our breakup. I'm not sure why I did what I did. Maybe I was a little afraid of Reign and Carver seemed more stable and dependable. On the other hand Carver and I had fun together, but I didn't like cutting things off with Reign or being told what to do either."

"Some years after Carver and I had the boys, I went shopping for groceries when the boys were at school and ran into Reign in the parking lot. He had driven all night relocating back home again after being gone for years. He said he knew he would see me when he got back. The last time I had seen him was the night I broke up with him.

Some years earlier, while I was away at college he had called my dad asking about where I was, but he was told it was best to leave me alone. That day at the store I felt very attracted to him and it seemed that the feeling was mutual. A few days later, he showed up at my front door. We talked at length on the back porch. I felt emotional for our lost years. He invited me to come see his new office down town and so, a few days later, I did. He sat behind the desk the whole time I was there and later told me that he had been afraid of what he might do if he left his seat. A few days after that visit he invited me back again, and I told him I would be out of town for a few days".

"Carver and I left that weekend for an annual business conference. I told myself that I would find a way to have a private dinner with Carver to discuss my recent meeting with Reign. I was feeling vulnerable and tempted; I wanted to talk to him about it all but our dinner never happened. Carver seemed to have been swept up into one group activity after the other and my suggestion for us to slip away for an evening alone didn't materialize. I decided right then that I would meet up with Reign after my return home and go from there. Maybe my resentment for not having a private dinner wasn't the best justification for my decision, but that is just how I felt".

"I called Reign after my return home and he suggested we meet in the mall parking lot. I parked my car and rode with him to his mother's house that had a little back house where nobody would see us. He brought Champagne, and we made love. We met like that once a week. I would go see him at his office, and sometimes I got so wrapped up in

sex...I must have been out of my mind, once I walked out with my dress on backwards and inside out. I was wearing it like that when I picked up the boys from grandma's house, I hoped she didn't notice".

"We were enchanted with one another. I was obsessed and I think I recognized something in him that was similar to me. He was unpredictable, spontaneous, and quirky, sometimes he was dangerous. I knew from almost the beginning that he could influence me to do things that I wouldn't otherwise have considered.

He had some strange ideas about how we would manage our affair, like telling his wife all about what was going on. Honesty is what he said his motive was. But then he suggested that I become friends with her and spend time with his family. I thought that seemed weird, but I went along with it. His wife seemed resigned to Reign's ways. She wasn't thrilled with the arrangement but she went along with it too. She wasn't hostile towards me, nor was she overly friendly. I felt awkward about all of it. Reign also encouraged me to let my Carver know but that wasn't a good idea at all. So I kept my secret. Carver didn't suspect anything, our sex life was invigorated by my affair, and he was still gone a lot of the time so he wouldn't have noticed when I was absent".

"Reign started telling me he wanted to have a baby with me. I was in love with him so the idea seemed romantic but also unrealistic and dangerous. I told him as much but he persisted in dreaming about it.

It was spring and I went to Reign's office for one of my visits, and he started making love to me. I had a diaphragm in but he pulled it out and in my passionate state, I didn't resist his advances. Afterward I felt frantic.

"What had I done?" I thought.

I convinced myself that just one slip up wouldn't result in a pregnancy but it did and on January 26th, four days after my birthday I gave birth to you. Before you were born I decided that no one needed to know about your conception. I decided that I could keep my two worlds separate —continue in my marriage and remain in my relationship with Reign". *"When it came time for me to have you, I started to worry about the birth, not the actual birthing process because I had breezed through two uncomplicated births before, but my fear was about how you would look. I thought you might look like Reign. Carver was with me as he had been with the boy's births. After I inspected you I determined that my secret was safe for the time being".*

"I never regretted having you, I was in love with Reign, and I love you..."

Mom stopped talking and let a silence fill the car. I only had a few more blocks to go until I reached the shop where I worked. I parked the car and let it idle, and let all the information my mom had shared sink in.

"I remember going to see Reign's mother when I was little with you, she always stuck in my mind, and maybe I even recognized something in her face that resembled my own." I thought about the lady who wore a thick bun wrapped on the back of her head, and how every time I saw her she had her back turned to the door, sitting in a high chair in the corner of the diner we'd go to. She seemed serious to me, but also very comfortable, in fact there was a part of me, even as a child that felt at ease around her, as if I knew that I had nothing to hide around her. We stopped going there around the time I started elementary school. About that same time I have no more memories of Reign coming around.

"One time I had a dream, about Reign's daughter, my...half-sister I guess she would be. In the dream she opened up the door to their house, and looked right at me, her face seemed so familiar, but I remember I was so young when I had that dream, and her face was vivid, it was real, like it carried a message, but I didn't have any way to understand that my dreams could communicate to me, or how to interpret their meaning. Now it makes sense why her face was familiar, she looks like me, in fact I look like Reign. I don't even know why I just said that about Reign, about me wondering if he was my father, but I did say it, like I knew it underneath everything, and somehow it's like I've known something all along, I've known that there was something amiss.

You've always said that you have psychic abilities mom, I think I do to. I think my dreams tell me things, and sometimes I have these visions of things and I don't always know why until later when life unfolds and I realize that maybe I was actually feeling into the future or I guess in this case, the past.

"Does dad know? About me? Does he know that I am not his biological daughter?"

"Yes. He's known for a long time." She paused for a moment, I figured she was searching for the details of how my dad came to know about Reign and my mother.

"Sometime after you were born, Reign wanted to get away with me on a trip. I didn't know right away how it would work, but he suggested that we take scuba lessons together so that we could explore the ocean together if we ever got a possibility to travel. We began the classes at the pool, then we had to do three open dives to get certified. We went out to the local lakes and Reign's wife came along for one of them. I told Carver that I had to go to the coast to finish my dives with some of the people from the class, so I got my opportunity to travel for the first time with Reign. We got to spend a night together and it was like I was addicted to him, we made love on and off all night long and I would feel euphoric, then it was like utter emotional exhaustion afterwards".

"Awhile after that Reign and I planned another trip to the coast. I told Carver I wanted to take my own trip there, and get away alone. I was surprised that he was fine with it, he said he would help with the kids and get his mother to help. So, we went and then even went on a couple of other trips...anyway, it wasn't the trips that made Carver discover our secret. One day Reign's wife came over to dig up some lilac starts to plant in her yard, and she ran into Carver. They were friendly to each other, and she was introduced to Carver as someone in my baby-sitting co-op. A few weeks later Carver was in his car stopped at a light and he looked over and saw Reign's wife in the same car with Reign. That night he confronted me about Reign, and he started to put it all together. He asked about you over and over, and at first I lied, but after a while I confessed the truth of it all."

"Why did dad stay?"

"Well, some of Carver's friends he confided in told him to leave me, but he was always loyal and stead-fast, that was one of the things I always loved about him. But at the same time I wasn't sure what was going to happen. I called Reign and told him that Carver knew about our affair and about you. I think he got the idea that he wanted to smooth things out a little, so he went down to Carver's office and said we could all live amicably in this manner or that he would figure out a way to support me if need be. Of course Carver was infuriated. Carver expected that I would either leave him, or give up Reign, but I didn't do either. I told him he had the option of leaving me but he didn't do that either."

"Anyway Reign suggested to me on the phone that the four of us go scuba diving together, I wasn't sure if Carver would go for it, but he did. Of course it was a disaster, Reign's wife sat in the boat making small talk, while Reign exhibited territorial rights to me, which were then reciprocated by Carver. Afterwards Carver was furious".

"I wasn't ready to give up Reign, and I told Carver that. I continued to live at home and still see Reign. I think Carver just figured that eventually I would get over Reign and things would return to normal".

"Well, what about me? Wasn't it hard for him to raise me after finding out I wasn't his?"

"Well, he had already raised you for three years, and he loved you, he had already developed a bond with you. He raised you, he really is your father you know?

"I know, of course he is." I said to my mother, and I loved him for it, but I couldn't help the feeling that stirred in me about a mystery that had stalked me for twenty years. I didn't know when or how, but I wanted to meet Reign again, I wanted to know more about the part of me that I had just realized I was missing. I wanted to feel some connection to the spirit that brought me into this world, maybe there was something in it that would help me understand the mystery of why I always felt so different from everyone else, and maybe he would have some answers to my many questions.

PART TWO

Shooting Arrows. Making Choices. Walking straight on that line, that glows and floats, but does not sink into mud, or rest on the ground.
Don't get caught in the tears of others, or the drowning of their self-pity. It is only a mirror of your own.
Turn the mirror around, and face the trail that your arrow made.
You have your dreams.
Make your choice. Shoot your Arrow. Experience it. Live it.
And suddenly you become the light. And those that were weeping, revel in the beauty of the shooting star.

3 years later

The tension of spring coming forth. Winter fading away tugged at my heart strings. I only had a couple of months left of school, and sitting down to do any kind of homework made me weary. I sat at the kitchen table in my apartment, staring at the computer screen, trying to pull out words to make use of. I stood up and put on a pot of water to boil. Maybe tea would help my process. I was finding another distraction looking for fingernail clippers, while the water boiled, and there was a knock at the door.

For a moment I contemplated not opening it, but I did and Corrine stood outside looking as if she was holding her breath, her eyes were big. I didn't say anything and just waited for her to burst out what she had come to say.

"I just watched Opera's finale, and she was talking about the show, you know how she has come a really long way since the beginning of it. And she said, you know, how it's important to just do the things you want to do, you've got to just do it. So, I am here to tell you we are GOING TO EUROPE!", she followed her announcement by looking up and around as if she had announced it to an audience of people, or as if there were a panel of angels floating above her. She looked up at me and boasted at how brilliant her idea was.

"We are?" I asked. I paused for a second, immediately thinking about how I could possibly afford to go to Europe. And then, I stopped figuring, "You're RIGHT. We do have to do what we want to do, right now! Don't we?" We both started jumping around the room and dancing, singing, "We're going to Europe, we're going to Europe."

We made plans to meet later in the evening to research plane tickets and destinations. By the time I got to Corrine's house, she had already gone and bought a map of European destinations. We sprawled out on the floor with our butts up in the air drawing a line from one place to the next, making a train route through nine different countries.

"I did some research on the Eurail pass and I think it would be the most economical to get a punch card of ten passes, then we can go to at least that many different places over 10 weeks." Corrine had been thinking about this, planning it already. For a moment I couldn't believe we were really going to do it.   Two more weeks went by and I received a credit card in the mail, which surprisingly gave me a $5000 limit. It was time to buy our tickets.

We found seats on the same flight going out of Portland into Georgia, then straight to London. The moment I pushed purchase on the computer screen, I felt a rush of power surge through me. I had stood over thousands of pepperoni pizzas over the years, counting meat and measuring mushrooms, thinking to myself how I couldn't wait until the time in my life when I felt I was really living the life I was meant to live. For the next couple of months I floated through every part of it, feeling so alive.
        ***

My school term finished and I packed most of my belongings into boxes to store at my dad's house while

I backpacked through Europe. I was sifting through books and clothes in my apartment when someone knocked on the door. I opened it and there stood Reign. Did I tell him where I live?

"Hey Baby, how are you?" he asked as he leaned into the doorway. I stepped toward him sinking into his chest and hugging him. He smelled like fruity yeast.

"I was thinking about you the other day", I said as I squeezed my head to his neck.

"You were?"

"Yeah, I have something I want you to hear, you're the only one I can think of that could appreciate it," I gestured for him to sit down and shuffled through the CD's below the T.V.

Out of the corner of my eye I kept a subtle note of Reign's energy. He had stretched himself out with his barrel chest puffed up and legs open, and his arms tucked behind his head, the way he liked to sprawl like a cat, almost purring, seductive and sexy.

The tango began, Astor Piazzolla's "Zero Hour". I sat still on the ground facing him, listening as the notes floated into the air; they put me in a trance, they pulled at my soul. Maybe it was the gypsy in me that felt the music in that way. Like my mother, I could feel the tension of chemistry between people, I could see the stories among them; it was our gift.

The music that moved almost eerily out of the speakers, connected me to the mystery of my mother and father's love, and I couldn't help but fall in love with my father too. He was a mystery that I yearned to discover. When I sat there with him, I wanted to jump into his arms, and then, I didn't know what...the idea stopped there, even so, I still had the feeling. I did know that I had an aching, and a deep desire to merge with him.

I turned and locked eyes with my biological father and we sat like that for three songs, the third had the ability to draw from my depths a movement that nothing else could touch, as if, in some other lifetime I had danced this Tango before. I knew he felt it too, this beautiful mystery. I crawled over to sit just under him and rested my head on my folded hands between his open thighs and looked up at him.

"This music moves me, do you feel it too? The accordion and the violin are such incredible vehicles for emotion," I watched him shift and smirk to himself, I smiled coolly at him, hiding all of my unknown tension sitting there with him. As though he saw right through me he raised his brow and smiled softly.

"Everything feels so sexual with you", I thought to myself.

"You're sexy," he said, as if I were my mother sitting there twenty-three years earlier.

"Oh yeah?" I flirted back without feeling, "how so?" The air around me stopped.

"You're so full of life," he answered. Suddenly, I felt awkward for putting on the music. I averted my eyes.

When I looked up again at him I saw power and sadness, unease and insecurity.   "I think it's time for you to go." I said looking right at him. He stood and wobbled slightly, then came in to give me a hug. I met his hug with a wall of armor and opened the door for him to go. He lingered there, grasping for an opportunity to make something right, but neither of us knew what that was.

"See you later," I said.

"Bye baby", he leaned in the doorway, the tango music played on,

"Bye." I closed the door on him. Anger came over me out of nowhere, I felt like a victim to something. I felt like a fool.

{19} —LONDON BRIDGES

"MAYBE I AM WHAT SHE ALWAYS WANTED, MY FATHER
AS A WOMAN…SHE WANTED THAT POWER. MAYBE
I AM THE WAY I AM BECAUSE SHE WANTED EXACTLY
THAT, WANTED THERE TO BE A WOMAN A LOT LIKE
HER, BUT WHO WOULD NOT HOLD BACK." WHY MY
MOTHER MADE ME, SHARON OLDS.

"Passport." I stood at the customs counter in London, England, with a very severe face staring me down.

On my back was a pack filled to the gills with what I was going to need for two and half months of backpacking through Europe. On my waist I carried a fanny pack with my passport and some other little crucial items for traveling.

I retrieved the passport and showed it to the serious woman behind the counter.

"How long do you intend to stay?" she asked with her brows raised.

"Until August 9th, my return ticket flies out that day." I held out the copy of my ticket to prove I wasn't lying.

"Mmmmhmm. And how much money did you bring?"

"Umm, well, I have $5000 on a credit card, and another $2000 on my debit card, and...$2000 cash with me."

"Are you aware that carrying $2000 cash around Europe is risky?"

"Oh, yes, I have been here with my mother before, and I have it in my underwear." The woman stopped without a flicker of amusement in her face. In fact, she looked angry like I was trying to play a joke on her.

"So, you're telling me that if I sent you over to that customs officer over there, and they took you to a private room, you would be able to show them $2000 dollars that you're hiding in your underwear?"

"Yes, I bought a special pair with a pocket in them so that I could keep the money safe." She looked me up and down and stared hard at me, trying to find some speck of dishonesty. Then without a word she stamped my passport.

"Enjoy your stay," she nodded at me with a smirking smile curling in her lips.

I found Corrine just getting through her line. Her entry into London was much the same as mine. We stood and looked at each other then looked around the airport.

We were in, our passports had been stamped.

"We're here, we made it to Europe!!" Corrine squealed triumphantly raising her eyebrows in excitement.

"I know, I can't even believe it!" We walked through a crowd of people making our way to the airport exit.

"Hey look it's a sign for the London Underground. COOL!" Corrine pointed out the sign with the big U that hovered above a staircase going downward.

"That would be great except my parents told me they would pay for a cab while I was in London. They're afraid it's gonna get bombed again."

"Oh yeah, well as long as they're paying for it." Corrine changed directions and started scouting to catch a London Cab. At the same time we realized it wouldn't be disappointing. The cab we called was a Hackney carriage, and ours was purple. Our cab driver had the greatest English accent which we got to hear the whole way to our hostel, while he told us stories and asked us about our trip. At the end it was 45 Euros, which equated to about $100 American dollars. We wouldn't need to take another taxi during our stay, the next transportation out of London would be on a train, which we were able to get to by walking.

We arrived at our hostel and were thrilled to find our bunk beds equipped with curtains to give us quiet and privacy while we slept. Corrine took the top bunk and I crawled into the bottom bunk. We fell asleep and didn't wake until the evening. After a little dinner at the hostel cafe, we went back to bed until ten o'clock the next morning. Jet lag demanded that we catch up with time, and the only way to do that was to dream and sleep.

In the morning I was refreshed and ready to get moving. Corrine was too. She had mapped out, her agenda, with all the tourist stops in London that she wanted to see, so we started walking.

First we stopped at the Tower of London, took pictures, and then took pictures of us in front of it.

I scoped out the people and I was especially fond of the thick British accents. We walked across the London Bridge, took more pictures, then crossed and went to see the National Gallery in Trafalgar Square. I was amazed when I stood looking at original Van Gogh paintings, in fact they were the ones I liked the most.

We then made our way to an older part of town where we went into an old torture chamber that had been made into a museum. There were all kinds of weapons and methods of torture; the place and the neighborhood reminded me of something out of a Shakespeare play. We covered ground from the moment we woke up until dark. By the time we arrived back at the hostel, my legs were so tired from walking, I lay down and didn't get up again until the next morning. With our enthusiasm for being in Europe quelled by a day of exploring, we decided to have a "mental health" day and rest, take showers, and get ready to go to Amsterdam on the train the next day.

***

I found my place on the train and settled in for a few hours of reading and writing postcards to let everyone back home know I had made it safely. Corrine dove right into her novel that she was reading, and I attempted to write a postcard to my mom.   What do I say to her? That I'm here? I couldn't get any further than Dear Mom, before I thought that maybe I needed to travel for another week or so until I wrote *any* postcards.

I watched the rolling landscape of the United Kingdom stream by me. This is the land from where my biological father's ancestors came. I knew nothing about it, but felt like my mother did about Italy, that something about it made me feel at home.

***

I sniffled as the wind blew softly over us. We were surrounded by overgrowth of wild bushes, birds camping out in every tree that filled his garden. He wore a cloak to protect him from the chilly wind and stirred the tea cup that sat beside us steeping Earl Grey. He pulled out the tea bag and added a squeeze of lemon and a bit of honey, something familiar to me. Even as a child I loved black tea with honey and lemon. He handed me the cup, then lit a pile of dry Eucalyptus leaves on fire, wafting the smoke toward me, saying that Eucalyptus is good for colds.

He sat cross legged, bent over the small Eucalyptus fire. His face through the smoke made me see him as if he were a beast in a fierce land. I felt comforted and strange, his movements intrigued me. I wanted to listen to him, to listen for him to tell me something magical.

He looked up at me,

"Hold your hand up like this," he held his hand with his palm facing me. I copied him.

"Okay, move it close to mine but leave just enough space that you aren't touching mine.

I moved it, just as he said until our hands were half an inch apart.

"Now wait." I waited for a moment wondering what we were doing, then I started to feel heat on my palm. The heat got warmer and warmer until it was hot and I finally moved my hand away.

"That's the energy we have between us. We are connected, you know?

"Wow that was cool."

Reign reached down and added more Eucalyptus to the pile. I sat quietly, wrapped in an orange and pink wool

224

blanket, the smoke swirled, and the trees beside me rustled. It had been awhile since the first time we met each other after mom had told me the truth about him.

***

May 2003

"Nice Shoes." I looked over at this man, who I now understood was my biological father. His face was familiar. His dimpled chin I used to have when I was young, it was a clue, and his nose too. The bridge of it was a shelf, where a wizard might place an important stone. Neither my mother nor Carver showed that characteristic.

The shape of his cheeks and lines of his face were very similar to mine, and his eyes especially struck me, because they were blue. As a child I had the bluest eyes, and no one else in my family had them. My mom had green eyes and my dad had hazel, even my brother's eyes didn't match mine. But my eyes were bright blue, and for a long time I thought the intensity of my eyes made me look goofy. My brothers and my parents all had intelligent or stoic looking eyes, but mine acted sometimes as if they were bobbing or dancing or performing. I couldn't help it, sometimes they even pierced through people. I think I was afraid of them in that way.

And here next to me was the man I got my eyes from, his eyes too had a hypnotic way, they danced, they laughed, and sometimes they became the eyes of a predator.

"Oh, these are alligator skin." He said looking down at his textured dress shoes. "I have never seen alligator skin shoes in my whole life Reign, where did you get them?" I stopped misstep and stared down at them.

"Oh, I got them when I was in Australia." I bent down and ran my fingers along the leather, feeling the tex-

ture of the skin. It was bumpy, but the shoe was soft. My first thought was that this man was a true eccentric, like my mother's father, only the two of them were very different men.

He and I walked along together down the road. I could tell he was leading me into the forest to get away from people, he seemed a bit secretive about meeting me.

"So, how did you find out about me?" he asked. There was something about his voice, a voice that I had heard in my dreams, or in hidden away memories from my childhood. I never trusted his voice, it always brought out a little warrioress in me, it made me stand up to protect something, maybe it was my family or my father, maybe it was the secret or my mother. I couldn't know. But, as I walked along in this quiet forest with him, I wanted to know the mystery of it. I wanted to discover the part of me that felt like everything made sense when my mother had told me about him that day in the car.

"Well, it's a little bit of a story. Mom actually told me when I was fifteen that she had had an affair with you. And the same day she told me, we also talked about Italy, about the trip she took with her dad there, and we decided that we wanted to go together, so we saved up money, and finally went last summer. When we were there we met a man named Pietro, who traveled with us, and I could tell my mom just loved him, he had these really broad shoulders, and a swagger, a lot like you. He reminded me of you, or at least what I remembered of you. She said he reminded her of her grandfather, because he had a gravelly voice. And he really liked me, so my mom was really excited that I might marry someone from her culture. Anyway, He came back here to America, because I was convinced that I loved him, but I didn't, well I didn't want to marry him.

Then, after he left, my mother told me. I said something like, Pietro reminds me of Reign, and then something like, I always wondered if he was my father, because we

both have dimples in our chin, and no one in my family has this nose. And mom said, 'he is your father'.
And then you know she filled me in."

"*What did she tell you?"*

"*Oh, well she told me about how she came to your office one day, and that she was wearing a diaphragm, but you came over to her and pulled it out and threw it across the room, and told her you wanted to have a baby with her."*

"*I did. I could smell her, she smelled different when she was in heat. I knew that if we made love that we would make a baby".*

We walked alongside the Aspens, the same ones he used to take pictures of my mom in. She would wrap her arms backwards around the trunk and pout, her short bangs and bright lipstick were a modern contrast to the grey bark and glittering green and yellow leaves. Each time I hear the aspens I imagine they are chattering in the wind, telling me about the infatuation of my parents when they were younger. The aspens know, they were there. They might even indulge more secrets if I asked them.

"*Does your dad know that you know?"*

"*No, I don't really feel like he needs to."*

"*That's better I think. He raised you and loved you like his own daughter."*

I looked down at his shoes, then at my sandals. The morning sun was beaming through the trees along the pavement. I had thought about talking to my dad, but there was a part of me that still didn't totally believe that it was real. Was it real? Was this man standing next to me part responsible for bringing me into the world?

"*Your mother was the love of my life," he said. "We worked very hard to keep you protected".*

"*When your father found out he was not happy. He calmed down after a while and we tried to all make it work together..." Reign trailed off. "Your mother is a unique woman, sometimes we were out of control, we would make*

227

love for hours, then she would leave not knowing which way was right," he chuckled at his clever remark.

"What about the consequences though? It's like you and my mom never thought about the consequences," I knew that my mom could get lost in her own world of dreaming, she and I were a lot alike that way, so it was interesting that I was being the Devil's Advocate, as if I needed some boundary from Reign.

"Well, we were in love, are you talking about logic? I am sure there are a lot of people, who think that affairs are reason for punishment, especially in your mother's upbringing, where you get married into the hands of God, to be manipulated by the rules and expectations of civilized living. But, love doesn't always work like that. It wasn't like that for her and me."

"Was it a Karma thing?"

"What do you mean?"

"Well, mom told me that she was seeing you in high school, but my dad gave her an ultimatum about him or you. Do you think it was his Karma that made my mom want to have an affair with you?"

"Mmm, maybe," he said contemplating my train of thought, "but I think that nothing can stand in the way of energy that needs to move between two souls. She and I may have had Karma together, maybe even your father was a part of it. It wasn't something that could be made sense out of. I don't believe we did anything wrong."

"But, my mother lied."

"Did she lie?"

"Well, yeah, she lies all the time about where she is going when she goes to see her boyfriend now, but I know about it, and I am not going to tell my dad, because it's not really my place to say anything."

"Maybe she didn't feel like she could tell the truth, maybe nobody wanted to hear it."

"That's true, but that doesn't necessarily mean that

she should not be honest. She was using my dad to be se-
cure, when she was loving you."
"She loved him too."
    "Yeah, she did love him too, just in a different
way huh?"
    "Yes," Reign answered. I was surprised at his will-
ingness to share her with my dad, he seemed to practice
beliefs of an entirely different culture, and his version of
things certainly didn't fit into the virtues of the culture I
grew up in.
    "Well, why are you able to accept her loving him,
where he has a hard time accepting the relationship that
you and my mom have?"
    "Social conditionings and laws are very strong. If
you marry someone, you belong to them. You have created
a kind of prison around you and that person. Of course you
can choose that, some people really like it that way, it's safe,
it's defined, and it makes things easier in some ways"
    "Yeah, I think my mom chose to get married because
it's what people did. She told me that my grandmother
would have had a fit if she knew she were having sex before
she was married, because it just wasn't acceptable. I think
that was part of the reason why having an affair was so
attractive, because she was finally able to feel in control of
something, well I don't know if control is the right word,
maybe more like the freedom to do something without hav-
ing to have approval by mommy, daddy, God.
    "As far as your dad goes, he trusted in marriage and
the nostalgia of what our culture promised about it. He
trusted that your mom loved him and that when she agreed
to marry him she wanted to be with only him. I think your
mom had convinced herself of the same thing, but then
we change don't we? As we grow, we don't stay the same,
and sometimes people grow apart, or they learn new things
about themselves and need to explore. With your mother
and I it was like a force of nature, what we felt for each

other was beyond us."

"Life isn't really clean cut is it? It's messy and unpredictable," I said, trailing off.

"It's an adventure," Reign chimed in. "Some people might say that what we felt for each other was lust, and not love, but no one can define love for another person. Your dad loved your mother, he accepted that she needed to explore relationships with other people and... your mother wanted freedom".

***

"Reign wanted me to marry him, he wanted me to leave dad and run away with him, but that's not what I wanted. I didn't want to break up our family, plus I never knew what Reign was going to do."

"I told you about Tahiti Wrenna. Right when we got on the plane he started talking about how in love he was with this seventeen-year-old. I walked into his office one day and he had pictures of her laying out all over the place, he was obsessed with her. You can imagine how that made me feel."

"Yeah, that is weird. But, why did it matter? I mean you were both deciding to have a relationship while you were both married."

"I know, but he would just go on and on about her when he was spending time with me, it just made me feel like he was done with me."

"Was she pretty?"

"Well, that's the weird thing Wrenna...she looked just like you, Oh! You know what?! I think I have a picture of her somewhere." She got up and opened the top drawer of her dresser. Inside a plastic bag were pictures of Reign and her in Hawaii, a few old looking letters, and a folded pamphlet. The pamphlet had a picture of Reign's lover, he had used her as a model for his advertising agency. I snatched up the

picture and looked into it. It was like looking in a mirror.
"She does look like me mom...only she's a tiny bit
more round faced, but...wow. Do you think he liked her
because he's a narcissist and he likes things that look like
him? Or, do you think maybe he was finding a connection
with her that he didn't have with me?"   *"I don't*
know...." my mother trailed off.

I woke up from a dream trance pondering the intermittency of events that took their course with Reign and my mother and my conception. Wherever I tried to find an explanation, nothing made sense.

I recalled the way that Pietro had just appeared out of nowhere, and how he so easily became a part of our trip and our life, then became a messenger, unearthing buried secrets from my soul. I had felt so guilty about stringing him along, though it seemed that there wasn't any way around it, it was as if mom and I had created Pietro, he gave us a way to talk about all the things that went unsaid.

Ten languages announced our arrival over the intercom of the train. I looked groggily out the train window as we pulled to a stop in...

Laura Marie Parker

{20} - AMSTERDAM.

Our hostel was located in the Red Light District. Supposedly it had been cleaned up a bit for the sake of tourists. I expected to see prostitutes on every corner, and drug dealers hiding in the alleys, but aside from a few food carts selling Greek food, a couple of women, *who did look like prostitutes*, and a few marijuana shops interwoven between tiny boutiques and bars, the scene was fairly tame. We decided that we would have to go explore those sometime after we settled into our room.

The Flying Pig had a symbol of a big pink pig on the sign outside, all lit up, it was hard to miss. When we arrived we had to press a doorbell, so they could check us out and let us in. As soon as the door opened we were met with a cloud of skunky smoke coming from a group of settlers lounging in a big cushioned chill out area right in the bay of the front window. Everyone looked dazed and half baked, or just really baked. The girl behind the counter had tattoos covering both of her arms, and wore big plugs in her earlobes. Her demeanor was dry, but kind enough to help us find our room, which was down a flight of stairs and filled with 12 bunk beds, half of which were occupied by passed out people. Corrine and I luckily had a bunk bed to share, she took the top, and I took the bottom. I liked sleeping in the cave of the bottom bunk, I felt safe in there, like I could hide and watch what was going on without being seen.

We tucked in and rested the best we could for a while, unsure of where to go or what to do. Traveling had taken a lot out of me.

After some hours of sleeping I awoke, unsure exactly of where I was. Our room opened up into a little courtyard. It was mainly a place where people went to smoke cigarettes, and upon waking I was confronted with tobacco smoke blowing in from a man who'd just been roused and was smoking on the patio. All the doors were wide open in attempt to air out the musky hungover, old cigarette butt smell. I wanted to get out of there, but I didn't know where to go. The only food in the hostel was bar food, and greasy breakfast food, the kind of food you want after a night of drugs and partying.

I decided to wait for Corrine to wake also, so that we could venture out and find food together. In the mean time I watched the smoker on the porch, he had a shaved head and an earring, his movements reminded me of my brother Dante, slightly on edge, and always ready to deal with something or make a deal.

I remembered my first meeting with my half-brother. I was warned to steer clear of him as if he carried dark demons, but my curiosity and a familial magnetism drew us together. I was driving my car through town on a Friday night and I saw him move across the street. I recognized the way his body moved, like Reign's and I followed him without caution. I needed to know who he was.

October 2003—from my journal
    *"I met him tonight, like a love story, like a movie.
I waited, talking to my mother after work, stalling, I don't
know why. It was a moment like ones I might have pined
away for in bed, late at night when I was thirteen. I never
imagined that two people who'd never really met could look
in one another's eyes and know each other so well. I've
been keeping my eye out for him, I couldn't help my curiosity. I couldn't help falling in love with the mystery of him.
Just last week I saw a picture in a family album that belonged to my half-sister, an album covered up, dusted with
layers of history in the locked attic of my life. The album
that I never knew existed until six months ago and when
his picture flashed past, I memorized it, etched it into my
mind, because I knew that was the only way. It seems like
people want to protect me from who I really am. It seemed to
me that staying away from him would be denying a part of
myself.*
    *I saw him walking down the street and recognized
how similar he was to that picture. I parked, got out of my
car, got stuck chatting with an acquaintance, and I thought
I had lost him. I went in the direction he was walking
caught sight of him, boring a hole through him, watching
only him, everything around me was lost, only props on the
stage where we were about to act out our first scene together.
I strutted, legs wide, walking as fast as I could in red 4 inch
heels. I closed in on him. Twelve feet away, he turned and
looked right at me...*

    "Excuse me, what's your name?" I looked into
his blue, deep eyes, and I already knew the answer, the
answer I had been unsure of while I chased it down the
street.
    "Dante." He furrowed his eyebrows, but

smiled softly and I walked up to stand and stare into him. My brother. I smiled and put my hand out.

"Hi. I'm Wrenna."

Our hands connected first and then he tilted his head a bit to the side, like a dog when they examine a sound coming out of you that they aren't familiar with. Then everything registered, and he nodded, our eyes connected still. I nodded back, and he pulled me into him, a gesture that was stolen from me for twenty-one years. I fell in love, with the connection, with loss that was found. Where had he come from? I had brushed by him last Saturday night and wondered if that was him, but shook it off because the timing wasn't right and I didn't think such a coincidence would be so likely this early in the game. There he was, in front of me, like a newborn baby, so fragile, so new, so innocent and already too wise.

"How did you know it was me?" he asked shaking his head.

"I saw your picture last week at Bernie's, we had dinner. I wasn't sure until I saw your broad shoulders and then I knew it had to be you."

"How long have you known?" he asked.

"Since September. My mom told me." I wanted to tell him so many things, and listen to anything he had to say. "I hope you don't hate me." I said.

"No, not at all, I've wanted to tell you since I found out. I don't hate you at all," he smiled and pulled me in for another hug. "Hey we gotta hang out sometime, I want to know you." Yes, I want to know him too. If I didn't already know that he was born one and half years before me, I would think somehow we were twins of the universe. I didn't even know what that meant, just that I already recognized a kindred soul. Maybe it was how my mother felt when she met Pietro, it was like we all fit into a giant puzzle, each of us a piece just waiting for the spirits to drop another clue in our path to get closer to knowing who we are.

"I agree," I replied. "I'd love to hang out and hear your side of the story."

"Let me get your digits." He pulled out his cell phone and I told him my phone number as he keyed them into the memory of his phone.

"I'll call you, we'll get together." He promised.

I wanted to take him in my arms and hold him, like he was mine, like someone had stolen him from me. I was afraid to let him disappear.

"Yeah, I'd like that." I studied him again, but this time in person. He didn't look much like our father, but just like Reign he had a big energy, and he could lead you with charisma, drawing you in with a certain sureness he projected. Dante's head was shaved, and his face, strong and handsome. His chin I noticed was not like the dimpled one I got from our father, but his eyes, like mine, they were blue, and deep inside there was a sadness, but also a wonderful curiosity. The blue in them made me sad for all the time I never knew him as my brother and glad he was no longer a kept secret. "Hey, take it easy." I said.

Just as I had approached him, shaky and excited, I smiled and turned, waved goodbye, and walked away. I walked in a fake-confident gait, tipping my head and letting tears fall into the cowl of my dress. He was gone. I knew I'd see him again and I longed for it. I wished I could have gone with him, but I didn't know how or if I was ready. One thing at a time I told myself, one thing at a time.

Tears kept streaming down my face as I made my way to the cantina where my friends awaited my arrival. I could only think of seeing Corrine and telling her everything, but I didn't think she wouldn't understand, or she would be too involved in her evening to want to care.

I collected myself and walked in to the restaurant, but the minute I saw my girlfriends, Dante's image flooded into me again, our exchange of glances, our silent forgiveness of each other, and all the history that we felt with each other but didn't actually know. I felt my breath taken away. I dabbed my eyes and hung onto Corrine for a brief moment, as she gave me a partially embarrassed, partially compassionate, partially confused look.

"Hey, what's up?" she asked with concern in her voice.

"I can't talk about it now. Maybe later. I'm okay," I said shortly excusing all of it as if it were no big deal. I left it alone, because I wanted it for myself. I sat for a while, staring, like I do sometimes when I'm in another world, and could hear Corrine and my other friend Fina talking about a boy that had broken her heart, but after some time I tuned her out and turned away. Corrine focused on her and ignored me. Finally, a thought of my brief encounter with Dante dipped into my mind and I squinted to keep tears from falling.

"I'm sorry, I'm gonna go home, I'm not doing well." I glanced at them with wet eyes and they graced me with sympathetic ones. They kissed me goodnight and I ducked out into the cool evening. When I left I had no intention of finding him, but I found myself walking the opposite direction of my car, leading myself to where I thought he might be, where I saw him last Saturday.

I spotted a few familiar locals standing outside the bar where most of the people I knew frequented. I didn't want to appear that I was looking for anyone. I wandered over to the DJ table where my friend Chris stood, and we playfully flirted with our eyes.

Then, I felt him looking at me. When I turned, Dante waved. I walked over and plopped myself down next to him. Infatuated. That's what I was, infatuated with the idea of him, with my own brother. And I wanted to saturate myself with everything he had to say, good and bad.

"Hey, mind if I sit here?" I asked laughing, knowing that he would never refuse, I am his sister after all.

"No, not at all." His friends said a quick hello then made their way over to the bar and started flirting with the single gals at the counter. "I can't believe you just walked up to me like that, I had no idea you knew about everything."

"I've been wanting to meet you for quite a while now, but I kept receiving warnings from people. Plus, I do still want to protect my father from all of this. I don't know if that's fair or not, but I feel like I need to."

"You know your dad already knows."

"Yeah I know, but he doesn't know that I know and I want to keep it that way for a while, he's been dealing with a lot of shit lately." I trailed off and we sat there silently, taking each other in like new lovers who had recently found one another. He curled toward me and I mimicked his body language. He sat protectively and intimately, we didn't want anyone to ruin this new connection, just like a toy that you just can't share until it's been broken in a little.

"I can't believe we haven't met before. I mean I know everybody in town", I told him.

"We went to the same kindergarten, I used to flirt with you and I remember going to your house and hangin' wit you. And it's like, where were our parents you know?" He laughed at himself.   "The same kindergarten huh?

"Yeah, crazy huh? So you write, like our dad? He's a really good writer you know, he's really creative. He's a fucking' idiot though, shit he has six kids. He wasn't a very good father to us, we're all fucked up. Mattie, she's got a good thing, a family, she's happy. She got away from all of it. Well. A lot of it. You look like her."

"Our baby pictures are identical. And our silhouettes even more of a trip. When I went to dinner at Bernice's we looked through her album, and it was weird seeing all of your faces when you were little, it was like my family, but I wasn't there. I don't know if I belonged there or not, but what would it have looked like if I was in those pictures? I can't even imagine. My memories are so full with the family I did grow up with."

"I used to get jealous when I saw your family, you guys were always so happy," he reached up and dabbed a tear out of his eye.

"We weren't perfect," I commented.

"Yeah, neither were we, you know I was doing meth when I was thirteen. I had sex for the first time when I was nine. I was all fucked up. But, I been clean now something like seven years. Bernie, she was always there for me. But now I got my music, and it's good you know?"

I didn't know and I didn't know what else to say, I had no idea what his childhood was like, and I was afraid to know. It was already so strange thinking that he was my brother, but I didn't know anything about him, for all of my memories I had none of brothers but the ones I grew up next to. I was still at a loss for how to connect with Reign or where to begin knowing him even though I tried from time to time. Was I supposed to go backwards and dig up all the history, to understand something, to know something? Or was I to just go forward and let it all unfold?

The one thing I wanted explained was why I felt so in Love with this brother who sat in front of me, and why my love felt sexual, emotional, and spiritual and brought a part of life to me that I had never before experienced. I wanted more, but for that moment I was full.

***

Corrine stirred above me. The man with the cigarette was gone.

"Ugh," Corrine poked her head down at me from above, "It smells in here, and I am so hungry."

"Me too, let's get outta here and go see what we see."

We were both groggy and needed more sleep, but sleep wasn't very regenerating in a room congested with post party humors. We both tucked our belongings tightly inside our sleeping bags, assuming that they might be safer in there. There was a separate lock box at the desk for our passports and extra money, which was reassuring, but in the back of my mind I felt nervous that I didn't have them right on my person.

Once we retreated to the streets, we started off in a direction that took us away from the red light district. We headed to something familiar, the Van Gogh museum, which we found closed for the evening. Nearby there was a little pond that had stones you could hop on across the pond. It was a gentle retreat. We were both still hungry though. Corinne had told me that one of her goals was to find Banana ice-cream, she said her mother had always talked about how good the banana ice-cream was when she had come to Amsterdam in the 70's, so we set out to look for some. With luck we found one, not far from another food cart, and had dinner and desert in one sitting.

"I don't want to stay here any longer," I said, licking my dripping cone. "Me neither," Corrine agreed. "I do want to see a couple of things before we go though. Maybe we can change our hostel reservation in Berlin to a day earlier and leave the day after tomorrow. That would give us one day to walk around and see weird things, so that we can at least say we did weird things in Amsterdam."

"Okay, sounds good. I am kinda dreading sleeping at the Pig palace tonight, but I guess it's only like 36 more hours and we're outta here." Corrine finished her icecream and I hopped across the little pond. The sun was setting. We both figured an early night would be good, maybe all the partyers would be out and we could get sleep before they drug in their detox fumes. On the way back though, we both a spotted a three story building, lit up and flashing with a Diner type sign that read "The Sex Museum".

"We gotta go there," Corrine said. I giggled, wondering what could possibly be inside a sex museum, or if it was anything like the porn stores back home.

The first floor was a lot like the sex shops in the bigger cities that we had popped into from time to time to check out the vibrators, or the random other sex toys that were on the market. Upstairs, an entire history of erotica and pornography was presented; there were rubber statues, posters, books, and all kinds of paraphernalia. We wandered through for an hour, commenting, giggling, and grimacing at some of the images. By the time we left it was completely dark outside, I carried a few "sex museum" bookmarks with me to give away as souvenirs.

In the morning we walked through the mysterious city that was the subject of so many Van Gogh paintings and the home of Anne Frank's hide away from the Nazis. The street we walked down had numbers of head shops, bars, shops stocked with varieties of cannabis, and a few shady restaurants. I felt the farthest away from 'home' since I jetted off in an airplane less than a week earlier.

"Psst, Psst," I ignored the sound and so did Corrine. We had been followed once by a couple of trouble maker boys in Mexico, who tried to sell us jewelry, and when we got close enough one of them reached out and pinched my nipple. Since then we were both more cautious to turn and give attention to any kind of notice of strangers in foreign countries.

The sound behind us persisted, and finally a man swooped in front of us, coaxing us, and saying, "I have the good stuff, you like?"

Corrine sluffed him off, "No Thanks", and she kept on walking. We walked on, all the while hearing his "Psst" for another couple hundred meters, until he finally gave up.

"Did that guy just try to sell us some crazy drugs?" I asked.

"Yeah, I think so. I'm glad we lost him," she said, with her head pointed directly ahead of us.

The city changed as we went away from the hostel, and all the beauty of Van Gogh's paintings came around us in the shapes and the light. There was an eerie light in the sky, a pinkish grey haze that didn't clear much as the morning went on. I stopped on a bridge overlooking a canal and looked over the buildings, trying to imagine the war that had gone on sixty years before. It was amazing how the rocks and the buildings could tell that story. I had felt a similar feeling about the structures in Italy when I first came with my mother. Somehow there was life and memory in the city, each city we went to had its own essence, its own history, and its own secrets.

We arrived at the Anne Frank Museum and were guided through and given a synopsis of who lived there and what there life was like during their years in captivity. When we came to the bedroom Anne had lived in, we were shown the window that she hid behind with her family. Outside was a tree, a tree that was alive back then. I found it interesting that the apartment had been saved, not fixed up and rented to someone new when the war was over, but saved for a story to be told, and that the tall tree outside the window was its keeper, still living to tell the story of a young girl, who made the most of her young life as a captive.

We were taken through the famous bookcase that kept that family safe for so long, and down at the bottom of the house was an open room, the end of the museum route. A television was mounted to the wall playing a movie of Otto Frank, Anne's father, speaking about her and her diary, which he read after getting out of Auschwitz. He was an old man now who spoke about Anne tenderly, expressing his amazement that a girl her age could feel as much as she did and the way that she did. He cried as he talked about her in his interview, and I was moved at the thought of the father that I didn't know. I wondered if he felt the same things I felt, a deeper connection than time spent together in this lifetime, as if we had known each other once in another life. And then I thought of my father who had brought me up and cared for me all along, and how tender he was with my own innocence and strong knowing of the things that went unspoken and unseen.

I walked away from that exhibit, deeply aware of the fleeting opportunities we have in a lifetime to forgive and try to understand the stories of the people around us. I wondered somehow if I was missing something with Reign, if maybe there was something more that we were supposed to learn from each other.

{21} - GERMANY

After almost a week of traveling, I stayed up all night roaming through Berlin with a friend I met in the hostel. I slithered into bed at 5 a.m. and when I woke close to noon, my throat ached. I was exhausted.

Corrine asked me if I wanted to go along with her to look at some monuments from WWII, but I was already fighting my own war with my body. I needed a day of rest. I felt guilty that I wasn't well enough to accompany her, but I couldn't motivate myself to move out of my sleeping bag. I had a fever and felt awful. Corrine packed up her things and left to explore.

The room with eight beds remained empty and quiet all day. I came in and out of consciousness, falling into hazy dreams and waking up sweating. I couldn't get away from my mind or myself. Reign, my mother, my father Carver, all of them were invading my dreams. I wanted to scream but my throat was so red and sore that I could hardly make a noise.

I still wondered why, even after three years of knowing about Reign, nothing seemed different. When my family got together in the summer, it was the same as always, no one mentioned Reign at all. Keeping secrets is the nature of affairs, and seemingly the nature of my family as well. I was a love child born out of the kind of Love that doesn't make sense, it's not the reasonable kind of love, and it doesn't adhere to any religion or laws. Right from the beginning my very identity challenged the conditionings of the culture I grew up around.

Just as much as I wanted to keep playing the game, pretending that Reign was only a lover to my mother and nothing else, I couldn't lie to myself. Something awakened the day my mother told me about Reign, something in my soul was set right. Reign was a part of me; without accepting that I deprived myself from being whole.

***

It was Friday night again, the season for red wine and steak. Dad always liked to get 20 ounce Ribeye's, of which, I would consume the majority of, sometimes down to the bone, washing it all down with a glass of Australian Syrah.

Dad poured me a glass of wine, and slipped out briefly to check the steak on the BBQ.
The steak smell wafted out into the late fall air; the cold never stopped him from grilling meat.

"Well, looks like a couple more minutes," he said swooping in the door. With his winter parka still on he slid over to the cabinet next to the fridge and found his pack of Marlboro ultra-lights, shook one out of the pack and retreated to the threshold of the door. He stood on the porch with the door slightly ajar so that we could continue our conversation.

As he paused, taking a suck of tobacco I went on with what I was saying about mom, "I think it had something to do with the Catholic Church, she always talked about the nuns telling her how sinful kissing and sex was." Dad took in another long drag and let it out.

"There were other things from when she was young that she still deals with," dad stopped there, he seemed to be protecting my mother somehow. "I also think she is bipolar." I squinched my eyebrows at him, I never liked when anyone used psychological terms to define someone. Dad would use the term bipolar often when we had Friday night dinners, especially when the topic involved mom choosing to have more than one lover at a time.

I had a hidden agenda to help dad understand my mother, because I felt I knew her better, I thought that I was special and that she had told me things she hadn't told anyone else.

I don't know why I wanted him to change or why it mattered if he understood my mom. I didn't understand the part of either of them that wanted the other to be something different.   In my childhood-eyes the two of them were always romantic, I idolized their relationship. They always kissed in the kitchen when they made dinner. Some nights I could hear them making love. When they went out to dinner on a date, she would dress up in an elegant dress, and wear a pearl necklace with 24 karat gold earrings and a little splash of Lily of the Valley or Opium perfume. Dad put on a suit and shaved. I sat on the toilet and watched waiting for him to put a little dollop of shaving cream on my nose. He put on after-shave and the two of them would leave us at my grandmother's or with a baby sitter, exiting with a trail of scent and a look of classy romance. They always appeared to be the perfect couple.   Dad finished his cigarette, stumped it out in an ashtray outside the door, and went to tend to the steak. He came back and slid a juicy ribeye onto my plate. We both cut into our meat, taking a break from talking for a moment. The topic of mom gave us something to talk about but it could only go so far before it became somewhat uncomfortable. We both knew where she really was on those Friday nights.

After we came back from Italy, mom began a ritual

of taking a night away, she said she was going to her little house, the one where Pietro had stayed when he came. But, dad and I knew that she wasn't there, she was at her boyfriend's house. David became her lover after Reign and my mom's relationship dissolved. For a long time I would say nothing, I never wanted to rat out her whereabouts, but then dad had brought it up one night, he inserted David's name into one of our Friday night dinners, and I realized that he knew I was aware of her affairs, in spite of mom's bent for deception.

"Dad..." I paused for a moment, "Mom told me about Reign," he looked at me as if he didn't know what I had even said, so I continued, "After Pietro left; he reminded me of Reign... you know? And somehow it came out...that...he's my biological father."

At first his face went serious and stoic, then his eyebrows bent and he began to cry.

"Oh," he moaned with his face in his hands, "I can't believe she told you that, I can't believe she told you, ohhh, hujhu, oh oh oh" he cried from a deep place inside of him, a place where he had hidden the truth for years.

I wept without restraint, feeling relieved, feeling for him,

"Oh, daddy, you are my father, you," I choked "always took care of me when I was sick, and always treated me so much like your daughter, and I am your daughter." I stood up from my seat and collapsed back down into his lap, letting him embrace me. My head tucked into his shoulder and I curled my legs into his lap, wrapping my arms around his neck and crying, "I love you daddy." I sunk into him, feeling this man who was my friend and my provider for so many years of my life. I noticed how I had never really known him, I only knew him through mom's experience of him. She kept me so close to her.

I felt a connection of love with him, a connection that I felt for the first time in my life without holding back.

And just like that Carver and I became allies, we could relate with one another because we both loved my mother, we had both learned how to love the steps of her tango.

Corrine came back to the hostel late in the evening. I stayed inside my sleeping bag, pretending to be fast asleep. For some reason I had nothing to say to her, I didn't want to rain on her parade and bring all of my family drama into our trip. Once she was sleeping, I fell asleep again and awoke feeling much better and ready to get on the next train to Interlocken, Switzerland.

{22} - INTERLOCKEN

The Alps jetted up around us, and we walked through the melting ice-cream bowl of the mountain's valley, along the quiet road from the train station, watching parachutes bobbing and dipping in the sky. We followed their trail to a large field, not too far from the hostel we were seeking. There were a couple of parachutes landing when we walked by the field.

"Let's go check out the paragliding schedule when we get there, I want to do it first thing so that I can face my fear of heights and have it over with", Corrine said. "Alright," I was happy to follow, because it meant that we got to explore. We arrived at Balmer's Inn, checked in, dropped our bags in a quaint cabin room overlooking the street, then immediately heading down stairs through the lobby to a desk where pictures of skydiver's and people sliding down canyons were advertised.

"Hi," Corrine announced herself to the man behind the counter.

"Hi!" he said cheerfully back. He turned his head toward me and locked eyes to acknowledge me.

"What can I help you with?" He asked. We stared into each other's eyes, connecting them like magnets. I was surprised by his intense presence, but still, I was intrigued.

"We are here to book a paragliding trip", I said, looking over the pamphlet to see how much the trip was going to cost me.

"Here you are," he handed me a printed slip, "Meet here tomorrow at 9:45, the shuttle will pick you up and take you up the mountain." His brown eyes looked into me softly and he smiled.

I stared at him, expressionless, not wanting to give in too much, he probably liked to flirt with a lot of girls who came traveling through. It was most likely just a game he played.

I handed him my credit card to pay the 300 Franks for my ticket up the mountain. He ran my card and returned it to me. "Here you are" he paused reading my name…"Wrenna," he smiled again at me.

"Thank you," I paused looking at his name tag, "Marco".

Corrine and I walked into the courtyard where other travelers were sipping beer, hanging out playing chess and chatting or reading.

"What was that all about?" Corrine inquired.

"Yeah you noticed that?" I asked a bit dumbfounded.

"Yeah, he was majorly flirting with you".

"Huh." I was surprised because, I didn't come on this trip to flirt, I had no intention at all to meet a lover, I was traveling to get away from myself and the way everyone knew me, and the way I knew me. I sat down on a fold out lawn chair.

Corrine opened her pamphlet about paragliding, surveying the pictures and reading the captions.

"I have to do this Wrenna..." she trailed on about excitement and conquering fear, but I wasn't really listening, I was thinking about the way that adventure desk guy had looked at me and how it made me feel whimsical, and alive.

***

I woke to the sound of our hostel-mate brushing her teeth in the sink by the foot of my bed. It had rained hard in the night and the smell of cool earth steamed up in the morning sunshine. The day felt magical already. I dreamed of flying, a recurring dream where I would go to the top of a hill near my house and start running down, then dive parallel to the ground and catch the wind. The wind always held me, and it felt so real.

Corrine sat up slowly and squinted at me with a groggy look on her face.

"You ready to fly?" I asked her.

"No. But I have to do it, I have to face my fear," she said convincing herself.

We walked down to receive our complimentary breakfast in the dining area.

"Good morning!" greeted the adventure guy as we walked by his desk. I found myself acting a bit skeptical, but underneath the act I was charmed by his enthusiasm. Someone else approached the desk and I was tugged away by Corrine's hungry belly.

At 9:35 I saw a van back into the Balmer's Driveway. Corrine and I both shoved the rest of our toast into our mouths and gulped a bit more coffee, then proceeded to the loading area, where we checked our bags for snacks and filled up on fresh spring water.

"You all ready?" I heard a voice ask me from behind. I turned and saw my adventure man, the way he looked at me was like nothing I ever experienced. It was a look of knowing and friendship, like he was waiting for me to remember the time we spent once upon a time. I gave him a look that asked, "What is it that I have forgotten?"

"Come by the desk later and tell me how the flight goes." he told me.

"Okay." I felt a flutter of excitement, but my attention was quickly averted to the shuttle loading; we were about to climb the mountain. On the bus ride we met our guides. There were four other people on the trip and just as many guides. Each of us would have our own partners to help us with our parachutes. I ended up with a comical Swiss guy, who was in his late twenties. Everything he said was laden with a thick Swiss accent that made me laugh, merely because each word had so much emphasis and seemed so boxy and loud, but he was gentle and fun, which made me trust him.

The van parked alongside a steep grassy hill where we waited while the guides laid out our parachutes. Corinne and I looked out at the landscape. Cascading hills with rich green forest filled the canyon which we were about to dive into. The sky was overcast with splotches of blue. An eagle flew in the distance, a plane flew overhead, most likely toting skydivers, and Corrine sat beside me, a bit shaky, and dramatic, but genuinely humbled in her choice to participate in such a daring sport.

Finally, we were harnessed and instructed in our

tasks of how to take off and how to land. I had thoughts of landing and wondered how it was even possible without breaking a leg. I didn't ask, I just trusted that I wouldn't.

Corrine went first in line. She and her guide were harnessed and their parachute lay stretched out behind them. I stood back waiting my turn.

"Ok! You ready?!" her guide shouted into the wind.

"Yeah!" Corrine said now fiercely conjuring courage and allowing her scared act to dissipate. They started running down the short steep grade, and all in a swoop the parachute lifted and their feet ran off the cliff, they were floating gently out over the forested hills.

It was my turn. I felt ready, especially after hearing Corrine's triumphant whoop when she was lifted and held upon the air.

The harness was clipped around me, I felt the presence of my guide supporting me from behind. And we ran pushing feet into the grassy earth, pulling forward with our upper bodies, playing with the tension of air and parachute and gravity.

My feet lifted off the earth, and they no longer needed the security of being rooted. I was a cloud, floating lazily in the air, with many feet of nothing below me.

We swooped gently around the trees and fell slowly.

I relaxed with the sensuality of the flight, my guide controlled the direction we went. We were cradled lightly in together and I wondered about him as a lover—though his staunch Germanesque quality did not synthesize with my spirit.   That adventure guy though, he was like spring water, a sweet fresh curiosity I wanted to jump into.

"Do YOO Want to Stee-ar?!" my guide dipped his hand into my grip and rolled the steering handle into my palm. He did this with both grips.

"Ok. NOW! Pull with your right hand." I tugged the right handle and we quickly dipped down.

"Whoa! Ok pull with other hand, softer this time."

I laughed and pulled gently with my left hand. We evened out and started feeling and listening to the wind. There was a dance between our bird and the wind's wings. I thought of nothing but soaring, I felt suddenly alone in the sky and peaceful and connected to Spirit.

We floated down and down and I only woke out of my dream when I glimpsed the city below. The guide took the reins again and instructed me to start running in midair. I did this and, so slowly it seemed, we approached the earth until my feet collided with the ground and the inertia sent me running 20 or thirty feet until the parachute slid along the field and everything stopped. We unharnessed, Corrine and I ran to each other - she was ecstatic, "I did it! I flew! I faced my fear!" She faced up at the sky with a proud face, joking at her triumph.

We thanked our guides, took pictures and went into town to find some lunch. The rest of the day we wandered around looking at coo-coo clocks, elaborate beer steins, and garden gnomes.

***

Back at Balmer's I sat down on the curb next to

the spring water spout. The sun occasionally came out from behind a cloud and warmed my hair.

Our hostel was quaint and peppy, and well kept. It had a comfort like my grandmother's house, dressed with curtains and shutters, adorned with silly knickknacks, and it was attractive to those looking for a shelter from the storm. I sipped on spring water and watched bikers and hiker's looking at maps, or coming back from a day's adventure. The more extreme adventurers compared notes about their excursions; many were Americans or Australians, but there were a few travelers from Japan and other European guests which were fun to watch and listen to.

Never before had I felt the presence in myself that I did sitting there. I had no place to be, or time to be there. I did not know anyone other than Corrine, who had gone to nap before dinner. The nature around me had a life to it that I never noticed before. Somehow everything seemed to be speaking to me, the plants, the rain, even the features of the Inn, it felt like a dream but I wasn't sleeping. Spring water bubbled out of its spout, singing to me. The birds danced a ballet in the sky, never tiring. Even the Garden gnome smiled at me and laughed, he seemed to have a spirit emanating from him. Without thinking I stood up and wandered right over to the desk through the front entrance of Balmer's, and there was the adventure guy helping someone sign up for a skydiving jump the next day. I stood and waited, as if I too were about to shell out 300 franks to go skydiving, but when I stepped up to the now empty counter, I was greeted with a hello that held nothing in-between us. Again, like we were friends already. How did he do that?

"How was your trip?" he inquired sincerely.

"It was great, I am so glad I went, definitely addictive, I could go a bunch more, but, well once is enough- if I were rich I'd go again." I answered.

"Have you ever done any of those things?" I gestured over at the board with pictures of all the activities advertised.

"Yeah, I've been working here for a while, after that long I have had a lot of time to explore around and experience what this place has to offer," he turned for a moment and put some receipts into a box, then turned back and looked right into my eyes, "I'd like to give you a tour," he said matter-of-factly.

"I have tomorrow night off. I get done around 6:30, we could have dinner and I'll show you around." For a moment I was speechless, just like that he asked me out. Back home it took forever to play the ask-out game and usually it was me asking out someone, not the other way around.

"Um, yeah, I think it sounds fun." I wondered what Corrine would say, she had rolled her eyes at me a few times over after I spent the night roaming around Berlin with a guy I met at the hostel. I was out until the sun came up talking, just having time with someone, and Corrine didn't know until the next day when I told her. I felt weird leaving her, because we were supposed to be traveling together, which I guess meant we stayed together all the time like being married in a way. But, I had little itches to explore certain opportunities when they came my way, and this was one of them.

"Is this like a date?" I asked boldly.

"Yeah, it's a date." he chuckled. "Meet me here at six-thirty."

"Ok, I will see you here tomorrow night." It was so spontaneous, I didn't even have time to get worked up about rejection, and he asked me out, just like that.

The next day Corrine and I meandered and lounged. Interlocken was a wonderful place to do just that. So far we had only been to large cities, which seemed endless in exploration and ways to spend money. There were restaurants and museums, historical sights, entertainment and transportation from one place to the next. The little village of Interlocken slowed everything down. Nature and the town and grocery store were all in walking distance, and unlike the city, people stayed in and tended more to their gardens. I relished in the opportunity to spend more time relaxing, like sitting under a shady tree reading the copy of Jane Eyre that I found in a 'take one, leave one' book shelf at the last hostel I had stayed in.

I laid back in a lawn chair mid-day waiting until 6:30. Corrine sat beside me clipping her toe nails. The little Balmer's courtyard had a shady corner of bushy trees, a milieu of varied lawn chairs spread about and some picnic tables where people could sit and eat. I read a few paragraphs before I realized I had not comprehended any of the words, I was fantasizing about the evening ahead.

My eyes closed. The sun lit my eyelids and warmed me into a dream nap. When I woke the sky had greyed into a cloudy afternoon. Corrine had her nose in a book.

"Hey. I think I'm gonna go change clothes before I go out. It looks like it might rain."

"Okay, I'm just gonna be bored and read my book."

"Sorry," I said, knowing well that she was hoping for a bit more excitement than a town that has a 10 o'clock curfew. If she had it her way, she'd be salsa dancing with a sexy guy that could really lead.

I dressed in the only pair of jeans I had and a cute silk/cotton tank top without a bra. Around my waist I tied my blue lightweight pullover sweatshirt. I wore flip flops and felt so in my body. Downstairs I hesitated for a moment, trying to look casual so that I didn't get Marco in trouble; any job I had ever had discouraged dating the clientele.

I caught his eye from the doorway where I leaned patiently. He gestured that he would be a moment. I felt special. I acted like I was just hanging out, maybe waiting for a friend, and secretly snuck glances at him. He was focused and intent on passing on his post to the night closing employee. Finally, he walked my direction and very directly instructed me to meet him out front. I walked out to where I suspected I would be out of the eye of any Balmer's employees. A few minutes later he met me and without stopping led me away and down the street.

"I have to stop by my place for a few minutes to change out of my work clothes, do you mind?" I was walking briskly alongside him.

"Do you walk fast because you're from a big city?" I asked.

"Oh, am I walking too fast?" he slowed his pace.

"I don't mind going to your house, this just feels like a great adventure." We walked many blocks until we came to a brown graveled road. I was hungry, and feeling a bit fatigued, so my legs were happy when we

finally reached the two story cottage.   "I live upstairs, there is an older guy that lives below me. I have a
couple roommates right now, a married couple that are
having marital problems," he made a face, "they might
be home." Marco explained as he unlocked the door
that opened to a staircase.

The air at the bottom of the stairs was cool,
almost cold, stepping into it from the balmy evening.
Marco turned and told me to wait at the bottom of the
stairs. I waited for a few minutes, then slowly scooted
up one step at a time, growing a bit impatient; When
Marco found me again I was half way up the staircase.

"Let's go get some pizza," he said. We went outside and he led me to his car, where he turned on "The
Dark Side of the Moon", and drove me to town to eat.

After eating, we drove with the windows
down toward the hills as the sun set. We didn't
talk about much, but listened instead to music and
breathed in the fresh evening air. After the heat of the
day it was nice to simply receive the cool night.

I wondered where Marco was taking me, and I
wondered if I would regret going out with a man I had
only met the day before. I wanted to trust in the magic
of the night.

We pulled up into a parking lot of a touristy
nature spot. There was only one car in the lot, which
made me wonder if I was setting myself up for a dangerous situation. I reasoned that even though I was in
Switzerland it really wasn't different than going on a
first date back home, in fact it was probably safer, because I knew Corrine would know if I'd gone missing
and with whom, so I let that go and decided to trust
him.

He led me up a path that grew steeper and narrower. The path ended at a pile of light grey boulders. A full moon beamed down at us for a moment before it ducked back again behind the clouds. We climbed around what I guessed were ruins of an old structure.

Almost to the top and rounding a corner into a rock room without a roof, I was surprised to find two lover's cuddled and kissing near one of the corners. We said a polite hello, as if we hardly paid them any mind and turned back down the steps of the ruin. I giggled a bit under my breath once we were down a level from the lovers. Marco took my hand and we made our way to the edge of a lake. Mosquitos bit at me and my flip-flops kept getting stuck in the mud. I was falling behind until Marco came back to me and told me to hop on his back. He carried me to a dock, and gently placed me down on the muddy bank. I took off my flip flops and dipped my toe in the water.

"You wanna swim?" he asked, raising his eyebrows flirtatiously.

"Yeah, let's." Without thinking about it, we both stripped off our clothes and ran into the lake. He dove in and began swimming in the dark water. I had no idea where I was, but I remembered the peace my mother had when she would disappear into the lake when I was a child, and felt a similar calmness about the water here. We bobbed out, Marco swam confidently toward the middle of the lake. I hesitated and waded out a little bit at a time. He turned to me and yelled, "Come on! It is great!"

We were both laughing as I came close to him. We had made it as far as we could go, the rest of the lake was separated by a divider in the water, placed for safety so that people did not swim into the dangerous part, I assumed.

I could touch the bottom with my shoulders barely above the water. The water and the crisp air brought me into my body and out of my head.

Marco reached for me, and pulled me into his body, which floated so smoothly next his skin. The moment my body touched his all my senses woke up as if they'd been sleeping for a long time. Lightning struck in the distance, and a loud clap of thunder boomed. We began to swim toward the shore and it started raining big drops. By the time we reached the shore it was pouring. Marco had brought along a wool blanket from the car, and we climbed up into a lookout deck and huddled together under it. The wool rubbed on my skin and kept the rain out. We were held inside the womb of the storm. Marco held me, wrapped his arms around my tucked up legs, our bodies were in balls, our skin pressed against one another. It was electric, and the rain poured down around us, thunder rumbling, lightening exploding one bolt after another. We kissed until the storm let up. With nowhere to go, I contemplated making love right under the blanket, tickled by wool and soothed by skin.

We kissed until the rain passed, then crawled out from our den to search out our clothes in the dark. I looked all over for my flip-flop but it had washed away with the rain, so Marco carried me back again to the car. It was after curfew by the time we arrived in town, so instead of making a fuss, he offered for me to stay at his house.

His roommates were up watching an episode of a 70's British sitcom. We watched a few minutes then slipped away into Marco's bedroom. We wrapped up in each other. He told me about his family from the big city, his Italian blood, his sister, who still lived in New York; it sounded so worldly and big to me. I told him about my mother and her affair, about how I was a love child, and about my radical conception. He didn't seem too phased by it.

I didn't know if I was in love with Marco, but I was intrigued and infatuated. I loved the adventure, and I loved being with him. He sat up and slid his hands down my waist, he was sure and direct. Something inside of me let go, a voice that had always been there stopped speaking.

***

Dreamy morning waking up. Mmm...his smell. I stuff my nose into the pillow to get more. I pull up the blankets to my chest, moving my breast into the bed.

The energy inside my body is ecstatic.

A soft light from the morning sun through the shade says, "keep some, hold it within you, it is yours." I feel it move down to my center and swell up in my sex.

Ahh...I lay back remembering the kiss, upon waking in a dream I kissed him, and to my surprise he kissed me fully, he met me and we swirled in some dimension different from the one I live in every day. When our lips parted my head was light, I went immediately back into a dream, from the most real feeling of the dreamed of kiss, it was whole, there was no clinging, only pure experience.

This is an awakening.

I am awakening to the morning of my soul...

The next morning Marco was gone, he woke up to an alarm, hit the snooze button four times and snuggled up closer to me until he finally disappeared. I had to find my way back to the hostel, where I found a very pouty Corrine waiting for me in her bed.

"Where were you? Corinne asked hastily.

"I stayed over at his house. Oh wow! Corrine, I think I am in Love."

She looked at me squinting her eye, trying to be stubborn, but there was a hint of smile coming across her lips. We went down to breakfast and I filled her in on every word and detail since the night before. "Hmmm," I sighed. "I want to see him again. I ripped a small piece of paper off of a nearby bulletin and wrote the words, "When do you get off? Do you want to hang out?" I put the paper in my pocket. When we finished breakfast I walked over to where Marco stood at the adventure desk and slipped the folded paper to him. I stood by for a moment until he had a chance to read the note. He slid it back to me. It said, "21:30, yes."

At 9:30 that night I made my way down to meet him, and again like the night before we left, this time we got into his car and decided to go directly back to his house, lingered briefly with his roommates until they left, then watched some episodes of the British sitcom again. Finally, late into the night we made our way to the bedroom.

At first we lay tired and spooning in underwear, pressed together sweetly, then he moved my face toward his and kissed my lips, pressing and tender, our tongues intertwined.

I loved the tossed blankets, I loved his bachelor way, I loved that there was no time or commitment to anything, no responsibility, no fear.

I got up red in the face, sweating, made my way to the bathroom, feeling drunk on sex, then back to

Marco's arms where we both fell hard into sleep.

I woke with Marco in the morning and he drove me back to the hostel.

Another night passed in a similar manner, it was the first section of the trip that Corrine and I were away from each other. I felt a little guilty, that I was choosing to go stay at Marco's again, but it was our final night in Interlocken and I was addicted, I was in love, and tomorrow I would leave, possibly never to see him again.

We went straight to bed and made love three times over, sharing stories and pillow talk about working in hostel's, traveling with friends, family, and ex-lovers. As we lay tangled in each other, he looked at me suddenly with inspiration in his eyes.

"Come back. Will you come back and stay with me? I want you to come back. My roommates are moving out in a couple of weeks so you could stay here." He wasn't wearing his glasses, which always gave him a sweet look. His brown eyes were dreamy with sex and presence and desire.

"Yes, I want to, I don't know how, but I'll try." I couldn't believe he had just asked me to come back to see him, a summer fling, the summer fling I had always wanted, and it wanted me back.

In the morning Marco drove me back. I spent my time with Corrine folding clothes and packing our belongings perfectly to fit in our backpacks. When we finished we went down to breakfast. I saw Marco reading the paper, and I walked right by him. He didn't look at me or say anything.

Suddenly I felt awful. I felt like a fool. I asked Corrine if she thought he was ignoring me because he was at work.

"Oh honey, I don't know, maybe he just didn't see you."

"Yeah maybe."

I walked right over to confront him, now slightly angry at how easily I trusted him. He looked up from his paper and smiled across his face.

"Hey!" he said, obviously happy to see me.

"Hi." I stood there looking at him, feeling suddenly that I wanted to cry, and knowing well that I missed him already.

"I'm leaving in twenty minutes or so." I said not knowing what else to say in the middle of the outside cafeteria.

"Come to the desk to check out, I have to get into work now, but I will see you at checkout.

Twenty minutes later, I lugged my backpack into checkout. There was another girl working behind the counter with Marco and I was struck with jealousy, wondering if he'd slept with a lot of guests or co-workers.

I checked out with the girl, then Marco came over to me in the lobby. He put his hands on my shoulders and looked at me, I gave him a hug and he kissed me, right there in front of his co-worker, "I guess I am special", I thought. He didn't say much, but when I pulled away from him a tear was streaming down his face.

I walked to the shuttle and jumped onto the bench that went along the inside of the van, holding six people on each side with all their backpacking backpacks. I was the last one in. My eyes were wet from crying and I felt an emptiness filling my inside.

Then, Marco appeared out of nowhere at

the back of the shuttle.

He thrust his arms out and dropped two handfuls of complimentary Swiss chocolates into my hands.

"Come back," he said and he stepped back and let the doors close.

Laura Marie Parker

{23} - SHOOTING ARROWS

"SEX IS THE SEED, LOVE IS THE FLOWER, COM-
PASSION IS THE FRAGRANCE" OSHO

"Put your hand up like thise," he gestured how I should hold my arm and hand. "Now, think about the tension, there is tension between us, No?" His Italian accent drew me into him. He stood straight, poised, and serious. I was turned on by his persistence.

"Giovanni, turn the music on!" he yelled to his friend across the activity hall.

We were staying at a campground just a bus ride away from Rome. We rented out a tent for 25 Euro a night, so we split the cost and felt pretty happy to be by Rome for five days. I thought about Marco a lot, but he was days behind me and who knew if I would ever see him again. Here was Antonio, an Argentine Italian, who worked for the campground, he let me smoke a bit of his hash the first night we were camping, and each time I saw him, I was drawn to him. When he said he was from Argentina, I asked if he knew how to tango and if he would give me a lesson.

He held my waist and pressed into me, always keeping a space between us, as if he projected his energy out so I could not collide with his body. He led me, with the right tension in a Tango. He taught me a few configurations with my leg flipping back, it was slow, then quick, and always there was tension. We danced one full dance without a word, but focused in on each other's eyes.

After the dance we escaped outside into the warm night. He invited me back to his cabin. I told him I would walk with him for a bit even though I was hesitant. I thought of Marco and wondered if I was betraying the special time I had spent with him.

I walked slowly under the Full moon, still high from the adrenaline of dancing. We went along a path toward all the employee cabins, and Antonio had little to say to me. My stomach started twisting into knots. I wanted to play, but I realized I was not interested in getting too serious with this new man, who had an air of danger about him.

We arrived at his cabin, he let me in and guided me directly to his bed, where he offered me a seat, and immediately dove into me for a kiss. He pushed me into the bed, and took off his shirt. I looked at him, his chest full of dark hair, his body not right, his eyes flaring with desire and a fierceness that was uncomfortable.

"I have to pee," I said, gathering my loosening clothes that Antonio had begun to lift and shift about. I stood up, sure to have my belongings, and went into the small bathroom, where I peed and panicked. I knew that I had to make a quick decision and play my cards right, I didn't know what to do, but I was afraid I was about to be raped. Maybe he thought we had passion or connection, but I was scared, in fact, I couldn't think of a time where I felt more trapped and afraid for my life.

I gathered my breath and walked out of the bathroom, my heart leapt up, and I started shaking, even my voice quivered slightly,

"I have to go, I just remembered my friend Corrine, she doesn't know where I am and we agreed to always let each other know. I will see you tomorrow, thanks for the dance." Before I turned to walk out I saw a dark glare come at me from Antonio's eyes, I was his prey. I put on my most innocent smile, as if I had not seen his eyes, as if I was still caught in his trap; it was just enough to throw him off my scent, and I made my exit. Had I lingered for a second, he would have had me for dinner.

I walked around the corner, then ran for a minute, tucking into a path I was sure to be away from him, and making sure that I went toward people's voices. I stopped running and caught my breath, my legs were shaking.

The moon was bright, right above me. I felt her protecting me. I became invigorated, not scared at all, I had escaped the grasp of a horny camp employee, I was sure he had played that game many times, I felt strong and clever getting out of his grasp. I laughed up at the moon.

I still felt a little icky from being touched by the guy, but then I thought of Marco...I couldn't fall in love with someone else, I couldn't let all that goodness I had in Switzerland be overridden by some creep out in the boonies of Italy. Oh how I wanted to feel Marco again, right from the start he felt safe, and good.

I went back to the hot tent and lay down wide-eyed and trying to fall to sleep, but the high full moon lit up the shadows outside and my mind chattered away. I thought about Ahron, Marco, Pietro, and Antonio. How could I be so boy crazy? I thought I loved Ahron, I thought about him all the time, and he was the one I wanted to marry, the one I wanted to have a family with, but I didn't like waiting around for him to finally want to settle down, what if he never wanted to marry me?

***

July __, 2005

    Corrine and I went into the city on a shuttle bus early in the morning. She wanted to explore some parts of Rome that I had missed the first time I went with my mom. We visited the Trevi Fountain and I made a wish that I would see Marco again, I can't stop thinking about him. Corrine hasn't mentioned anything about Marco, I think she wrote him off as my summer fling, but I think it was more than a summer fling for me, I think I'm in love with him. Sometimes I question if he really cares about me, I mean, just that every time I ever had sex with someone in the past so quickly, they were usually gone so soon, but Marco told me to come back. And what if I don't? I will go back to America and he will for sure forget about me. I don't even know what could come of us anyway. But somehow it doesn't matter. I just want to see him again.

    After the fountain we saw a few more sights then we headed to the Vatican where we had to stand in a huge line. It took almost an hour of waiting in the sun to get in. Our turn finally came and we were shown a long arched hallway, painted with Angels and clouds all the way across the entire length of the ceiling. There was so much to see.

    We got in to see the Michelangelo Frieze, where Corrine snuck a few pictures inside the packed Cathedral. She shimmied her way up to get a certain angle with her camera and I lost her. I stood for a bit waiting to see if we would find each other again, all the while observing the curves and angles of the painting that covered the entire ceiling and wall. It was remarkable and a miracle that any one person could create such intricate art. I finally got swept out along with a crowd of people and found myself in a small temple with a few pews and the Mother Mary statue holding her hands out in a receiving gesture. I sat quietly, wondering what to do. I didn't remember any prayers other than the "Our Father" prayer, but I wasn't called to say it. I thought about asking God for something, or for praying about something in my life that needed help, but nothing came to me, so I just sat in the silence.

There were only women in the room with me, seven women, all sitting alone. They were quiet also. The woman next to me sat with her eyes closed, her face looked sad, or serious, maybe both. I closed my eyes and rested. When I opened them, the Mary statue seemed to be looking right at me, so humble, and motherly. Without knowing it, I began to have a flow of thoughts enter my mind. I thought about Marco and his touch. I thought about Ahron and my longing for him to pursue me. I thought about my mother and how confusing she could be. I thought about Reign and how I felt like such a victim with him, but then I also wanted something from him too, and the only way I knew how to get it was through a flirtation, or something that felt sexual, but it wasn't sex, it was a disconnection with...something. Just as I wondered what that something was, I was drawn into a light, I felt Spirit in the room.

The light warmed me and in the space where my heart beat I felt an expansion, a full energy extending from my chest and moving outward and around me. I couldn't move, but was held in the pew by the energy. The women that sat staggered with their rosaries and their bowed heads, seemed to glow different colors. So many things came clear to me, unconditional love filled me, a love that went *beyond the religion that was practiced in that temple. I had come to Europe to experience my life for myself, to lift the veil of illusions and see the truths of existence. My conception was not about cuckolding and sin. I was conceived out of love, an abundance of love, and I came to earth to be a symbol of unconditional love. I began to weep.*

Reign was foolish, but so was I. I couldn't rationalize our behavior or my feelings when I was around him, but I felt that we both had great yearnings and big dream worlds. Something beyond Time and Space connected me to him, something Soulful. My mother had her wounds with him, and there were enough stories told for me to create him into an awful predator, but he held up a mirror for me, only he could show me the part of myself that is like him, and from there I had a responsibility to choose my actions. I forgave Reign's foolishness, and my own. I forgave my mother for her own human path and experiences too. Or maybe it wasn't forgiveness at all, I don't believe either of them did anything wrong, maybe it was compassion I felt for them, compassion and understanding for their human-ness. My heart swelled with compassion for them, Reign, my mother Sylvie and Carver. I beamed and wept in the quiet of the temple.

Whatever guilt that I carried with me about my decisions to make love to Marco and not wait for Ahron lifted off of me and burned away with the smoke of the candles on the alter. I wanted to love and be loved, as the old saying goes, it takes two to tango, and if Marco wanted to tango with me, I would tango. Maybe Ahron would never put those dancing shoes back on with me again, but that was up to him, I would never stop loving him, he had made up his mind, I couldn't change him, he had already made his choice.

All the women around me did their rosaries, over and over and focused on their prayer, no one paid any mind to me, the one who sat sobbing in the pew, no one worried about me, or wondered if something was wrong, they just continued on their path, focusing on their prayer, feeling their feelings. We did not need to speak the same language. They wouldn't have talked to me anyway. But, somehow, it was as if they were angels, all of them, looking right at me, though each one had closed eyes, whispering Hail Mary's in Italian, praying for their families, praying for love, praying for peace, praying to be safe and alive. I was not different, and there was no need to speak. I wept for happiness and I wept for the journey.

We returned to our camp site on the last bus and went to our tent to rest our feet. Corinne wanted to get a start on packing for our departure the next day, but I was restless, so I stepped out and followed the moon-lit path to the computer lab, where the campers could book hostels or write emails to their family. I decided that it might be a good time to finally email my mom. I kept an eye out for Antonio and was happy to slip in the door to the lab without any confrontation.

When I opened my email, I was surprised to see a message in my inbox from Marco.

"Wrenna,

My roommates will be gone by July 26th, the house will be empty and available for you to come stay. I would love to see you again. Think about it, the invitation is open."

Marco

My heart was racing, and at the same time I began to cry. When the doors to the van had closed, I didn't know what to think about going back to see

Marco, and I still didn't know how I could do it. Corinne had our entire trip mapped out for us. Next we would go down through Italy and then to Greece, back to Italy, to Spain, France, and finally London again. I clicked on the reply arrow and sat wondering and dreaming, then I wrote my reply:

Marco,

Our time together was so juicy, I would love to see you again too. I am not sure how though. I don't know if Corrine will want to come back to Switzerland with me. Even so, I will think about it, and see what I can maneuver. I can't imagine leaving Europe and not having another time to be with you."

Wrenna.

I sent it, then contemplated writing to my mother again, but I didn't know how to tell her that I was considering going back to see a lover in Switzerland, I may have forgiven her, but I still wanted the freedom to make my own decisions without her voice getting in the way, especially when I was supposed to get on a train the next day to go to Naples, where I planned on seeing Pietro.

{24} -"BACK IN OL' NAPOLI"

"BE PATIENT TOWARD ALL THAT'S UNSOLVED IN YOUR
HEART...LOVE THE QUESTIONS THEMSELVES. DO NOT
SEEK ANSWERS. PERHAPS YOU WILL GRADUALLY,
WITHOUT NOTICING, LIVE SOME DISTANT DAY INTO
THE ANSWER." RAINER MARIA RILKE.

I had mixed feelings about seeing Pietro again. I wasn't sure why I had even made plans to see him, other than the fact that I would be in the neighborhood. It was strange, I had this feeling that my mom and I had created him, in a sense, out of our own imaginations, as a catalyst for my mother to tell me about Reign. I did love Pietro, a part of me did. There was something about his soul that connected to mine, as if we were ancestors. But, when it came to loving him like a lover, or considering having any more of a committed relationship with him, I wasn't interested. Without my mother in Italy with me, I had little attachment to him. Pietro had come to do what he was meant to do in our lives.

"It'd be nice to go dancing. Even in Rome there

wasn't any Salsa, ugh, why are we here Wrenna?" Corrine asked as she lay on the cot in our small room.

"Hmmm, I was just wondering the same thing. I came here to see Pietro, but alas, I don't want to see him. I just don't know what I should say to him". I wondered if I owed him anything at all.   "Let's go, Corrine."

"You mean leave this place tonight?" she perked up.

"No, I mean let's go out."

"But, aren't you supposed to meet Pietro in like an hour?"

"Yeah, but I can't, I just can't, let's get out of here and just be out until there is no chance that Pietro will be waiting for me."

"Okay!"

I felt petty, like an irresponsible silly girl, and at the same time, it felt good to make a decision for myself, and know that it was my heart speaking, and not someone else's.

We went out, and hours later returned to a very quiet hostel. We were getting dressed and a light knock at our door surprised me. When I opened it, the lady from the desk stood outside. She informed me that my cousin had called for me numerous times during the night looking for me.

"My cousin?" *Pietro*. "Oh yes, I don't want to see him."

"Ah, yes, I understand, have a good rest." The lovely woman turned and walked away, unfazed or burdened by my burden.

I settled into my cot that night, perplexed at how I continued to change my mind with Pietro. He was attractive, but I wasn't attracted to him. It seemed like each time I would think about giving him another go, I would meet someone who would bring me alive. I felt okay though changing my mind, I realized that I couldn't expect myself to always know how things were going to be, and maybe it was okay to change directions.

In the morning I took Corrine to the Castel dell'ovo, and for the first time on the trip, I felt like the tour guide. It was an odd feeling to be the leader. Corinne was two years older than me and ever since high school I had looked up to her, and let her lead me.

When we arrived at the Castle, I had a feeling like I was living in a lost dream. I missed my mother suddenly, for the first time since I left. I had refused to write any letters or even call her to tell her I had arrived, I wanted to be able to hear my own thoughts without her influence. Standing by the castle made mom's essence palpable, her laughter rang out from the harbor bar, and it was nice to hear her voice again. I remembered getting locked into the bathroom at the Zi Teresa restaurant, and the two of us panicking and trying to figure out how to get out. Our trip was an adventure and we were in it together; we shared that story, it belonged to us.

I didn't even know why I brought Corrine to the castle. Maybe I had to come back to remember who I was the day I met Pietro; the girl with a mother and one father and two brothers, the girl who didn't know much about herself.

Pietro's charisma danced me up the ramp to the courtyard. I didn't know that first day with Pietro that

I was looking into a mirror. He was the fourth child of his family. When he was a young boy, his mother and father could not afford to take care of four children. His mother sent him to live with his aunt, she cared for him for many years, all the while he thought of her as his mother, and his mother as his aunt. Nobody told him the truth, it was to be believed that his aunt was his mother. It wasn't until he was an adult that he found out his cousins were really his siblings. He went back to live with his real mother again, and when we met him, he still lived with her. Pietro became a moving force in my life, leading me to the truth about my father and helping me to unlock the secrets of my family. A part of me imagined that he would just appear there in the courtyard of the castle. I would turn from looking over the edge at the wild waves crashing on the wall of the egg castle, built half on land and half in the ocean, and there he would be. Would I apologize? Would I justify something? Would I tell him about my father and how he was a part in that mystery, the way that I was a part in the mystery of his own daughter? Nothing I could say would make any difference, Pietro never asked me about who I was, it was hard to say if he even wanted to know.

Corrine navigated us back down and away from the Castle to the dock where we boarded a ferry to the Island of Capri. I was finally going to see the Blue Grotto.

When we arrived we had to find the travel guides that would sell us tickets for the boatmen who would take us out to the Grotta Azzurra cave. It was easy enough to find because there were many other tourists doing the same thing. Corinne was happy when we got on a boat with four Roman traveling men our age. One of them was a pretty boy, just the type that Corrine loved to chase after. She was happy we had a game to play while we rode out in the Gulf of Naples. We arrived at a meeting place in the middle of the water, where small row boats with men singing Italian Folk Songs were waiting to take a small group of people into the cave. The caves could only be entered for a certain amount of hours during the day while the tide was low enough not to cover the opening.

We climbed carefully out of the bigger boat onto the row boat, only four people at a time, and we rowed away serenaded by a jolly Italian. At the entrance of the cave we waited until the waves drew back, and the rower ceased his music to concentrate, reaching up for a chain that was bolted into the rock lentil of the cave. He used it to anchor himself then let the coming wave push us through the hole. Inside, the water was calm and the light glowed bright blue. I was surprised that I didn't feel more moved by the experience, I thought something would ignite me there. It was lovely, but nonetheless filled with the essence of a tourist attraction, it didn't hold the treasure that I thought I would find.

"Get out and swim, eh?" The boat man raised his eyebrows and his smile stretched across his face, he was excited to watch us swim. We both jumped overboard into the pool of glowing water, and took our tops off. We were giggling when the boat rower started making faces and chuckling at us. Swimming in the pool topless was freeing, I lay back and let my breasts bob above the water in the dim lit cerulean cave.

Reign stood on the edge of the pool, his broad shoul-

ders and belly hovered above me, held up by strong legs; he reminded me of a frog about to hop onto the lily pads that lined the rim of the pool. I bobbed about surrounded by large fronds of tropical plants that filled the inside of the conservatory, while my mother waded seemingly shy at the other end. Reign jumped in, swimming to her confidently, and took her into him, pulling her by the small tide made with their bodies, they swam together in an embrace. The fire that once was between them was now cooled off by time. What once was the fire of creation now radiated with a humble cautiousness.

For a moment Reign held my mother, nothing else in the world seemed to exist.

We were swimming in No-Time, a stretch of space my mother had discovered in order to escape the reality of her physical world. It was the first time the three of us were together in the same place since I was three-years-old. I kicked to the other side of the pool, holding a kick board and peered over my shoulder, my bare butt bobbed above the water. I felt like a small child, separate from Reign and my mother. They were engulfed in their own wonder like Adam and Eve, naked and taken in by desire.

My mother was free again like when we traveled in Italy, like a nymph in a pool of magic. She was a wild woman, an animal who never knew a cage. She had arrived home again, to the home where laundry wasn't daunting, where dishes were not her burden, a place where she could love as she wanted to, without permission or guilt, without jealousy or royalty.

She kissed him messy, she kissed him searching for that time they knew each other's darkness, like the time they revealed their shadows and their light to each other. In a way they destroyed each other, but in another, they found wholeness.

I saw how they loved each other, how they could only love each other in the world of dreams, but never in reality.

I saw that I was created by that dream, I was created to have a connection to the dream world, to be the bridge, to bring people back to their dreams, and out from their conditionings. My two fathers, my mother, they are human never-the-less, and as angry as I wanted to be at all of them, I saw that we all chose our paths, we were not victims to our Fate. The pool was our spring of life, like a source that we were all born from. In that moment I was connected to the very source from which they created me, I saw for the first time an image of where I came from. There was no changing my parents, and what they chose was theirs.

"Wrenna, the boatman says we should get back in, it's time to leave the cave." I came back from my memory of my biological father's blue pool to the mystical blue cave off the shore of Capri. Maybe the treasure was in me all along. Maybe Pietro, leading with his heart, eventually showed me how to lead with mine, maybe I wasn't meant to see the bending light of the Grotta Azzurra until now, suddenly it didn't seem so boring after all.

Upon our return to shore, we found a clump of ocean boulders that were right next to the sea where we each laid out and took a nap in the sun. After a bit I was toasting and wanted to get into the shade or cool off. Corinne looked content, stretched out next to four handsome boys, so I let her be and hopped down to find a place I could swim. Not too far away, a small bit of beach beckoned me. The waves lapped gently onto the sand, and I was the only one there. In the distance, tourists were eating and laughing, men were working on and off of the boats in the harbor, and a summer kind of busyness moved around me, but where I stood everything was quiet and peaceful. I stepped into the water and was surprised at how warm it was. I walked farther in and finally let my body slide all the way under. The buoyancy of the water lifted me up like a balloon floating in the sky, I became one with the sea, the same oneness I felt in Marco's embrace, making love in Switzerland. I couldn't deny the magic of floating in the Tyrrhenian Sea, there was no drawing back. Even when I let my breath out I still remained afloat.

I was inside my own womb, listening to my heart, feeling my body, aware suddenly that I could create anything. I forgot about Corrine and her agenda and about the city's constant busyness, I forgot about the guilt I carried over my father's willingness to raise me as his own. I realized that my heart was calling out to me to break the pattern of always living to please someone else. I had followed my mother and Pietro where they wanted to go, and never really stood my ground about what I wanted. I had finally made it to the Grotta Azzurra, and let the cerulean blue light fill my pores, and now it was my choice to keep following my heart. I wanted to go back to Marco, but I was afraid to, I was afraid to break Corrine's heart, or afraid to abandon her. But this was mine, my trip, it was for me to decide where to go next.

I would go back to Switzerland, I didn't know how yet, but I felt it in the song of the water, I would make it back to the mountains one way or another.

{25} - WHERE LOVE CAN BE LOVE

We boarded the ferry to Greece, which was stocked full of the Greek men, who smelled of the machismo of their warrior ancestors. They followed us with their eyes, preying upon the vulnerability of travelers.

We entered immediately into a mini casino, where men in uniforms waited behind the bar ready to pour drinks. Corinne and I both focused our attention on finding our way around the ferry, and we discovered that there was no actual sleeping area other than a sleeping deck where people found a spare rectangle of space to throw down a sleeping bag and pillow. The ferry ride was fifteen hours, in which the majority was nighttime and seemed like a good time to sleep, though we had taken the advice of a traveler we met in Italy to buy a couple of cheap bottles of wine and drink them as we sat on the open deck of the ferry, and after realizing that we didn't have our own private sleeping area, I was happy to have the wine. We shared a bottle with a man named Patrick and finally curled up in our bags at one in the morning.

Water misted over us, and the moon glowed down on our faces. By 2 a.m. my sleeping bag was wet and I had not slept at all, so I moved inside the covered part of the deck and found an empty bench where I arranged all of my clothes into a pad to sleep on. Everything felt damp and the big boat motored through the water toward Greece. When the sun came up over the water, I awoke, sleepy and a little sore, but loving the feeling that I had embarked on a short journey through the Adriatic sea to the Ionian sea, and finally to a country I had only read about in literature classes. We had to run to catch a bus that took us to Athens, where we had booked a room in the middle of the city. It was late in the day when we arrived and once we were shown our beds, (bunks again), we questioned if they were infested with bed bugs. The room was the shabbiest of all, still somehow more comfortable and quiet than Amsterdam, but shabby none the less.

Even though we were tired from traveling, we only had a night in Athens before traveling on to the Isle of Santorini for a week of reading and beach time. We walked that evening to the Acropolis, it wasn't a far hike from the city, and after indulging in a Gyro, we followed the map up the hill and found that the stage of the Theatre of
Dionysus was lit up, it was set up for a concert that would play later in the evening.

As night fell over the edges of the Acropolis, Lovers came out of nowhere, holding hands, finding their places dotting the jutted rock eruptions, and falling into each other's arms. Nothing else in the world seemed to exist for any of them. I remembered Rome and the way the men would look past their kiss to see if anyone was looking at them, but here in the dusky starry night, overlooking an ancient city, these lovers were drunk on the love of youth. It was like the stories my mom and dad had told me about when they were in high school, going up to the butte and making out after dances or on Friday nights.

I watched in delight at the freedom of it, and was happy that there is a place in the world, up on a hill, where love can just be love.

Santorini, Greece

"Mind if I sit and serenade you?" asked a young musician carrying a guitar. A woman walking with a wobbly gait plopped into the beach chair next to me. They were drunk and laughing. The musician stumbled a bit as he found a place on the sand, and pulled his guitar out of its case.

"My name is Demitri," he smiled revealing purple wine-stained teeth. He began plucking strings and tuning his guitar, then his angelic voice streamed out into a pop song. The lyrics were all in Greek, and they sounded lovely coming out of this twenty-year-old musician wearing his black leather jacket, singing the soft tune. The air outside was perfect and the island wasn't lit like a huge city, so the stars shown all across the sky. The constellations seemed different, though I didn't know exactly how. Demitri played three songs then got up and thanked me for letting him sing. He wandered away down the beach alongside the tipsy lady.

I got up and was drawn toward a strip of lights, where I found a small group of gypsies that seemed a little older than me, but bright and full of smiles, hanging out together. One woman struck me. She wore a Labradorite crystal around her neck. I complimented her on it. "I sell them," she said back, "would you like to see?"

"Yes." I was intrigued and delighted, I felt as if magic was pulling at my feet. The girl led me to her friend, who pulled out a flat suede box and handed it to her. She looked at me, her eyes glittering green and sapphire. She wore layers of light silk and thick dreadlocks. She had a wide belt wrapped around her waist, and bangles around her wrists. Her canine teeth rounded her upper lip, giving her a wolf shaped mouth, and her voice played musically, stamping and dancing.

"Here, you choose," she said holding out the box for me to see. I looked over the crystals, each one hung from a different strap, some were wound up in hemp.

I scanned pendants shaped like tear drops and others like icicles. One simple quartz crystal pendant, called to me, I appreciated how light and strong it was. Most jewelry got in the way, but this one would fit right in the nook between my breasts, hovering over my heart. I wanted it tied with a green leather strap, just a 1/8 diameter little rope.

"My name is Destine, you are beautiful," her looks were hypnotizing. She reached up and wrapped the green twine around my neck and I paid her my Euros.

"Thank you," I said, holding my hand over the quartz against my chest. Destine's eyes flickered and I felt a power emanate from her. I didn't even know her culture, or what her life was like, but I loved her style, and how unique she was. I loved that she chose to be so bold.

As I walked aimlessly back down the beach, I felt mesmerized by the gypsy woman. She was enchanting. I wondered why I didn't know her, or why I wasn't friends with her all along. I felt such a fierceness in my own soul, a longing for something more passionate. I thought about my mother and Reign, and how they seemed to follow a thread that led them through to the truth of their soul, regardless of what others said life needed to look like. Regardless of church or marriage, regardless of their parents or anything else, they chose to listen to themselves.

The crystal hung around my neck as a reminder of the gypsy in me, the one who walks alone and decides for herself, the one who decides the best direction in the moment and listens to the wind, the one that knows whatever happens becomes her wisdom. I sat down in the sand, sifting the grains through my fingers, and my thoughts drifted over the waves...

He has a barrel chest of a Welshman, wearing cloaks and pointed feather hats.

He bobs cool-like the oceans rising and falling, like a fish in its waters.

Everything is more comfortable in slow moving heat...she opens like blooming lilies, he lays back like cats—-

Nowhere to be, total primal, only existence calls on his attention.

Earl Grey, English Breakfast- Lemon tea. Giant leaves caressing cheeks,

And every hesitation,
Holding back love, because our love is so big, too big for those
closed-hearted superficial Pan Hating, God fearing !?$.

Like the oceans rising and falling, riding trains, staring out into
space, seeing compositions of shadow and light,
Seeing spirits who only see black and white.

I met a black lady who lost a baby to death in her first year, and
I told the lady she was important,
She spoke to me, sang to me like the base note of all music,
she was the anchor that life floated upon, the mother knowing
darkness,
The mother knowing love is everything, not just pretty things.

I came through him into my mother, where she dreamed me into
being with parts of her and all the magic she felt when she was
with him.
So, I'm part Welsh and part Witch, and part Gypsy, these
things are my wholeness and I have far away, other-life dreams of
standing on great cliffs,
All of my straight dark hair hanging down to my butt, whipping
in the wind, catching all the power of the
Spirits that live there. It's my deepest connection. I am
that wind, I fly like the eagle that catches the upward drafts,
That circles and circles like a great spiraling,
The spiraling of death and life, that heals us into
light.

***

Marco,

I'm coming back. I will be arriving on the 29th
of July and staying until August 7th. When I get closer
I will let you know the time and station that I will be

arriving at. Let me know if this works for you.

Wrenna

{26} - CINQUE TERRE

"UNCERTAINTY AND MYSTERY ARE ENERGIES OF LIFE.
DON'T LET THEM SCARE YOU UNDULY, FOR THEY
KEEP BOREDOM AT BAY AND SPARK CREATIVITY." R.I.
FITZHENRY

"Where is number 45?" Corrine held a map that she had gotten from the train station showing the streets of the five terrains, otherwise known as Cinque Terre.

"Where are we?" I slid my finger along the map, "this is the right street."

We both stood dumbfounded, not saying a word, looking at the building in front of us. There was a 42 and a 44 and a 46. We turned around and looked at the building behind us; 41, 43, and then the next block started. There wasn't a 45 anywhere.

"But this is the street, what's the address again?" Corrine asked. I showed her the printed paper with our reservation. She looked it over. We were standing in the beating sun, with our backpacks still weighing on our shoulders. We had walked down a steep hill from the train station, it was the longest day of travel yet, and neither of us could wait until we had a meal in our bellies and a bed to lay down in.

"Oh no, what is the name of this city?" Corrine asked. "I think we may have gotten off one city too soon, we are staying in the one at the very end, the last stop, weren't you counting the stops?" I sunk at her accusatory voice.

"It was hard to tell what was going on, there were like 50 stops in the last hour!" I said defensively. We were both getting tired and edgy. Corinne lugged her backpack tighter on her hips and started walking back up the hill from where we had come. I followed and we didn't speak a word to each other.

Once we arrived at the train station, we discovered that we did in fact get off at the wrong stop, but luckily a train would be coming in five minutes and it was the last one for the night to the next village. I tried not to think about the what-if we hadn't made it in time to get the train.

The entire city of Riomaggiore jetted up from the ocean. I had a thought that it would be fun to take a ball up to the very top and roll it down, watching it bounce and find its way to the very bottom like a Plinko game, to finally see the ball roll into the waves and bob away.

It was six o'clock when the train dropped us off at the bottom of the hill. The heat made my feet feel heavy. Corrine and I had very little to say to one another, we just wanted to get to a place to put our backpacks away, and rest, and eat.

In order to fulfill our needs though, we had to climb up a steep hill through the city to the hostel office to get our room key. As we started up, with backpacks weighing us down, I made notes of the things around me. There was a little market just a little way up the hill, and I promised myself I would go there and get something for dinner. Every building around me was a stucco material painted with bright colors, making the city shine like a rainbow. Behind me the water was painted with the reflection of the buildings, it was like walking in a watercolor painting.

We climbed higher up the hill, looking for the right number on the building, and there on my left sat five very old Italian people, lined up on a bench with no expressions on their faces, but eyes that were lit up and curious. As we walked past them, they turned their heads very slowly to watch us walk by, I chuckled under my breath.

One more level of hot concrete and beating heat and we finally reached an air conditioned office, where we were given our keys and directed back down to the very bottom on the hill. We both wondered why we hadn't just left the backpacks down there in the first place.

As we came back down the hill, I noted the laundromat, and a couple of fun eating places, then the old people again, watching us, and this time turning their heads the other way, all in unison very slowly, watching us in amusement.

The building we were staying in was painted pink. Inside the main door was a cool stone staircase that wound up and up for many flights of stairs. Our room was on the third floor, up six flights, and one more flight up was the community kitchen.

We had three keys, one to the door outside, one to the kitchen, and one to our hostel room. The bathroom was next to the kitchen. I stopped a few times climbing the stairs. The day's journey had left me exhausted, but somehow after I made it to our room and dropped my bag, I was motivated to go back down to the market before it closed to get some things for fixing dinner. I also figured that Corrine would be happy if I made her some food. I sensed that our hunger was keeping us quiet.   The market was so quaint, with fresh vegetables and cheeses. I plucked up some salami, basil, tomato and mozzarella, along with a bottle of wine. The store was busy with people focused on what they were doing. I purchased my goodies and went back upstairs, all the way to the fourth floor, to prepare a salad for us. Inside, the kitchen was quaint and functional, with a little table to eat at and a small oven and sink. There was a cutting board, a chopping knife, and a few plates with silverware. I found a cork screw and opened up the bottle of wine, poured myself a glass, and took a sip, sitting down for a moment to rest my swollen feet.

Outside the window was a building across from me. My window looked right into someone's apartment; it looked like the 'someone' who owned it and had lived there for some time. An older lady, I guessed she was eighty something, came out of her patio door with a basket tucked under her arm. She turned toward a side wall next to the balcony and began to climb a ladder with her basket hooked into the crook of her arm. She climbed right to the roof of the building, where she bent over and gathered up lettuce, tomatoes, and other veggies from the garden that took up the square of roof above her house, then she tucked the veggies into her basket and made her way back down the ladder. Inside she washed and prepared her rooftop salad. I sipped my wine and thought, "I want to be like that lady someday."

Corrine had joined me and we took joy in watching the show across the gap between buildings until dinner was over, and they closed their shutters. After we ate Corrine did the dishes, insisting she do her part, and we made our way back down to our room to read and finally fall asleep.

The next day I opted to rest and relax, and explore the town a bit. Corrine went for a long hike by herself and didn't make it back until almost sunset.

I returned to the market and bought fresh oregano, a box of pasta, two tomatoes, a bottle of cheap wine, an onion, olive oil in a small bottle and a tiny carton of crème. I had carried a little container of salt along with me from the last store I'd been to. I left the store feeling full in my heart, and stood looking down the steep hill at the ocean. "This town is something from a child's painting", I thought. The buildings were stacked in many colored boxes, splashed with bright pastels, like strokes of paint falling into the ocean.

I climbed the three flights of cool stone steps inside our hostel then went on to another flight, where I unlocked the kitchen and put my things on the table. I started a pot of water to boil.

Across at the other building I heard clattering and went to the window to see the old lady from the night before now fixing dinner. I watched her preparing food like a choreographed dance, imagining she had rehearsed her moves a hundred times. Into a bowl went gently rinsed salad greens. She steamed fish in a delicate pan and out of the icebox came a cooled zucchini dish, which she grated parmesan all over.

She served her petite family, two grandchildren, whose voices carried through the corridor between buildings. She drank her glass of wine and smiled lovingly at her children, chattering in Italian, very excited while she listened intently, until the climax of the story when she broke out in to a smile. Finally, she whisked dishes away, closed the shutters, and then all I heard were the clattering of dishes once again.

I sat aware suddenly that my heart was fluttering at what a beautiful movie that was, a window of real life, how I yearned to be ordinary in that way! Deeply inspired I finally stood, and threw my noodles into a now boiling pot of water. I chopped onion, grated cheese, and sautéed and deglazed, I wanted to make a cream sauce for Corrine after her all day hike to the other towns of Cinque Terre.

I sang Dean Martin songs, because they had Italian words, and I felt at home with myself. As my sauce simmered, I chopped some fresh oregano to add, and the smell reminded me of Pietro, it was romantic, the way he was, the way he wanted to love me. A life with him though, he was so pushy at times, and he was like a young boy at 32, still expecting his mother to care for him. A sudden overwhelming feeling rushed over me. I remembered the feeling I had when I traveled with my mother and Pietro, always going, always keeping up, always serving my mother or Pietro's whims, and giving of myself. I supported everyone in their dreams, but hardly took time to really think about what my dreams were, it just seemed easier to go along with what everyone else wanted to do.

I heard the lady again outside the window

who was out on the veranda and watering her potted flowers. She put down her watering jug and grabbed a basket and climbed up to the rooftop to the garden. She bent over, her rumpus poked up toward the sky, her apron flowed over her knees as she tugged up weeds and unwanted extra growth, then picked up a watering can and sprinkled the shadowy garden as the sky dimmed. Right as the first star lit the sky she gathered her vegetables in her basket and climbed down the ladder slowly holding one rung in one hand and the basket in the other. Her feet touched the cement balcony, where she set down her basket for a moment, adjusting a few pots, then she lifted it into her hip again and went inside. Her doors closed, and everything was quiet.

Corrine arrived just as the last light faded from the sky. She was grateful for the cream sauce and told me about the scenery on her hike.

"Corrine?" I knew it was finally time to fill her in on my decision to go back to Switzerland. "I have been feeling really tired and worn down, and I've been thinking a lot about wanting a place to slow down. I have decided that I am going back to see Marco, he invited me to stay with him and I just want to go read Harry Potter and sleep and process my traveling. You can come if you want, it is not that I want to leave you, I just want to rest, and I want to see Marco again." I heard my self say the words and knew they were mostly true, though deep down I did want to go alone, I wanted to have the time to fall in love.

"What would I do there?" Corinne asked in voice erupting with anger. "So, you're leaving me? In the middle of Europe? This is supposed to be our trip Wrenna," her anger mixed with hurt expression. I started to cry.

"I'm sorry Corrine, I don't really know what I am doing, but I'm exhausted going from one place to another, I just want to slow down, I really don't want to hurt you or abandon you, I mean you can come if you want."

"What and just stay in a hostel while you hang out with Marco? No, I think I might just go home, or, I don't know what I'm going to do now, you can't leave me." She fell silent, I felt a lump welling up in my throat—I didn't know what to say, I had to leave, or rather I wanted to leave, the desire was so clear in me and so true, I realized my indecisiveness had come from my fear that Corrine would be mad, and she was! But, it was okay because I knew what I wanted and I was going for it.

Corrine scooted her chair back and stood to leave. She stomped away and left me to tearfully clear the plates from the table.

I sat in the tiny kitchen at the little Formica table and let my guilt go out the window and away to the sea. I rejoiced in the pleasure of knowing that I would see Marco in only two days. It felt as if I broke up with a longtime lover at the same time. Corinne and I had been friends for seven years, chasing boys, going dancing, and experiencing our emotions, our changing bodies, and our sex.

Here I was saying goodbye, maybe forever, to my best friend, so that I could say hello to myself. My tears felt freeing, the lump in my throat released and I moved to the sink, my limbs feeling weak and tired, and I looked forward to sleeping. I felt a pang of guilt and worried about Corrine, but I had to let her go, I couldn't take care of her. I thought about Ralph Waldo Emerson and all the things he said that inspired me, "We have to stand on our own two feet", "You will always find those who think they know your duty better than you know It.", "I do not wish to expiate, but to live. My life is not an apology, but a life". She will be okay, I assured myself, she is a strong woman; besides, there comes a point when we must make decisions that color the way of our lives. I had let everyone else determine my path before, now it was time to choose my own.

{27} - A RECKONING

"THE WOMAN WHO DOES NOT REQUIRE VALID-
ATION FROM ANYONE IS THE MOST FEARED INDIVID-
UAL ON THE PLANET."—MOHADESA NAJUMI.

I woke in the bottom bunk, sore and tight. After a long stretch of my legs, I sat up, groggy, puffy eyed and unsure of what to expect. The room was empty. Corrine packed early, before the sun and left, she had nothing left to say to me.

"Was I wrong?" I wondered. I opened the shutters and surveyed the ocean and the street below. The morning was quiet. All was still save for the waves that lapped gently to the shore.

"Good morning waves," I said aloud. It felt nice to be heard and not judged. They swooshed a good morning back to me. The beauty of the day and the shock of aloneness welled into waterfalls and poured down my cheeks. "I am alone. I am alone now." I spoke aloud to no one.

"Oh Marco, I am coming back, I am doing it! I can't wait to see you. Oh, but why do I feel so tight and so crazy? What am I doing? Wait that is your voice mom." I said aloud to the empty room.

"My voice, what do you mean my voice, I am not even here." she said back.

"Yes you are," I said to my mother who sat mirroring me. She was wearing a blouse with buttons that looked like they might pop open over her C-cup breasts, and a shin length jean skirt pulled taut between her knees and the ground. She leaned back on the dresser, I leaned on the wall and we faced each other.

"Oh mom, I think I am in love with Marco."

"Are you?" she asked with doubt, cocking her head slightly.

"Well, does it matter to you? Why does it matter?"

"Are you being safe?" she answered my question with a question.

"Who are you to talk about being safe mom? You, who sneaks around stalking your boyfriend, you, who lies to dad about where you're going or about having a boyfriend."

"I don't lie, he knows that part of me, he just doesn't want me to talk to him about it, I don't want to be hurtful," she reached up and wiped away a tear. "Anyway that's me, I just want *you* to be safe, sometimes I just think you sleep with guys too fast, then the mystery is not there anymore and they lose interest, you've gotta know how to play the game Wrenna," she said matter-of-factly.

I sat taking this in for a moment, the image of my mother faded away. I came back to the room in Cinque Terre with six empty bunkbeds surrounding me. Seagulls were beginning to scout for their morning fish.

It was my mother's voice that was gone when I

was in Switzerland, she was too far away for me to hear her worry. And now I sat alone, and I grabbed at her, questioning my decision for a moment to go back and see Marco.

"What game?" I said to myself. "What game? There is no game here, I am only here for another twelve days and then, and then, I go...back to America. I don't have time to play any games with Marco, he asked me to come, I am coming, I don't want to play games mom."

He licked me to a deep orgasm, made love to me, kissed into my Kundalini, I can't play games with him, he is just him, and if he asks me to go and it doesn't work, where I will go, I will go find the next adventure, the next quiet place to rest. I am free to do that now, I have no one to answer to, I am alone, my mother can't keep me safe anymore, and that is my responsibility now.

"Mom?"

"Yes, I am here"

"You've got to let go of me and trust that I can live my own life and make my own decisions." Saying those words out loud to her cracked my voice and choked me up with tears.

"I have never told you how to live your life mom, I am not always excited about your decisions, especially when I am torn about not being honest with dad, and I may not make the best decisions in my life either, but it's my life. I am twenty-three, I can't take care of you anymore. I can't keep your secrets anymore, it's not fair. I get so tired of having to think twice about what I said to dad because it may or may not have coincided with your story," my voice heaved, I was weeping, tears streamed down into the cracks of my neck, and I felt my mother crying too, I remembered the way her neck would get wet from crying and I would come away from hugs damp on my shirt. "I am just so tired of lying, I want to be in love, and I want to be honest about Reign and you and who I am. There are so many secrets I can't keep track! Why can't you just be honest? Why can't you just accept who you are and love it? No one is going to hate you, they will probably be happier because they don't have to dance around all your secrets that they already know half the time anyway."

"You don't understand Wrenna, it's not that easy. I did try to tell dad before I had an affair that I was feeling vulnerable, I tried to tell him a lot, but it never worked. I just don't even think he wants to know, so I've just kept it for myself, until recently I haven't told anyone until I confided in you , and I guess I did that because I assumed one day I would tell you about Reign."

She closed her eyes to rest as if she was sleepy or just done trying to explain herself.

"But, I do understand."

"No, you're angry at me."

"But, I'm not angry at *you*, I am angry because I'm sick of *lying*, I just want to be who I am without having to hesitate to make sure I have all the facts straight. I am always protecting someone's feelings. Remember when we were driving though Italy and you sat in the back seat of Pietro's car listening to that dance movie soundtrack, I feel like that was the first time I ever saw you, the you that lived at the center of the mom that made sure everyone was happy and that everything looked as it should."

"It's complicated Wrenna. I love dad, we are friends, we've made a family and raised kids together, we've known each other for a long time, but there are parts of me that he just doesn't get, and there are parts that I don't think he will ever understand, even if he wanted to."

"Like what?"

"Like the part of me that comes from an immigrant family; the part of me that is like this Italian culture that you are surrounded by right now. It's hard to describe, it's more of a feeling. My soul resonates with the way of the gypsies and the people of the Old Country, but when I was young, my dad stopped speaking any Slovenian, because it was safer to blend in. We were still pretty fresh out of WWII, when Jews and Eastern Europeans were being killed because they were different. It wasn't easy for my father being an immigrant."

"Carver and I come from very different cultures. He is tolerant and intelligent, so he is able to accept me and he loves me, but there is just something about my soul that I don't think he will ever understand, it's something I can't describe or explain. There is no reason for it, it's just a part of me, and it's not his fault that he doesn't understand, it's just that we are different. With David there is a familiarity and an unspoken knowing of something, maybe because he is from this culture too."

"What about Reign mom? What was the attraction with him?"

"We didn't necessarily come from the same cultural or religious background, but we *were* drawn to one another, and in a way we were working out some of

our deepest darkest parts of ourselves. But, there was also a creativity that came out when we were together. And you know, I really can't say why I felt the way I did about it, but
I did love him Wrenna, I loved all of them, just in different ways."

My mother's image began to fade away, and I became aware of my aloneness, sitting on the ground of the hostel room next to the empty bunkbeds, I sobbed. When I finally got up, I felt lighter, as if all the tears I had shed were layers of myself. I was ready to get moving, I wanted to pack and leave that room and my aloneness. I began gathering up my clothes and refolding them, like I had done at every stop, in order to fit them into my singular backpacking pack. As I folded my skirts and shirts, my one pair of jeans, my coat, and my light sleeping bag, I laughed. I had been carrying a coat the entire trip in weather that was ninety degrees and humid. I picked it up and hung it in the closet, then took my sleeping bag and tucked it into the closet on the ground. They would be gifts for the Universe. My backpack zipped up with ease and the lightness was a relief.

Nothing stood in the way of my path. I was alert of all my surroundings, and aware of my natural instincts to avoid danger and find magic. When I arrived at the train station, it was so quiet, there were very few people waiting to board trains.

It was only an hour until I caught my train. Just ahead of me as I entered into the station I a man with lion dreadlocks, they were haphazardly wrapped with a cotton tie. He wore patched linens, and toted a guitar, a viola, a didgeridoo and a bag of magic tricks. He was a gypsy. He walked through the doors into the station, looked around a bit and walked back out, settling down on the ground next to his belongings. His intense eyes followed me patiently and mystically. His home was where ever he was, and it was apparent. He embodied his space and looked like it was where he was supposed to be.

I studied him from a distance, as voices of what I had heard in my life about gypsies tried to sway me from my curiosity. When I walked past him, his eyes spoke to me. I sat down facing him, and pulled my arms out of the straps of my backpack. He was a traveler who had dropped his ego, somewhere along the train tracks seconds from where he started, and from that place he was able to shape shift and move like water.

"Are you a musician?" I asked nodding at his instruments.

"Yes, I am a performer. I am traveling with my friends, but they got behind, I am not sure where they are. I have been waiting for them to come on the next train. We got separated." I sensed that he was slightly worried for his friends, but hopeful that they would arrive soon. His accent was thick and unrecognizable to me.

"Where is your accent from? I mean...where are you from?"

"I come from Jerusalem."

"Really?" I paused. "Wow. What's your name?"

"Ori. Ori means 'My Light' in Hebrew."

"Oh, that's beautiful."

"What is your name?"

"It's Wrenna, like the Wren bird".

"And where do you come from?"

"From America."

"What brings you on your journey?"

"Oh, well, my friend Corrine, she came to my house one day and said she wanted to go to Europe with me. Well, I guess that's how the trip started, but now I realize that I wanted to get away from who I was at home, even though I didn't really know who I was. Does that make sense?" I paused and Ori didn't say anything so I went on.

"I came to Italy three years ago with my mom, and we met this guy from Naples. He traveled with us, and finally he came to America to see me, he was pursuing me, but I wasn't in love with him. When he left I told my mom that he reminded me of a lover my mom had years ago, and my mom confessed that the lover was my real father.
It's kind of confusing and kind of crazy."

Ori let me finish and then contemplated my words for a moment.

"I am a gypsy. I meet people from many places, and we all live differently, but we are all here working on something, we are the same you and I; I go because my heart tells me to go. This is my law, to listen to my heart. And my heart always leads me home."

A train that wasn't ours pulled up behind me, but I ignored it. Ori's eyes memorized me.

"I have a gift for you," Ori said pulling out five crystal orbs, each one big enough to fill the palm of his hand. He began to roll them up and down his arms, twisting and bending them to roll in all directions. He was hypnotizing me, giving me a gift of remembering magic. When he finished, I offered him the last of my Swiss Chocolates, he took one and unwrapped it. I used my wrapper to fold an origami crane and gave it to him, "my gift to you", I told him.

Ori accepted my gift and we sat silently for a moment.

"You are traveling alone?" he asked.

"Well, I am now, I just left my friend, I wanted to go somewhere different than her. It was difficult to leave her, I felt guilty about choosing my own direction, because I'm afraid that I abandoned her and made her traveling more challenging".

"We like to think that don't we?" he laughed, "when in truth, all paths lead to the same place eventually, and the more we follow our hearts, the more others will have the freedom to follow theirs".

Right then my train arrived.

"Oh, I have to go." I stood up and heaved my backpack up on my back again.

"Thank you".

"You are welcome," Ori said, "Here, take this, it is from Jerusalem". I reached out and he slipped a tiny cross into my hand with a metal mold of the crucified Jesus attached to it. On the back was etched 'Jerusalem'. "So you don't forget me", he said. I put it in my pocket and ran to board my train.

Sitting in the window seat where I could see Ori across the platform. Another train pulled in on the other side and just before I departed, I saw Ori's friends arrive. They were travelers, Gypsies, they lived on the trust that their hearts would always bring them to where they needed to be.

***

The countryside swam by as I listened to two German women talk to one another about things I did not understand. I looked out the window, the first train ride alone in my whole life, it wasn't far, but what awaited me on the other end was such a mystery. What if he wasn't there? What if he is late and I have to wait pathetically or try to call him?

The open country showed signs of becoming more urban, the houses got closer together, and I sensed we would arrive soon in Spiez. "I suppose if he isn't there I will just have to find a place to stay," I thought. "No that is just your own worry Wren, that nothing is ever easy when you are following your heart."

We slowed down, the train station came into view, but I did not see Marco waiting on the platform for me. I was ready to get off when the train stopped, as it was a very brief stop, and only a few on the train were departing, the others were headed for Zurich. As I stepped off, I stood still and took a breath, not knowing what to expect. People passed by, I lugged my backpack onto my back and secured it.

"Hey!" I turned around and there stood Marco, in a bright red shirt, his olive tanned skin looked so warm next to it. He hugged me and slid his hand up behind my neck bringing me into him for a kiss.

"I am glad you came back." he said and smiled. My unsureness melted away into disbelief. This was by far the gutsiest decision I had ever made, and here I was walking again with a man I was falling in love with.

{28} - MISTRESS OF AUTONOMY

Not forever and a day: Not for eternity, or any time like it.
I'll promise nothing beyond this moment.

— TONY TOPOLESKI

29/07/05
Day 1—Marco's house

    I have found a muse. I feel as if I am reconnecting the lost pieces of the greatest pyramid in the world. Am I simply high? Is this what so many before me have been inspired by? Oh, I awoke tonight dreaming, and continued to dream dreams of flavors, sauces, foods, I had to climb through cellophane blankets to reach some kind of reality which then was just a continuation of the dream—but I wasn't dreaming, he was whispering, "What do you want?" in such a way that I thought it could only be a dream. Then, without hesitation or second thought I was, 'the honey comb suspended in the jar of honey', buoyant, bobbing, waiting for the bees to arrive back to their nest and take pleasure in what they had created, that's when it hit me, it is the creation. MY Creation that I am striving for. I want to stop living in my mother's shadows. I want to create some-

thing for myself.

Marco worked most days and came home to me at night, some nights he studied for a major test he was preparing for. On the first morning after I arrived, I awoke in a nest of blankets, the light was dim and I could hear soft rain pitter pattering on the rooftop. My body felt stretched in a different way, parts of it were pulsing and tingling, there was so much sensation, and the rain lent a moodiness to it that sent me deep into a feminine creative space.

I dreamed up a plan for my day until Marco returned from work. First, I would walk and find the little grocery store to buy supplies, there wasn't much in the house except milk and frozen chicken, and that just wouldn't do. After that, I would drop off groceries and go hunt down a copy of *Harry Potter, The Half-Blood Prince*, which was released less than a week before I arrived. I dressed in my favorite travel skirt made of green silk, and decided that jeans might be more appropriate, the air was much cooler after the rain. Maybe just a comfortable outfit would do. I would have to get some breakfast in town, so I opted to get Harry Potter first. I grabbed my satchel and slipped on a pair of sandals. As I left the little cabin and skipped outside, I was filled with a spirit of magic. The trees were all heavy and wet and Pthalo green moss sparkled on the rocks; every path felt as if it would take me into a dream.

I walked down the gravel road until I reached the highway, where I headed toward the town. I thought about stopping in at Balmer's to say hello to Marco, but decided to find a croissant and coffee instead.

The houses in the distance each had rows of flags

that hung from the rafters. Around me there were decorative buildings painted with bold lines, and colorful shutters. Rain dripped from the shingles above a shop window. I recognized where I was and remembered the bookstore around the corner from where I stood. Inside the window to the bookstore I saw the hardback copy of Harry Potter, my heart fluttered with excitement. I went in and used my credit card to buy it for forty-seven franks, it would be my friend and companion for the rainy days spent while Marco worked. I happily tucked it in my satchel and went out to find breakfast.

I found my way to a lovely coffee shop and ordered a cappuccino and croissant.

I opened up Harry Potter to indulge in the first page.

Rain dripped outside the cafe window and the streets shined a grey black. I sunk into the book, captivated by the story; I felt that I had arrived to a home I had never known, full of magic, and rainy days with books and a warm fire, "Ah, this is me" I thought.

When the rain let up, I packed up my new heavy hardback and wove my way through town to the COOP several blocks from Marco's house. I searched for eatables to make meals with. I loaded up my basket with mushrooms, onions, ginger and some oranges, then picked up a bag of rice and went to the counter to check out. There were a few people in line in front of me.

I finally moved up to the front of the check stand and the woman checking my groceries stood quietly looking at my bags full of peppers and tomatoes. She asked me something in German that I could not understand, then when she realized I could not communicate back, she put a sign up at the cashier stand and took all of my veggies with her. She was gone five minutes. While all the people behind me waited in line patiently, she weighed and marked all of my bags. I figured out that I was supposed to weigh and sticker my own produce, which was the Co-ops system for efficiency.

The cashier returned and smiled at me then finished my transaction.

When I walked outside the sun was shining through the clouds and the mountains glistened, there was a rainbow stretching across the sky. I was at first embarrassed that I didn't know about weighing my produce, but the woman had not reprimanded me, she met me with compassion, which made me appreciate our human interaction.

***

I searched for a wine bottle opener all over the kitchen, but couldn't find one, so I dug into the cork with all the sharp objects I could find. The cork popped into the bottle and I filtered some wine out for cooking with.

I put on a pot to boil and measured rice, then set to work to make stir fry with sweet and sour sauce. I wondered if Marco liked different kinds of foods, or if he was going to be picky. All I had seen him eat was microwaved chicken pulled out of the freezer when he got home late at night. I wanted to nourish him and make him a meal for my gratitude for inviting me to stay.

I squeezed orange juice, and mixed it with honey, set it aside, then grated some ginger into an oiled skillet. I cut up some of the chicken I thawed in the microwave and tossed it on the hot oil. I began to feel the excitement of cooking. As I chopped veggies, my mind drifted to the way Marco kissed me. It was straightforward, no thought or guilt or question lie in-between, he would scoop my lips into his, and each time he kissed me I would stop thinking and give in to his lead.

I loved that no one in the world could find me, not a soul knew where I was in that moment. I was absent from my identity and transformed into a mythical creature, a muse, a goddess, being fed pleasure and love and desire. For the moment I was removed from the expectation of being proper, or well-raised, or educated. I was exempt from being in the middle conversation between my mother and father. In Marco's cottage I could be Reign's love child and Carver's daughter, and Sylvie's female creation, here I could be a Goddess and a witch, I could make magic however I liked, and I could feel the spirit in my bones; I could be whatever I wanted to be.

The chicken soaked up ginger and onion flavor and I tossed in the rest of the cut up peppers, mushrooms and zucchini. I found soy sauce in the cupboard and added a few splashes along with a dash of hot sauce. In such a limited kitchen I made it work.

The clock on the microwave read 6:30, Marco was getting off work. I set the table, turned everything down to low and sat down to read a bit of Harry Potter while I waited for him. Half way into a chapter I glanced at the clock, it was 7:04, he probably just had to wrap things up, or had to stay a bit late, I forced myself to not worry or think too much about it. At 8:00 o'clock I could no longer focus on reading at all, I felt foolish and hurt, but again justified that he must have had to stay late. I paced back and forth through the bedroom, into the kitchen and the living room. I considered calling him, but felt silly like a housewife. I felt like my mother, who would add water or broth to the gravy for chicken and dumplings and sauces in order to keep them from drying up when company was late, or for my dad who would often come home late from hunting.

As a family we were always coming in and leaving at different times, and mom always had some dinner prepared. Every night, she cooked a wholesome and nourishing meal. Sometimes the meat would still need cooking or certain parts of the meal were not ready, leaving my mother hungry and feisty. She would finally give in and just eat salad, trying to hold herself over until the food was ready.

I sat down at the kitchen table, feeling defeated. I wanted this dinner to make Marco fall in love with me. I suppose I was looking for someone to share dinners and life with, I was looking for a partner. I didn't know for sure if it was Marco, but this was the first time I had ever stayed with a lover, it was the first time any of my lovers let me get so close.

At the moment of my defeat, Marco unlatched the door downstairs, about to catch me disarmed and vulnerable.

"Hey!" he said with his face lit up and his eyes wide.

"Hi." I paused, as Marco put his things away in his extra room, "Are you hungry?" I called from the kitchen, pretending to be reading my book. "I made you dinner". He came back in and pulled the lids off the rice and stir fry.

"Mmm," he whiffed the still steamy food that waited for him on low heat.

"I already ate." I told him looking down at the table so he wouldn't see that I was still wondering why he hadn't come home earlier.

"Oh good. One of the guys had to leave early so I finished his shift. I would have called, but I didn't think you would answer my phone," he said as he sat down with a plate full of food. I looked up at him, happy at his excuse mostly that he had been thinking about me. I forgave him and let go of my moments of paranoia. After all, he invited me here, of course he wanted to hang out with me. He didn't say anything about the meal being tasty, but he did eat all that was left. I wondered if he was happy it was something other than plain micro-waved chicken. I wanted to erase his mentality that "food is fuel" and add a little passion to eating.

As soon as we cleared the table, Marco came to me, sliding his hand around my waist and pulling my body to his, again we were in a tango, I followed his lead. He said nothing, but dipped his face down to kiss me, it was as if he had put a spell on me; I loved surrendering to it. He lifted off my shirt, I unbuckled his pants, he pulled at his shirt, I unbuttoned my jeans, and he caressed my skin exploring me. He was not discovering sex for the first time, but feasting on it. He did not play a game of teasing, but understood that many hours away from one another brought a lusty hunger. I felt like a woman, not a girl in a quiet game, but a woman meeting a man who could hold my power next to his. I was there to express myself, to find a part of me that I never knew, and he was there to receive it.

***

Marco drove me up through the mountain roads, he finally had a whole day off. The day was a bit brighter, still cloudy, but sun poked through occasionally and the rain only sprinkled here and there. We listened to The Wall, which I laughed to myself about and secretly wished we could listen to something other than Pink Floyd for a change.

I glanced at him, and for a moment I saw Pietro, driving down the Amalfi coast. I had a sinking feeling, I didn't really know Marco any more than I did Pietro. I wanted to go back to how it felt when I had just arrived at Marco's, back to the beginning of the mystery.

The car climbed the mountain, weaving around and around. We finally arrived at a fancy burger joint, it was the only building around for miles, set up in the mountain top where any moment I expected Heidi to come trotting down the hillside.
Tiny purple flowers matted the silvery grasses at the base of the giant hill next to us.
The rain had ceased and everything was left pristine and shimmering.

Marco ordered a bottled water and I had a chamomile tea. We both ordered burgers.

We looked at the sky.

We looked at the people.

We had nothing to say. Our time was coming to an end. We finished our burgers and drove back to the cabin. Marco set to work on studying for a test to qualify for Grad school. I settled in with Harry Potter for a couple of hours, then took a break and stepped outside.

The late afternoon light and gentle breeze blew across me, I could smell fall coming, in mountain towns, like my hometown, the yin of fall came early. Where I stood I could feel the intensity of the melted glaciers, the water that swells the rocks, the force of precipitation and how the earth was beginning to break down, ready to transition to another season and transform the body's and spirits around it. Storms were coming, but for the time being, it was peaceful, I was peaceful.

***

The forest to the north of my little lover's cabin called to me each time I passed it to go into town. There was a path that led up into the woods where it seemed that no one ever entered and I heard the birds singing their songs, and the wind whispering to me, "come in".

I woke in the morning to a sunbeam dashing along the wall of the bedroom, and birds rejoicing in the deep summer. I felt compelled to pack myself some snacks and go explore the forest trail that beckoned me.

At the foot of the trail I paused closing my eyes. Even in summer the smell of cool ice melting and mingling with dirt and rock filled the air. A soft wind blew from the direction of the lake; it smelled of algae, mud and decaying leaves. I glanced up at the clouds moving silently, changing slowly, drifting off, they had no opinions. And there in front of me loomed the path through trees that weathered storms cast upon them by the soul of the Alps, the trees that sang the song of the mountains. I took a breath. "I am alone, there is no one on this path, and I am walking it alone." The gravity at my feet tugged at a sadness that had welled up inside of me.

Visions of all the people in my life swirled around me. There were so many endings. When I began this journey, there was so much possibility, I couldn't even imagine what it could bring, other than perspective. I had wondered if I might meet Pietro again and fall in love with him in a new way, maybe I would feel differently about him since my mother wasn't along, but when it came that time, I discovered what I had known all along, that I wasn't in love with Pietro. I knew that I would never see him again, he was now a whisper in my memory drifting off in a ship across the sea.

Reign, I related to the way he moved through the world, not concerned about consequences, but more interested in the experience of existence. I figured that my mother had loved that about him too. He was powerful in the way he never really seemed to care what anyone thought about him.

I sat down with my back against a sun warmed rock and closed my eyes. I thought about Carver, the man who gave me a father. There were monuments of father-daughter moments we shared throughout my life that held sentimental value for me, and I felt a loyalty to him for giving me a foundation to stand on. But any time I wanted to be honest about Reign's connection to my existence, I closed my mouth. To recognize Reign as any part of me, whether it was positive or negative, seemed to make all of those memories with Carver seem like a lie, even though they were real. I did not know how to move forward in totality. How could I possibly be the daughter of two men? The only way

I knew was to live in two worlds like my mother did. One in a secret fantasy life, and one in an illusory reality. But did I have to choose that? Couldn't I choose to live as me? Honestly?

Ahron and Marco. My lovers. I loved them, but something was missing, neither of them saw my wholeness, only parts, and they only showed me parts of them. There was a fierceness to the Woman that lived inside of me that Ahron could never look at, and Marco seemed to have other aspirations, he lived so far away, and he wouldn't be coming back with me. The sun beamed into my eyes, then a cloud passed over the sun and I stood in a shadow. I packed up my things and began walking deeper down the path. After forty minutes of walking and getting lost in my thoughts, I came to a ridge where a large boulder blocked the path, marking an end to easy walking, if I were to go farther I would be merely breaking my own trail unsure of where I would end up or how to get back.

I sat down on the huge boulder and rested, my body tingled. I saw flickering lights before my eyes that always appeared after a long walk in the sun. "They are fairies", I thought, blinking and seeing their light still. The forest was still until a grey squirrel with a pinecone in its mouth jumped from log to log below me. He made his way up to a rock near me and began tearing away at the tough peel of each pine nut shell.

I looked up through the tops of trees, into a mystical forest filling me with a sense of power; a power from a different paradigm. There were no men to take me away from myself, my mother was far away, and even my best friend for years was somewhere in Spain.

I could hear everything the earth wanted to tell me that I had never listened to before. I fell asleep dreaming in the sun.

I jumped down off the boulder into the cushion of matted leaves and needles on the forest floor. What went beyond this point? I would find out. I cut through trees and climbed over rocks and fallen logs. Moss and mushrooms speckled the ground and layered the bark of dead trees. I could be committing suicide, walking so far into an unknown forest, how will I ever get back? The forest floor tilted downward, and I started running to keep up with the slope. I came to the bottom of the hill, the sun shone brightly between the trees and I could not see beyond it.

The wind picked up a pile of dirt and swished it into my eyes. I felt my spirit lift up slightly with the branches of the trees. They rustled and the light between the leaves were like sequins glittering before me. The wind came like waves of the ocean and I saw all the birds come out from wherever they had been, flying in all directions, getting ready for a storm. I blinked the sand out of my eyes and saw that the sky had darkened, the sunlight vanished from the tree gate, allowing me to see through the veil, the truth of what I had not seen before.

I was at the Lake. Stepping down to the shore, a stronger wind ruffled my hair, but the clouds parted and the sun shone again. Out in the distance, an orange and black snorkel stuck out of the water and moved around the rim of the lake. Carver sat on the beach reading a book. Reign dove in, splashing water into a rainbow and swimming toward my mother. My brothers and sisters were all along the shore, swimming, looking at tadpoles, catching snakes. We were on our own island. Where was I? Just standing and watching? Ahron was at the farthest end sitting in a boat with his fishing pole. I wanted to swim to him, but I was afraid I'd scare the fish. Then, from behind me I heard a rustling from the forest. An arm reached out and took my hand. Inside of that touch, I knew myself. It was her, the Goddess of the forest, inside of her I was inside of myself, inside where the greatest treasure waited to be unburied, the discovery of myself, a treasure that never runs out.

As I turned to go back, I looked out at the lake one last time, my mother was walking out of the water, and Reign was gone. She stood in her swim suit, breathing in that mystical world that no one could follow her to.

She told me the truth about Reign, a truth that freed my voice to speak about the things that I had always felt. She had opened the door for me. Her life was hers, she had chosen her path, like we all do, and that became her story. She was a Goddess creating her own world, healing her own sorrows, inspiring her own joys. There were wounds I carried, never having a voice to speak about what I knew, about my mother's secret life, about the truth of who my biological father was, but I could no longer blame my mother. Inside the forest I knew my true identity, and I didn't have to lie about it anymore.

Marco stood on the platform. He kissed me. I held on for a few more moments and smiled at him, then lifted my bag onto my back and boarded the train to Paris. As the train started moving I looked out the window at Marco. We were moving apart like two sides of a Rubik's cube, he stayed on that platform as I moved onto another one.

Paris, France

Laying on the grass under the lit up Eiffel Tower, I wondered, "what now?
Where is home for this gypsy girl?"
I watched a kite flying and dipping in the sum-

mer evening breeze. Down on the grass a girl stood harnessing the power of the wind to make her kite fly. She was the kite's anchor.

"*What do you want? What do you want?*" Marco's words whispered in my mind. I whispered back, "I want to write my own story Marco, a story where I meet my soulmate and nothing stands in the way of us spending lifetimes creating together, a story where pain is nourished into love and transformed into wisdom. I want to live in a world where love can be love, where no one possesses another's freedom. I want to own my choices, stand on my own two feet, listen to my heart and follow it, and... Marco?

He didn't answer. The sky was dark now, the curfew for my hostel was coming up and it was time for me to get back. I let my last words to him slip off into the Parisian stars,

"I want to have a family."

***

The sun was setting, we were flying in No-Time, not rooted in the past, and unknowing of the future. The colors outside went from a rich yellow-green-blue, to a lavender grey, but instead of fading into dark starry speckled blue, the sky would oscillate back and forth from oranges and deep reds to greyed-out whites and purples. We were flying with the sun, every time it would begin to dip beyond the horizon, the rich orb would bob back up again and relight the sky with brilliant new colors. I watched this happen for what seemed like an hour until finally our plane could no longer catch the sun. We slipped into the blanket of night.

** (by Tony Topoleski)

        **Not forever and a
day: Not for eternity, or
any
Time like it. I'll promise nothing
Beyond this moment,

This single instant
In which my lungs draw
breath and yours as well, Beside me.

I'll tell you
To forget about all that,
And I will say it
While brushing away
That mischievous lock of
hair that has fallen So se-
renely upon your face.

Then, Perhaps, in the moment
That comes just after,
I will move my arm around you
While you lay your head
Upon mine. And with the perfect
Lightness of our two bodies,
Your skin soft against mine,
We can look into that same starry
Expanse, which lets some-
thing reminiscent of eternity
Drip down around us.

      Finito...per ora

Laura Marie Parker

Glossary of Italian to English Translation

1.Vaffanculo! = Fuck You!

2.Saldi = Sale

3. i miei piedi sono doloranti, le mie scarpe sono vecchie e irritabili come me=my feet are sore, my shoes are old and irritable like me

4. Queste scarpe, queste scarpe= these shoes, These Shoes

5. Devo comprare un nuovo paio, queste scarpe hanno fatto il loro corso=
I have to buy a new pair, these shoes have run their course

5. Beh, sarebbe bello per qualcuno aiutare una vecchia signora, potrei morire prima di arrivarci. Qui ti aspetto, aspettando e aspettando, quando guardi questi piedi, guarda queste scarpe, che sono nei brandelli, che stanno cadendo a pezzi. E devo aspettare, devo aspettare=Well, it would be nice for someone to help an old lady, help an old lady go first, I could die before I get there. Here I am with a little bit of paper and a very small number on it, waiting and in wait, when you look at these feet, look at these shoes, which are in shreds, which are falling apart. And I have to wait, I have to wait.

6. Aqua minerale gassata, vacanza = carbonated mineral water, holiday

7. Ciao, si bene= Hello, yes good

8. Pronto = Greeting, a way to answer phone; ready.

9. Non ti piace il cibo = You do not like the food?

10. Abbraccia me = Hug me

11. Arrivederci, ci video = Goodbye, I will see you

soon.

12. Fragola = strawberry; Fragolina = strawberry

Laura Marie Parker

Afterword

After all is said and done, I have written a book. I look over the adventure and still have a fondness about my travels and my discoveries along the way, but sixteen years is a long time from the start to the finish, and so much has happened since then. I can say that the person I was in this story is integrated into the person I am now, but she is only a part. I have since fallen wildly in love, birthed three boys, traveled more, learned to bake, found health through wild crafting herbal remedies, and written from start to finish this book. There was a time when I lived so fiercely in my fantasy world that I at one point called thirty pages of abstract poetry my novel. I took a webinar class with Shaman Lynn V. Andrews, and the one thing that stuck with me from that class was that she said it was important for me to finish something. My interpretation of her advice was that I needed to stop dilly-dallying with my book, and single-pointedly finish it. I considered burning it at least once a year, at one time I even did burn a lot of it, there were many parts that went to the flames. It was an effort, but in the end, I look back at it, and though it was a solo journey, I did not do it alone. My husband encouraged me as an artist to move through the uncomfortable parts, my children urged me on merely out of my desire to inspire them to follow their dreams. I loved writing when I was young, my journal and I were in constant conversation, (mostly about boys, but also about the unfairness of life and the beauties of life as well). Life is my art, the way all the things weave together is such a magnificent tapestry to me, and so I wanted to invite others to peak into what I see, I

334

wanted to share my story, because I love telling stories. So now, after all is said and done, I have written a book, to begin the story, of a gypsy girl, turned gypsy lover, turned gypsy mother, turned Shaman and herbalist and homesteader. This is only the beginning. As my Qi Gong teacher said to me the day I met her. "You look like you have a lot to say," and it is true, I have *so much* to say.

Made in the USA
Middletown, DE
17 July 2021